THE POLITICAL IMPORTANCE OF REGIONAL TRADING BLOCS

The Political Importance of Regional Trading Blocs

Edited by

BART KERREMANS
Associate Professor, Catholic University Leuven

BOB SWITKY
Assistant Professor, State University of New York, Brockport

Ashgate

Aldershot • Burlington USA • Singapore • Sydney

© Bart Kerremans and Bob Switky 2000

All rights reserved. No part of this publication may be reproduced, stored in a retrieval system, or transmitted in any form or by any means, electronic, mechanical, photocopying, recording or otherwise without the prior permission of the publisher.

Published by
Ashgate Publishing Ltd
Gower House
Croft Road
Aldershot
Hants GU11 3HR
England

Ashgate Publishing Company
131 Main Street
Burlington, VT 05401-5600
USA

Ashgate website: http://www.ashgate.com

British Library Cataloguing in Publication Data
The political importance of regional trading blocs
    1. Trade blocs 2. Trade blocs - Political aspects
    I. Kerremans, Bart II. Switky, Bob
    382.9'1

Library of Congress Control Number: 00-133524

ISBN 0 7546 1107 8

Printed and bound by Antony Rowe Ltd, Chippenham, Wiltshire

382.91
P76

OC 44101779
Feb. 2002

Contents

List of Figures and Tables

List of Contributors

Sherry L. Bennett received her Ph.D. from Michigan State University. She is an Assistant Professor of Political Science at Rice University and currently a Visiting Scholar at the University of California, Berkeley. Her current research interests include the examination of domestic constraints on international trade policy and the resolution of trade disputes in domestic and multilateral organizations.

Erick Duchesne is an Assistant Professor in the Political Science Department at the University at Buffalo, SUNY. He also taught at the Faculté St. Jean of the University of Alberta and Michigan State University, where he received his Ph.D. in 1997. He specializes on the impact of domestic politics on international economic negotiations.

Bart Kerremans is an Associate Professor in the Political Science Department at the Catholic University Leuven (Belgium). His research focuses on international trade policies especially of the European Union and on EU decision-making in general. He has published in various journals including Governance, the Journal of World Trade, and Regional and Federal Studies.

Quan Li, Ph.D., the Florida State University, 1998; Assistant Professor of Political Science at the Pennsylvania State University, University Park, Pennsylvania. Specializes in international relations and international political economy in particular. Ongoing projects include regionalism, capital control liberalization, macroeconomic policy coordination among the major powers, and the effects of globalization on interstate conflict and democratization.

David A. Lynch, Ph.D. is an Assistant Professor of Political Science at Saint Mary's University of Minnesota. He received his Ph.D. from the University of California, Santa Barbara. His research foci are trade and American foreign policy. Publications include 'The WTO and Trade,' an annual contribution in A Global Agenda, published by the United Nations Association of the USA.

Rafael Reuveny is an Assistant Professor in the school of public and environmental affairs (SPEA) in Indiana University, Bloomington. He holds a double major Ph.D. in Political Science and Business Economics and Public Policy from Indiana University. His research deals with the political economy of international trade, the relationship between trade and conflict, the link between conflict and economic growth in the long run, and the relationship between conflict and environmental scarcity. He has published papers in various journals including American Journal of Political Science, International Organization, International Studies Quarterly, Journal of Conflict Resolution, Journal of Peace Research and Review of International Political Economy.

Bob Switky is an Assistant Professor at the State University of New York at Brockport. He received his Ph.D. from the Claremont Graduate University in California. His research interests include European Union politics and international political economy. He has written on European Union external trade policies and has a forthcoming publication of an international relations textbook (Addison-Wesley-Longman, 2000). He is also involved in a project on the determinants of trade policies in cultura industries.

William R. Thompson is Professor of Political Science at Indiana University. His most recent publications include Great Power Rivalries (1999) and The Emergence of the Global Political Economy (2000). Current research interests include strategic rivalries, North-South IPE, evolutionary approaches to IR theory, and modeling ancient world system dynamics.

Abbreviations

AAMA	American Manufacturers'Association
ACTWU	Amalgamated Clothing and Textile Workers Union
ACP	African Caribbean and Pacific
APEC	Asian Pacific Economic Cooperation
ASEAN	Association of South East Asian Nations
ATMI	American Textile Manufacturers' Association
BCNI	Business Council on National Issues
BQ	Bloc Québécois
CAFE	Corporate Average Fuel Efficiency
CEEC	Central and Eastern European Countries
COG	Chief of Government
CMA	Canadian manufacturers' Association
CU	Customs Union
CUSFTA	Canada United States Free Trade Agreement
EC	European Community
ECU	European Currency Unit
EFTA	European Free Trade Association
FDI	Foreign Direct Investment
FTAA	Free Trade Area of the Americas
GATT	General Agreement on Tariffs and Trade
GATS	General Agreement on Trade in Services
HST	Hegemonic Stability Theory
ILGWU	International Ladies Garment Workers Union
LAFTA	Latin America Free Trade Area
MFN	Most Favored Nation
NAFTA	North American Free Trade Area
NTA	New Transatlantic Agenda
NTM	New Transatlantic Marketplace
OECD	Organization for Economic Cooperation and Development
PTA	Preferential Trade Agreement
RP	Reform Party

RTA	Regional Trade Agreement
RTAA	Reciprocal Trade Agreements Act of 1934
SADC	Southern African Development Community
TABD	Transatlantic Business Dialogue
TAFTA	Transatlantic Free Trade Agreement
TBT	Technical Barriers to Trade
TNC	Transnational Corporation
TPL	Tariff Preference Levels
TRIMs	Trade-Related Investment Measures
TRIPs	Trade-Related Intellectual Property Rights
TEP	Transatlantic Economic Partnership
UAW	United Auto Workers
USTR	United States Trade Representative
WTO	World Trade Organization

1 Introduction

BART KERREMANS AND BOB SWITKY

The Importance of Regional Trade Agreements

For an increasing number of countries, it is difficult to resist the attraction of regional trading arrangements. It seems as if one of the first consequences of globalization is the regionalization of trading patterns. This is visible in both trade statistics and in formal regional trade agreements. Indeed, the patterns of trade and investment in the multilateral trading system have been regional for some time (Thomsen, 1994: 111-122; Lawrence, 1996: 17-19). Countries tend to trade overwhelmingly – and ever more – with their neighbors. As Table 1 shows, this is by far and foremost the case for the industrialized countries (cf. Anderson and Blackhurst, 1993: 5 & Appendix; Anderson and Norheim, 1993: 19). More and more countries are concluding trade agreements with their same neighbors and investing in a deepening of such agreements; this trend contrasts with trade agreements concluded on a multilateral scale (Wallace, 1990; Thomsen, 1994). As a matter of fact, of the current 134 members of the World Trade Organization, only three are not parties to at least one regional trade agreement: Japan, Hong Kong, and South Korea (see Table 1.1).

Despite (or maybe because of) the overwhelming presence of regional trade agreements (RTAs), economists have been challenged by the question of whether RTAs are beneficial or harmful in the long run (cf. Srinivasan et al., 1993; Smith, 1994; Deardorff and Stern, 1994; Proff and Proff, 1996; Wei and Frankel, 1998). The effect of RTAs on the multilateral trading system is also a major concern for lawyers, political scientists, and practitioners alike. Whereas lawyers have been debating the meaning of the relevant WTO provisions on regional trade agreements, political scientists and political-economists have been focussing on the effects of regional trade agreements on the willingness of political leaders to continue to support multilateral trade liberalization. Do such agreements reduce the willingness to support multilateralism because RTAs make multilateral

1

trade liberalization less necessary, as Bhagwati has claimed; or do RTAs enhance support of multilateralism because they pave the way for further liberalization on a wider geographical basis (Baldwin,1997: 865) or because they 'lock in' policies of liberalization (cf. WTO, 1998a: 29; see also Sapir, 1993: 432)?[1]

The answers to these questions remain controversial. That is why the literature on regional trade agreements has proliferated during the last decade or so. This has partly been a response to the renewed or new interest of many countries in such agreements.[2] One-third of all the currently existing regional agreements have been concluded since 1990. Factors such as the dissolution of the former communist bloc and the renewed interest in regional trade agreements in the Western Hemisphere have played an important role in this. A country like the United States, for instance, didn't show a lot of interest for such agreements before the end of the 1980s, but it started to develop a regional trade agenda from 1985 on, first with Israel and Canada (the 1988 CUSFTA), later with Mexico (NAFTA), and since then with the other countries of the Western Hemisphere (Pomfret, 1997: 110-111). Attempts at extending NAFTA (to Chile for instance) or to conclude a hemisphere-wide agreement (the FTAA) have absorbed a lot of political and administrative resources since the first half of the 1990s.

Table 1.1   Share of intra-and inter-regional trade flows in each region's total merchandise exports (1997)[3]

	North America	Latin America	Western Europe	Central & Eastern Europe	Africa	Middle East	Asia	World
North America	36.2	15.3	18.6	0.9	1.4	2.5	24.9	100
Latin America	52.1	20.5	15	1.2	1.2	1.1	8.6	100
Western Europe	8.3	2.5	67	5.6	2.6	2.8	9.3	100
Central & Eastern Europe	4.7	1.8	59.7	18.6	1.4	2.5	9.1	100
Africa	15.9	3.3	50.5	1.1	9.4	1.6	14.7	100
Middle East	12.5	1.7	21.3	0.8	3.8	6.6	52.5	100
Asia	23.8	2.5	16.5	1.1	1.5	26	50.7	100
World	*19.6*	*5.6*	*40.8*	*3.6*	*2.2*	*27*	*24.1*	*100*

On the European side of the Atlantic we see a similar development. The European Union reacted to the fall of the Berlin Wall by trying to support the countries of Central and Eastern Europe through, *inter alia*, the conclusion of regional trade agreements (the Europe Agreements). In the meantime, the integration of the countries of the European Free Trade Agreement (EFTA) in the EU through the European Economic Area Agreement was concluded as well as a Customs Union Agreement with Turkey. Trade agreements – as part of the negotiating agenda of the Cooperation and Partnership Agreements – with some of the republics of the former Soviet-Union are in the pipeline. But the European Union has a longer tradition in conducting its trade relations through regional trade agreements. What could be seen after 1990 was an intensification of this approach in response to the new political situation in Central and Eastern Europe.

In other parts of the world, regional trade agreements have recently gained in importance as well. In Asia, the idea of a ASEAN Free Trade Area (AFTA) was launched (Anderson and Blackhurst, 1993: 2). In Latin America, new such agreements were concluded (e.g. Mercosur) or old ones were revitalized (e.g. the Andes Community, the Central American Common Market). In Northern Africa, Morocco, Algeria, Tunisia, and Mauritania launched the Maghreb Union, and in both East and West Africa ideas about the creation of economic and monetary unions have been launched as well (cf. the WAEMU, the COMESA, and the EAC). Although these plans and initiatives still have a long way to go, it is a first step in the direction of regional trade liberalization for these countries. On the other extreme of the African continent, largely because of the democratic reforms in South Africa since 1994, the Southern African Development Community (SADC) is being renewed and reinvigorated.

Thus, despite the confusion on the welfare effects of regional trade agreements, it is difficult to ignore them and their obvious attraction to many – if not most – governments. It is equally difficult to ignore the increasingly important role of such agreements in the multilateral trading system in general and in the World Trade Organization (WTO) in particular. This is recognized by the WTO itself. But it is equally important to note the concerns that exist about the effects – economic, legal, and political-economic – on international trade and the international trading system. As former WTO director-general Ruggiero phrased it in his speech before the Institute for International Economics:

> No doubt regional agreements can be helpful to the integration process – providing an impetus to greater liberalization – especially for the developing countries. But in a world where the reality of global integration is calling for global solutions across a whole range of policies and issues, regionalism cannot provide an alternative to the multilateral system. [4]

In the World Trade Organization's 1998 Annual Report (WTO, 1998a: 22-23) a similar approach towards regional trade agreements can be found:

> Trade policy reform works best under a number of clearly defined conditions, including (..) a mutually supportive process of unilateral, regional and multilateral liberalization and deregulation.

This book addresses these concerns about regional trade agreements. From a variety of political and economic angles, it explains the emergence of trade blocs, their internal policies and politics, and their effects on global trade. Unlike most books on regional trade blocs, this volume will not provide sequential descriptions and analyses of each of the world's major trading blocs. The focus here is on a number of causal factors that help explain the emergence of trading blocs and the development of their relations to and effects on the multilateral trading system. In each chapter, attempts have been made to draw theoretical and case-based generalizations that may apply to other trade blocs than the ones used in the empirical analyses. There, of course, limits to this approach. Regional trading blocs are a relatively recent phenomenon. That should make us very careful about generalizing about existing ones, especially as far as their impact on the global trading system is concerned.

Definitions

Before looking deeper into the dynamics of regional trade agreements, it is important to clarify some basic definitions. In many cases, terms such as 'regional trade agreements', 'free trade associations', and 'regional trading blocs' are used interchangeably. From the perspective of GATT-based rules, the 'regional' aspect of a regional trade agreement only becomes relevant to the extent that such an agreement provides exceptions to the

MFN principle by granting trade preferences to a limited number of countries. It is the discrimination between those that are parties to the agreement and the 'others' that is the decisive criterion to talk about regional trade agreements. The reference to 'regional' may be misleading since that assumes that all the parties involved have to belong to one particular geographical area. Though this is the case for most such agreements, there are agreements for which it is not, and as Lawrence (1996: 9) has put it, 'geographic proximity is not necessarily the most important determinant of participation in "regional" agreements.' The EU's Association Agreement between with seventy so-called ACP countries – better known as the Fourth Lomé Convention – is an example of a preferential trade agreement, though not a reciprocal one, among parties that are not geographically close. But the defining characteristic of a 'regional trade agreement' is precisely that it grants preferential, and therefore discriminatory, treatment to a specified group of countries. This notion is reflected in Fishlow and Haggard's (1992) distinction between *regionalization* (which refers to regional concentration of economic flows) and *regionalism* (which involves a political process characterized by economic policy coordination among the cooperating countries).

This brings us to another point of clarification. The above definition of 'regional trade agreement' does not mean that the definition only refers to agreements covered by article XXIV GATT and article V GATS. In two ways, it does not. First, these articles basically only refer to two kinds of such agreements: free trade agreements and agreements that establish customs unions. Such agreements are far-reaching, and for some of the agreements that are considered to be regional trade agreements, it is unclear whether they would comply with one of these two possibilities. Second, a number of preferential trade agreements are not covered by article XXIV GATT and article V (and Vbis) GATS, since they are covered by the Enabling Clause (cf. Pomfret, 1997: 103). This clause allows developing countries to conclude non-reciprocal preferential trade agreements among themselves. The clause does not extend to agreements between the developing and the developed countries.[5] But since such agreements are preferential in nature, they can be considered regional trade agreements or the equivalent.

Therefore, in empirical terms, regional trade agreements can be considered agreements concluded among members of the WTO and that the

RTAs have to be reported to the WTO which scrutinizes their compliance either with article XXIV GATT (as interpreted through the Understanding on article XXIV), article V and Vbis GATS, or point 2 c) of the Enabling Clause. Such agreements create preferential access to particular markets and, therefore, discriminate among the WTO members.

The term 'regional trade agreement' could, to a certain extent, be used interchangeably with the term 'trading bloc', although the latter often has negative connotations. The term 'bloc' suggests both exclusiveness and power. Exclusiveness refers to the fact that blocs exclude as much as possible non-members from their markets. In addition, the term 'bloc' emphasizes the power of the regional grouping as a whole. It also asserts the existence of a collectivity that is capable to act as a unitary actor (cf. Henderson, 1994: 181). But such a collectivity only exists when the trade agreement that creates the 'bloc' includes provisions for the 'bloc' to act as a single actor in the multilateral trading system (cf. Rollo, 1994: 35). At the moment, only one of the existing regional trade agreements provides for this – Mercosur. If one also considers the European Union as a regional trade agreement although - it is much more than that – then there are just two of them. To conclude, the term 'trading bloc' used in the literature is an ill-defined concept, sometime creating more confusion than that it does clarity (Cable, 1994: 1). Since there does not seem to be an over-riding need to establish air-tight definitions – scholars use the terms loosely – this volume will, therefore, use the term interchangeably with regional trade agreement (RTA) and 'preferential trade agreement.'

Organization of the Book

This book attempts to combine and integrate the often insulated literatures on trade blocs, particularly from economics and political science. In Chapter 2, Bob Switky deals with the theoretical foundations of the study of regional bloc. He reviews the dominant analytical approaches to the study of trade blocs in addition to evaluating the potential for some approaches that have received less attention. The purpose of the chapter is to describe the analytical angles by which trade blocs are studied and to explore the possibilities for compatibility across academic disciplines. He also frames the critical questions raised by trade bloc scholars and the contributors to this volume.

In Chapter 3, Raphael Reuveny and William R. Thompson will explore the effects of the creation and existence of regional trading blocs on protectionism. The question they try to answer refers to the widely held assumption that regional bloc formation leads to rising protectionism, especially when a traditional leader in the multilateral trading system – such as Britain in the nineteenth century and the US since World War II – starts to engage itself in concluding RTAs. Their analysis starts by looking at the domestic political and economic consequences of NAFTA and proceeds by considering whether US trade regionalization necessarily implies a movement toward protectionism and trade closure. In doing so, the authors focus on Krasner's trinity of tariff levels, trade proportions (trade openness), and regional trade encapsulation (Krasner, 1996). The authors reject empirically the widely shared notion that regional trading blocs and protectionism necessarily go hand in hand.

In Chapter 4, Quan Li analyses the impact of regional trade agreements on bilateral trade. His focus is on the role of institutional rules. He argues that the degree of intra-bloc trade bias is causally related to the institutional rules of a bloc in three important ways; first in its coverage, second regarding implementation, and third in its dispute resolution mechanisms. Such rules affect the credibility of the RTAs. Li also shows this by comparing the institutional arrangements of seven different trade blocs.

In Chapter 5 Bart Kerremans explores the interplay between domestic factors explaining regional bloc formation, the interaction among different regional trading blocs and the propensity to liberalize trade multilaterally. Kerremans suggests that the fear that regional bloc formation in both Europe and North America will damage multilateral trade liberalization is overstated. In addition, he suggests that the effects of regional bloc formation and the drive towards regional bloc expansion need to be assessed through an analysis in which the interplay of (a) multilateral, (b) regional, and (c) domestic trade policies.

In Chapter 6 Kerremans extends the analysis of Chapter 5 by addressing the question of cooperation and competition between the world's two largest trading blocs: North America and Europe. It will show that cooperation between these blocs seems to have a strong appeal partly because of the increasing size and market power of the two blocs. It also indicates the extent to which regional trade liberalization, inter-regional cooperation on trade, and multilateral trade liberalization are complementary. Multilateral trade liberalization has clear political and economic limits as has cooperation among trading blocs. It entails the question to what extent the welfare effects of regional bloc formation have to be assessed in the light of an ideal world of complete free trade, or in the light of a real world in which regional trade liberalization – and to a lesser extent inter-regional cooperation – provides opportunities for trade liberalization until now not provided by the multilateral trade negotiations.

The topic of Chapter 7 by Erick Duchesne and Sherry Bennett is the domestic ratification process of regional trade agreements. Their case study is the debate on the NAFTA ratification. In their analysis, the authors focus on the interplay between several important actors: (a) official institutions such as transnational interactions, (b) national governments, and (c) different organized interests, particularly business interests.

In Chapter 8, David Lynch focuses on the formation of RTAs by looking at the NAFTA negotiations. He explains why in these negotiations, the outcome did not reflect the overall economic preponderance of the United States. Lynch focuses on two explanations derived from an analysis of the negotiations in two sectors: automobiles and textile and apparel. First, he finds that Mexican and Canadian negotiators tailored – whenever it served them – their demands to the interests of strong interest groups in the United States. Cross-border and cross-level processes were at work, and companies that produce in two or three of the NAFTA-countries played an important role in this. The second explanation highlights the importance of existing trade arrangements. The weaker partners could sometimes exploit the fact that existing trade institutions already gave them favored access to the stronger country's markets.

Notes

[1] Anderson and Blackhurst (1993: 4) have phrased this question in an interesting way: 'The fact that a key motivation of excluded countries [countries excluded from existing RTAs] to join an existing RIA or form a new one is their desire to safeguard their ability to pursue outward-oriented development policies suggests that RIAs can make a positive contribution to the liberalization of global trade. An important empirical question is whether that contribution is more or less than offset by possible negative effects of regionalism.'

[2] 'Renewed interest' refers to what Bhagwati (referred to by Cable, 1994: 2) has called 'the First Regionalism.' This regionalism refers to both the successful attempts by the West-European countries to form the EC and the abortive attempts elsewhere in the world – especially in Latin America, Africa, and Eastern Europe – to establish their own regional trade agreements based either on import substitution policies or on principles prevalent in centrally planned economies (cf. Proff and Proff, 1996: 84) Pomfret (1997: 99-103) gives an overview of the way in which the import substitution RTAs failed.

[3] Source: WTO (1998b). See Anderson and Norheim (1993: 22-23) for warnings on using shares of regional trade as an indicator for regional trade biases.

[4] 'The Future of the World Trading System', speech by Renate Ruggiero to the Institute for International Economics Conference, Washington DC, April 15, 1999, published on internet (www.wto.org/wto/speeches/bergen.htm)

[5] Cf. Differential and More Favorable Treatment, Reciprocity and Fuller Participation of Developing Countries ('Enabling Clause'), Decision of the CONTRACTING PARTIES of 28 November 1979, point 2 c).

References

Anderson, K., Blackhurst, R. (1993), 'Introduction and Summary', in K. Anderson, R. Blackhurst (eds), *Regional Integration and the Global Trading System*, Harvester Wheatsheaf, New York, pp. 1-18.

Anderson, K., Norheim, H. (1993), 'History, Geography and Regional Economic Integration', in K. Anderson, R. Blackhurst (eds), *Regional Integration and the Global Trading System*, Harvester Wheatsheaf, New York, pp. 19-51.

Baldwin, R.E. (1997), 'The Causes of Regionalism', *The World Economy*, vol. 20, n° 7, pp. 865-888.

Cable, V. (1994), 'Overview', in V. Cable, D. Henderson (eds), *Trade Blocs? The Future of Regional Integration*, The Royal Institute of International Affairs, London, pp. 1-16.

Deardorff, A.V., Stern, R.M. (1994), 'Multilateral Trade Negotiations and Preferential Trading Arrangements', in A.V. Deardorff, R.M. Stern (eds), *Analytical and Negotiating Issues in the Global Trading System*, The University of Michigan Press, Ann Arbor, pp. 27-94.

Fishlow, A., Haggard, S. (1992), *The United States and the Regionalization of the World Economy*, OECD Development Center Research Project on Globalization and Regionalization, Paris.

Henderson, D. (1994), 'Putting 'Trade Blocs' into Perspective', in V. Cable, D. Henderson (eds), *Trade Blocs? The Future of Regional Integration*, The Royal Institute of International Affairs, London, pp. 179-198.

Krasner, S.D. (1976), 'State Power and the Structure of International Trade', *World Politics*, vol. 28, pp. 317-348.

Lawrence, R.Z. (1996), *Regionalism, Multilateralism, and Deeper Integration*, Integration National Economies Series, The Brookings Institution, Washington DC.

Pomfret, R. (1997), *The Economics of Regional Trading Arrangements*, Clarendon Press, Oxford.

Proff, H., Proff, H.V. (1996), 'Effects of World Market Oriented Regional Integration on Developing Countries', *Intereconomics*, vol. 31, n° 2, pp. 84-94.

Rollo, J.M.C. (1994), 'The EC, European Integration and the World Trading System', in V. Cable, D. Henderson (eds), *Trade Blocs? The Future of Regional Integration*, The Royal Institute of International Affairs, London, pp. 35-58.

Sapir, A. (1993), 'Regionalism and the New Theory of International Trade: Do the Bells Toll for the GATT?', *The World Economy*, vol. 16, n°4.

Smith, A. (1994), 'The Principles and Practice of Regional Economic Integration', in V. Cable, D. Henderson (eds), *Trade Blocs? The Future of Regional Integration*, The Royal Institute of International Affairs, London, pp. 17-34.

Srinivasan, T.N., Whalley, J., Wooton, I. (1993), 'Measuring the Effects of Regionalism on Trade and Welfare', in K. Anderson, R. Blackhurst (eds), *Regional Integration and the Global Trading System*, Harvester Wheatsheaf, New York, pp. 52-79.

Wallace, W. (1990), 'Introduction: The Dynamics of European Integration', in W. Wallace (ed.), *The Dynamics of European Integration*, Pinter, London, pp. 1-26.

Wei, S., Frankel, J. A. (1998), 'Open Regionalism in a World of Continental Trade Blocs', *IMF Staff Papers*, vol. 45, September 1998, n° 3, pp. 440-453.

World Trade Organization (1998a), *Annual Report: Globalization and International Trade*, WTO Secretariat, Geneva.

World Trade Organization (1998b), *Annual Report: International Trade Statistics*, WTO Secretariat, Geneva.

2 The Importance of Trading Blocs: Theoretical Foundations

BOB SWITKY

Introduction

Determining the importance of regional trading blocs is a notoriously difficult task since their consequences for the global economy are far from clear and because of the relatively limited – but growing – scholarly research devoted to the issue. The traditional literature in political science and economics (with the exception of customs union theory) generally ignored the topic of regionalized trade. Substantive theorizing about regional trade blocs did not begin in earnest until the mid-1970s (see, for example, Preeg, 1974). By the late 1980s, however, preliminary perceptions about regional trade blocs had crystallized. In 1988, for example, the National Planning Association reported that both labor and business leaders in the US perceived a general failure of the General Agreement on Tariffs and Trade (GATT), and 89% of these leaders felt that the international economy was moving in the direction of regional trade blocs. Furthermore, seventy-six per cent of these leaders felt that this would hurt the U.S. economy, and 64% said that this trend would hurt the world economy (Belous, 1990: 173). These developments have led to a burgeoning scholarly literature on the topic in the 1990s.

In light of the actual and perceived changes in the nature of the international political economy, several key theoretical questions confront trade bloc watchers. For example, to what extent are trade blocs relevant players in the international arena? When do they have a significant impact on the multilateral trading system or, more simply, on countries outside of the bloc? Another series of questions revolves around the explanations for the *emergence* of regional trading blocs in the global economy. For

13

example, are trade blocs the result of a declining hegemonic international system or are they a next-best strategy for combining economic liberalization beyond the nation-state but without global-level competition? In addition, are trade blocs used as tools by domestic-oriented politicians interested in imposing unpopular policies on their countries? To what extent are cultural factors relevant; are blocs more likely to emerge, for example, when there are common cultural and linguistic ties? Another type of research question focuses on the cohesiveness and effectiveness of trade bloc foreign policy making.

A major function of this chapter is to examine these questions by drawing together the disparate literatures on trade blocs and organize them into useful categories. This is a valuable enterprise for two reasons. First, there is an undisciplined assumption, particularly in the popular media, that trade blocs are inevitably dangerous. While this may be a useful operating hypothesis, the theoretical and empirical reasons for such a claim remains underexplored. Second, the divisions across academic disciplines are quite pronounced such that each often ignores the insights of the others. A theoretical stock-taking is clearly in order.

The chapter is divided in the following way. Part II looks at the economic and especially political importance of trade blocs. It will be argued that the examination of trade and sometimes investment flows only provide part of the story. Complimenting any economic interpretation should be the study of 'trade bloc politics' because trade blocs generate unique political environments at the domestic, regional, and global levels. Whereas Part II generally focuses on the consequences of trade blocs, Part III explores the explanations for the *emergence* of trade blocs. The discussion is more of a review of major approaches than a presentation of convincing evidence in favor of one theory or another. This part of the chapter will also place in context the rest of the chapters of this book.

The Economic and Political Importance of Trade Blocs

Any debate about trade blocs should include some attention to how important trade blocs really are. It is possible that, like many topics in any academic discipline, the topic of regional trade blocs is an intellectual fad that will disappear in five or ten years. Many people remain skeptical that trade blocs are worthy of special attention. As will be discussed in further detail below, one could make the case, for example, that aside from the European Union (EU), all other trade blocs are tenuous enterprises. This chapter, indeed this book, explains why such a view is inappropriate. Trade blocs have important global consequences in addition to significant implications for the domestic politics of trade blocs members and non-members alike. In short, their presence can be felt in altered private trade strategies, regulations, and politics.

Economic Indicators of Trade Blocs

The most common starting point for assessing the importance of trade blocs is an examination of trends in economic data. Since World War II, economists have relied on a variety of measures to track the regionalization of trade. The most common approach is to track intra-regional trade, for example, and determine whether it has increased over time in a given region. A variation of this method evaluates whether a regional trade area is of greater importance for its own exports than it is as a destination for the rest of the world's exports. Another approach is to compare the ratio of intra-bloc trade to inter-bloc trade, or – in the case of some trade blocs that do not include the United States – the ratio of intra-bloc trade to trade with the US. Yet another approach is to analyze the ratio of total extraregional trade to GNP over time. The ultimate aim of each of these approaches is to determine the extent to which the multilateral trading system – or the health of particular sectors or companies – will be affected. For example, policies adopted by trade blocs can alter the behavior of multinational corporations. In anticipation of a perceived 'Fortress Europe' by 1993 (when the EU's single market program was to be completed) Japanese and U.S. firms appeared to rush into the EU before it closed up since some of the EU's proposed restrictions threatened to limit their access to European markets (U.S. General Accounting Office, 1990). Seiichi Tsurumi, assistant to the president of Mitsubishi Corporation, said that the investment push 'took off [in 1989] when Japanese companies decided Europe was serious about 1992 [the single market]. Now we all want to get in before protectionism keeps us out' (Revzin, 1990). *The Economist* reflected upon the sentiment outside of Europe: the 'message for outsiders is clear: it is safer to manufacture inside the community than to do it where business sense might otherwise dictate' (*The Economist*, 1989: 29). Consequently, some foreign firms invested in Europe and established European subsidiaries which they hoped would be considered 'European' after the completion of the single market. Balasubramanyam and Greenaway note, however, that the Single European Act was only one of several factors influencing foreign direct investment decisions by companies that were interested in Europe (Balasubramanyam and Greenaway, 1992). Greater market opportunities from a successful single market program was another, for example.

There are two complications with reliance on economic data alone. First, there is statistical evidence that the regionalization of trade is much less pronounced than commonly thought (see Thompson and Reuveny in Chapter 3). O'Loughlin and Anselin have looked at the extent to which exports are disproportionately sent to countries in a specific region and any patterns that have intensified over time. They actually find that between 1968 and 1992, there is little evidence to support the hypothesis of a world devolving into trade blocs. In particular, they show that the US and West Germany continue to develop strong trading links with their immediate neighbors, but these links were established before the mid-1970s and have been stable since then. Japan's experience is the reverse, that is, of *globalizing* exports (O'Loughlin and Anselin, 1996). Anderson and Norheim (1993) and Frankel (1991) come to a similar conclusion.

The central debate about this finding really revolves around the rate at which regionalization is taking place. In the studies mentioned above, the process of trade regionalization is underway, but not nearly as fast as most people assume. There also seems to be a disconnect between the trade patterns on the one hand, and the more formalized and more recent establishment of regional trade agreements on the other. The lack of evidence, however, for *rapid* trade blocs formation would lead one away from important economic and political dynamics that have evolved within and between Europe, North America, and Asia.

A second complication with reliance on economic data is that even when trade flows indicate some degree of regionalization over time, there are no explicit theoretical thresholds indicating what constitutes a significant trade bloc.[1] It does not make much sense to suggest that when a certain percentage of trade is 'internalized' regionally that we have an important trade bloc on our hands. There is also no comparable threshold that determines whether a trade bloc is dangerous or not. What is important or dangerous is, of course, a matter of perspective,[2] an issue to be taken up later in the chapter. Moreover, it is possible that considerable inter-bloc trade and broad mutual cooperation can exist between two blocs that have, nonetheless, individually exhibited increased trade regionalization over time (see Kerremans in Chapter 5). For example, trade and investment flows are significant in the relationship between the EU and the US (the main player in NAFTA) with two-way trade amounting to over $250 billion a year, largely in balance (Piening, 1997). Granted, trade disputes have often soured the Trans-Atlantic relationship. Examples include the chicken war of the 1960s, Airbus, Helms-Burton legislation, and the EU's ban on growth hormones. Such trade friction notwithstanding, as Christopher Piening notes, 'it is clear that disputes and disagreements have failed to have any major effect on the qualitative and quantitative progress that has been achieved' (Piening, 1997: 105). Furthermore, the New Transatlantic Agenda (NTA) signifies a willingness on the part of the EU and the US to cooperate in a large number of political and economic areas. In March 1997, the EU Commission unveiled a blueprint for a New Transatlantic Marketplace (NTM) which, its authors hope, will help transform the trade relationship between the US by creating an EU-US FTA in services and by eliminating tariffs on industrial goods by 2010.[3] The NTA was signed in December 1995, and the NTM as well as the Transatlantic Economic Partnership (TEP) are still evolving; thus it is too early to judge their impact (see Kerremans in Chapter 4). It should be noted that another NAFTA member, Canada, has a different relationship with the EU including its own trading patterns and disputes (such as the turbot war of 1995). The EU has, however, entered into agreements with the Canadians that are similar to those held with the Americans (Piening, 1997).[4] So, despite trends toward a greater regionalization of trade, the world's two most important trading blocs are highly dependent on one another, and despite the occasional trade dispute, have a major interest in the wider global trading system (Hines, 1992: 118) as well as mutual cooperation.

Political Indicators of Trade Blocs

Regional trading agreements (RTAs) that establish trade blocs are defined here as a group of countries united by treaty or agreement for mutual support or joint action with a political agenda. If regional trading blocs are indeed becoming important actors in international affairs, we should expect to see signs of unique 'trade bloc politics'. Such dynamics are already evident, and they take several forms.

Those who support the notion of trade blocs as 'building blocs' to a more open global system point out that some states may convey to outsiders that if a multilateral approach does not work, then the *negative* alternative of a regional trade bloc will be threatened. For example, the US used NAFTA in part as a bargaining chip during the final years of the Uruguay Round by calling on the Europeans to deliver important reforms (notably on the Common Agricultural Policy) under threat of 'going regional' through NAFTA and diverting EU trade.[5] In early 1999, there was talk of Argentina forming closer ties with NAFTA at the expense of its ties to MERCOSUR as a result of the deteriorating situation in Brazil (Lapper and Warn, 1999). There are many other examples involving the politically-driven interaction of many trade blocs or the interaction of trade blocs and individual countries:

(1) States may seek to enhance foreign policy objectives by forming or expanding a trade bloc. The EU effort to increase trade cooperation with the countries of Eastern and Central Europe was designed to cement political relations. As Southey has argued, the EU Commission – as chief EU trade negotiator – sees trade pacts as a symbol of a meaningful relationship with third countries (Southey, 1997; see also Chapter 5 of this volume).

(2) A country may seek membership in a trade bloc in order to enhance its political voice in multilateral bargaining fora. In some of the Latin American arrangements, for example, a group of countries has more leverage in accession negotiations to NAFTA than would individual countries. In Eastern Europe after 1989, the prior regional negotiations between Hungary, Poland and Czechoslovakia helped increase the leverage of each country vis-à-vis EU accession negotiations (Whalley, 1996: 16-17).

(3) The formation of APEC may be viewed as 'an insurance policy should the Uruguay Round fail and the world economy slip into competing regional blocs' (Kahler, 1995b: 16).

(4) Individual state may fear being blocked out of regional trading arrangements. Consider the following examples:

- What encouraged a number of Asian countries to take a more forthcoming attitude towards APEC was the concern that NAFTA would limit Asian access to North American markets (Hormats, 1994).
- One factor that encouraged the EU to be more accommodating in the Uruguay Round was the APEC summit meeting in Seattle that made the EU wary of closer US ties to Asia (Hormats, 1994; Kahler, 1995b).[6]
- The EU's interest in Eastern Europe after the collapse of communism encouraged Latin American states to push for their own hemispheric 'center'. Latin American leaders were particularly concerned about a diversion of foreign investments. In response to growing perceptions of the strength of European and Asian trading blocs, Latin American countries have sought to solidify ties throughout the Americas.
- The possibility of a Free Trade Area for the Americas (FTAA) has encouraged the European Union to seek closer trade ties with MERCOSUR countries. The move is also motivated by the fact that trade between the EU and Mexico fell during the 1990s – in part thanks to NAFTA. From 1993 to 1997, for example, trade between the EU and Mexico fell from 8.8% to 6.3%. From Mexico's perspective, this also opens up the possibility of being able to play off the EU and the US (*The Economist*, 1999).

(5) Greater inter-bloc cooperation has emerged as an important political dynamic. In July 1998, for example, the European Commission reported that a proposed free trade pact with MERCOSUR would lower agriculture prices leading to a cost of up to $15.6 billion a year for the EU to compensate farmers. In the case of beef, MERCOSUR prices are about half of those in the EU. After the planned enlargement of the EU to include five countries from central Europe, costs could rise another 25%. Not surprisingly, the French have been most skeptical of the FTA between the EU and MERCOSUR (Smith, 1998). This undoubtedly will lead to heated debate within the Council of Ministers.

(6) Trade blocs are also important in their interaction in the domestic political sphere. Trade blocs provide an alternative mechanism for aggregating different opinions in cooperative ways. Mexico, for example, sold NAFTA to domestic constituents (as well as foreign investors) as a way to get better access to the US market and as a way of breaking with the

stale, ineffective Mexican economic policies of the past (Kahler, 1995c: 21; see also Lynch, this volume).

Do Trade Blocs Matter? – A Matter of Perspective

The importance of trade blocs depends on the perspective of the country, firm, or politician. Almost every country around the world is now a member of some sort of regional trading arrangement, but the disparity in the size and scope of the different trade blocs suggests that only the EU and APEC, and to a lesser extent NAFTA, account for large shares of global trade. Among the small number of what could be considered 'large' trade blocs, which ones really matter? The answer depends on one's perspective and one's primary interest in the study of trade blocs. On the one hand, there is the impact of trade blocs on smaller states, particularly outside of a major trade bloc. Jamaica and other Caribbean countries, for example, have clearly felt the negative effects of being outside of NAFTA (Rohter, 1997). On the other hand, if one looks at the bigger picture – issues that affect the health of the liberal, multilateral trading system – then the sample size of relevant trade blocs is quite small. The decisions made by the EU and to a lesser extent NAFTA are the ones most likely to affect the global trading system. APEC is neither a cohesive nor highly institutionalized grouping, and none of the smaller trade blocs has either the political clout or the institutional depth to carry out significantly influential measures on their own.[7]

So, how should we judge the importance of trade blocs? Our findings are that trade blocs are significant entities and are not likely to be fads in the academic literature. How important the trade bloc phenomenon is, however, depends on the perspective of the country, the company, or even the researcher.[8] Global trade is regionalized to a certain extent, but this alone does not tell us the extent to which trade blocs matter. We can determine the degree to which trade blocs have resulted in trade creation or, more importantly, trade diversion, but we still lack guideposts for what constitutes a significant level of diversion. The work on economic trends is crucial to our endeavor, but the trade or investment data alone can not indicate whether the trends are politically relevant or not. The 1990s, as many of the above examples demonstrated, witnessed an increasing degree of trade bloc politics as countries used trade blocs for concrete or negotiating purposes. It is also important to remember that economic analyses suggest that the welfare implications of regionalism are varied across time and trade bloc. What helps account for there variations are political factors often downplayed by economists **(Mansfield** and Milner, 1999). We turn now to the matter of what explains the emergence of the most recent wave of trade regionalization.

Explaining the Emergence of Trade Blocs

There is little agreement among scholars about the importance and implications of trading blocs for the international political economy. The source of such disagreements is, of course, a function of alternative explanations for *why* trade blocs form in the first place. This section of the chapter reviews many of the competing explanations for the determinants of trade blocs. Tables 2.1 and 2.2 provide abbreviated lists of these explanations in terms of their levels of analysis. Table 2.1 focuses on the more macro levels such as global political and global economic forces. Table 2.2 lists the more micro levels which include domestic political factors, functionalism, and culture variables. The explanations at the macro level, or the 'top-down' approaches, assume that broad forces are primarily responsible for the emergence of regional trading blocs. By contrast, the 'bottom-up' approach in general assumes that local variables, domestic political, or intra-regional forces are the primary motivation for trade bloc formation.[9] The categorization method chosen here allows for a better distinction of *three* levels of analysis: domestic, intra-regional, and global. For example, Chia Siow Yue points out the *subregional* effects within ASEAN also have international ramifications (Yue, 1997). In addition, as Kerremans points out in Chapter 5 of this volume, intra-regional dynamics can ultimately influence the multilateral trading system and domestic political dynamics.

Below is a list of several other useful ways to organize the literature. There are strengths and weaknesses with each of these organizational methods; they will be discussed where appropriate in the rest of this chapter.

a. One can categorize trade blocs descriptively in terms of their level of institutionalization. Joseph Grieco, for example, compares blocs in terms of dimensions to the process of institutionalization including the locus of the institutionalization process, the scope of activity, and the level of institutional authority (Grieco, 1997: 165).[10]

b. If we assume that trade blocs are formed deliberately on the part of political leaders, then they may be formed for offensive or defensive reasons. For example, a motivation for forming a trade bloc may be to encourage or discourage free trade.[11]

c. The determinants of trade blocs may be categorized in terms of economic or political-military variables. Although most analyses of trade blocs are generally economic in orientation, some studies have highlighted the importance of political variables and military alliances in the regionalization of trade.[12]

d. One can categorize bloc members dichotomously in terms of those acting as engines of trade bloc formation (such as the US, Germany, Brazil), and those who tag along (the 'price takers' such as Canada and South Korea).[13]

e. Finally, another distinction can be made between advanced industrial countries and developing countries.[14]

Explanations for the Emergence of Trade Blocs at Higher Levels of Analysis

Classical Trade Theory and Customs Union Theory

The literature on trade blocs is, for the most part, quite recent. Classical economics, Marxist analyses, and even the interdependence literature virtually ignored the subject. The classical, liberal economic approach, for example, assumed that in a world capitalist system, economic relations will result in a division of labor that integrates all countries *on a global scale*. If there is a breakdown of an open trading system, the prediction is for a rise in protectionist, beggar-thy-neighbor policies. The possibility of various states banding together to ease the deleterious effects of a closing world economy had – until recently – received little attention. The choice was between an open system based on multilateralism or a closed (or closing) system based only on bilateralism. More promising economic work on regionalized trade has been based on Customs Union Theory which posits that when a customs union is formed, trade is both created and diverted. Internally, potential member states expect the combination of economies of scale and lowered trade barriers facilitate trade. Within such a regional trading arrangement, countries also achieve gains to trade through the reciprocal exchange of concessions on trade barriers and greater market access. Externally, the privileges to states within the union are not shared with those on the outside giving a *de facto* advantage to union members (Viner, 1961). Two recent examples of trade diversion involves NAFTA discrimination against the EU firms. First, European telecommunications equipment exporters face Mexican tariffs of 15-20% compared with tariffs of less than 5% within NAFTA. Second, European textiles and clothing exporters face a 35% tariff against zero tariffs for NAFTA-originated clothing (Crawford, 1998).

Table 2.1   Explaining Regional Trade Bloc Formation: Higher Level Analyses

---

1. Economic Explanations

- Classical Trade Theory & Customs Union Theory
- The Interdependence Approach
- Marxism and Neo-Marxism

2. Hegemonic Leadership & Military Alliances

- Global Hegemons
- Regional Hegemons
- Military Alliance Impact on Trade Flows

3. Blocs as Alternatives to Global Competition

- Blocs as Safe Havens or Temporary Shield to Global Competitive Forces
- Blocs as Tools to Force Open Closed Markets Outside of the Bloc / Securing Market Access
- Regional Arrangements as the Alternative to a Failed Multilateral System.
- Increased Diversity of GATT/WTO Membership

While an extremely valuable contribution to our understanding of trade blocs, there are limits to how far CU theory can be pushed. In the case of trade diversion, it may not matter if the amount of trade diverted is slight or is restricted to certain sectors. It also may not matter that intra-regional trade is increasing if inter-regional trade is still robust.[15] Brazil, for example, is a member of MERCOSUR,[16] but its exports to the US in 1996 (worth $9 billion) were greater than its exports to MERCOSUR, the Andean Pact countries, the Central American common market and Caricom[17] *combined* (Dyer, 1997). In general, however, CU theory has limited explanatory value for the emergence of trade blocs unless a political variant to this theory can explain how, and to what extent, trade diversion and trade creation play a role in the motivation of political actors to engage in the formation of customs unions or RTAs.

The Interdependence Approach

The traditional liberal economic approach, while helpful at explaining some of the economics of free trade areas and customs unions, does not provide a sufficient explanation for why and especially when states decide to pool their efforts instead of each going it alone or going multilateral. A similar difficulty emerges from the interdependence literature. According to Richard N. Cooper, interdependence is based on technological advances in communications and transportation which increase both the speed and reliability of moving goods, funds, persons, information and ideas across national boundaries (Cooper, 1972: 163). In theory, state autonomy diminishes as international economic links increasingly bind states' policies together. The rise of transnational actors and institutions should, presumably, also *inhibit* the development of trade blocs since it becomes impossible for one nation to sever its interdependent ties from other nations. In sum, as the literature originally formulated, interdependence over time should increase and make the possibility of protectionist policies and regional trade blocs *less* likely. This, of course, need not be the case. Interdependence could lead to a higher level of policy integration among a few countries than would be feasible on a multilateral scale. Regional arrangements thus may help countries cope better with the increasing pressures of interdependence. This issue is discussed at greater length in the section 'Blocs as the Alternatives to Global Competition' below.

Marxism and Neo-Marxist Approaches

Like classical economics and the interdependence literature, Marxist analyses were equally uninterested in the possibility of trade blocs. In the long run, the demise of capitalism was supposed to result from the struggle between the classes at the domestic level and, perhaps, by a violent revolt by the developing countries. Neither of these developments materialized. The process of communist revolution could have been facilitated by capitalist state competition, but, as with the other issues, the 'region' was never a unit of analysis. Recent efforts have been made, however, to apply neo-Marxist concepts to the emergence of trade blocs. They highlight the importance of transnational businesses and their desire, or need, for markets and sources of profit located beyond national confines.

The Marxist-influenced literature that does address trade blocs is based on several loosely connect ideas that form various 'social theories', particularly regulation theory. From a neo-Marxist perspective, regional trading blocs are the consequence of 'inherent rigidities' that have grown out of the post-War global capitalist economic system. The neo-Marxist analysis is still in its infancy and faces several challenges. Gibb and Michalak, for example, find that the countries in trade blocs are becoming the principal actors restructuring the international economy and that most countries involved in major trade blocs are using blocs to strengthen the multilateral trading system as well as the Fordist mode of international regulation (Gibb and Michalak, 1994). The regulation, post-Fordist and accumulation theories upon which the neo-Marxist arguments are built are not yet sufficiently developed – as many in this school of thought admit.

Most economic approaches, while helpful at explaining some of the economics of free trade areas and customs unions, do not provide a sufficient explanation for why and especially when states decide to pool their efforts instead of each going it alone or going multilateral. Political factors, among others, are crucial to the decision of states to form a customs union. Gowa (1994), for instance, argues that trade patterns follow military alliances. The next theoretical approach, Hegemonic Stability Theory, is often referred to because it links grand political and economic developments.

Hegemonic Leadership and the Impact of Military Alliances

In general, political scientists have done a more systematic job than scholars in other disciplines of developing the links between trade patterns and military alliances. The Cold War, for example, was a critical force in driving some countries to cooperate economically. In an effort to prevent communism from gaining a foothold in Western Europe from within and without, the US provided Marshall Plan aid and other assistance in order to shore up European economies as well as to re-establish and enhance

European and North American economic ties. This economic strategy was the accompaniment to the security strategy spearheaded by the North Atlantic Treaty Organization. Since the end of Cold War, some of the political and economic motivations for cooperation have changed or have disappeared altogether. The US and Europe still have strong ties, but in the absence of the Cold War context, the Europeans are, to some extent, freer to choose their own political-economic direction. The basic point, though, is that the political-security context should not be ignored when analyzing trade bloc dynamics.

According to Hegemonic Stability Theory (HST), a hegemonic international system is one in which a single country (the hegemon[18]) has a preponderance of military, political, and economic power and an ability to promote system-wide trade and monetary stability (Keohane, 1984). Indeed, as some argue, a liberal economic system cannot be sustained without a hegemon (Gilpin, 1987). Only a hegemon has the power, and undertakes the responsibility, to coordinate macroeconomic policies, ensure that countries facing balance-of-payments deficits will find the credit they need, and act as a lender of last resort. Although not explicit in the original formulations of HST, it is a logical extension that as the global hegemon declines in relative power, regional trading arrangements will become more attractive alternatives to unsustainable multilateralism. Trade blocs, thus, are hypothesized to increase in the phase of hegemonic decline.

There are two possible outcomes for the structure of global trade in the case of hegemonic decline. The first is what Gilpin calls 'malevolent mercantilism' which refers to the clashes of nations in the 18th century and in the interwar period of the 1920s and 1930s. The purpose of each state is to triumph over other states, and the conduct of interstate warfare is carried out by economic means (Gilpin, 1987: 404). Furthermore, 'exclusive blocs and economic alliances would signal a return to the lawlessness and beggar-thy-neighbor policies of the 1930s...International trade, monetary relations, and investment will be increasingly intra-regional. This regionalization of economic relations will replace the present American emphasis on multilateral free trade, the international role of the dollar, and the reign of the American multinational corporation' (Gilpin, 1975: 234-235). Under such conditions, regional trade blocs are supposed to become a quick and easy solution to a multitude of problems. One of the dangers of this eventuality is that in the absence of a global hegemon, *pluralistic* leadership will be required to keep the global economy open. As a result, the collective action problem becomes particularly relevant (Anderson and Blackhurst, 1993: 206-207).

The second possible outcome during a period of hegemonic decline is that of 'benign mercantilism'. In this case, a degree of protectionism safeguards the values and interests of the national society in a world characterized by the internationalization of production, global integration of financial markets, and the decline of national control. However, cooperation is achieved such that a deterioration of global economic relations does not reach the level of economic warfare. Benign mercantilism will stabilize world economic relations 'if greater regionalism is held to provide security and protection against external economic and political forces over which the nation-state acting alone has little influence or control' (Gilpin, 1975: 235). To some extent, one could argue that Europe has recently exhibited characteristics of benign mercantilism. Despite its originally inward looking Single Market program, the EU has shown preliminary efforts on two fronts to maintain a liberal economic order: efforts to improve the business (and by extension, regulatory) links with the US, and calls for a new round of WTO negotiations.[19]

The U.S. is still the world's hegemon (albeit in relative decline) and still holds the world economy together (Gilpin, 1987: 253). Despite rhetorical calls for a Common Foreign and Security Policy, Europe is still divided, and both Japan and Europe are still dependent on the U.S. for security. The challenge for the global-level version of HST is to specify which factors will lead to regional solutions and which will lead to a bilateral or more belligerent strategy in an era of declining hegemony.

A variation of the HST notion is that a *regional* hegemon may be necessary for the rise and maintenance of regional trade areas. Each trade bloc, it is postulated, hinges on the dominant strength of a regional political-economic power. The 'hub and spoke' notion parallels this idea.[20] The US is the regional hegemon for North America. In Europe, the argument is often that Germany is the hegemon. In Asia, most authors focus on the role played by Japan (see, for example, Kotkin, 1990).[21]

There are two areas in which both the global and regional hegemonic leadership theses need shoring up. First, building on the works of Gilpin, Stephen Krasner (1976), and others, Grieco's examination of the hegemonic influences on regional political and economic areas reveals that the presence of a regional hegemon is neither a necessary nor sufficient condition for the emergence of regional economic institutions. Institutionalization can be found, for example in the cases of the European Community and MERCOSUR but not in the case of the proposed East Asian Economic Community (Grieco, 1997: 174-175). Second, a complicating issue for proponents of regional hegemonic leadership is the selection of the hegemonic states. All analysts correctly assign the North American hegemonic role to the United States. In the European and Asian regions, however, analytical anomalies emerge when looking back historically or to the not-too-distant future. The choice of Japan in Asian is problematic for two reasons. First, Graham and Anzai argue that Japanese controlled affiliates in Asia are simply too small to constitute the basis for the regional hegemon expectation. Japan is also competing against a growing US corporate presence and foreign direct investment from other countries in the region as well (Graham and Anzai, 1994: 14). Second, Japan's legacy of imperialism has made potential Asian partners leery of Japan's foreign economic policy (Grant, 1993). Moreover, as China's economy and political clout grow, it will become increasingly difficult to sustain the argument that there is a single hegemon in Asia. The choice of Germany in the European case is complicated by the fact that France was to some extent the dominant political-military European player in the crucial ten or fifteen years after World War II.[22]

Trade patterns can be influenced by such things as geographic proximity (see below) and developments in the structure of a given industry. They can also be influenced by the presence of military alliances. Joanna Gowa, for instance, focuses on the influence of anarchy in the international system and the concern that countries have for their relative position in that system. In this context, states will pay serious attention to the potential impact of trade on the distribution of political and military power. In short, economic gains from trade will translate into increased military power (Gowa, 1994). Building on Gowa and others, Mansfield and Bronson argue that trade generates efficiency gains that increase the potential political-military power of states. Conversely, countries seeking to increase their power may wish to pursue regional economic arrangements. The authors compare the relative impact of preferential trade arrangements (PTAs) and bilateral and multilateral alliances. Their study shows that bilateral alliances generate more trade than multilateral alliances, but that *both types of alliances* yield greater trade than PTAs (Mansfield and Bronson, 1997: 199). The authors conclude that 'the security externalities generated by commerce create political incentives for states to trade more freely with allies than with other countries' (Ibidem: 205).

Another study that focuses on political-military variables is Grieco's work on the 'relative disparity shift' hypothesis (Grieco, 1997). Grieco contends that variation in contemporary regional institutionalization is the result of the existence of differences in the amount of change in the relative capabilities of partners in the different regions, and is the result of differences in expectations of partners in the different regions regarding the likely effects of enhanced regional institutionalization. For example, when the relative disparities in capabilities within a region shift over time, disadvantaged states will become less attracted to regional institutionalization. Grieco finds that this hypothesis is helpful, but in varying degrees, at explaining the moves toward greater institutionalization in many regions of the world.

Blocs as the Alternatives to Global Competition

Given the changing nature of international protection (from tariffs to non-tariff barriers which are harder to contend with), and the difficulties in achieving multilateral solutions, regional trade blocs are often seen as a preferred alternative to global competition. Richard V. L. Cooper considers regional trade blocs as a 'second best solution' to the 'deteriorating GATT system' (the worst being a complete breakdown of world trade).[23] In a position similar to Gilpin's, Cooper feels that regional trade blocs allow firms and governments to adjust to new realities e.g. declining hegemony. The trick for states in such a situation is to maximize the way back to a full multilateral trading system and to minimize the possibility that regional trade blocs could really hurt such a system (Cooper, 1990: 30-32). Taking a slightly different tack, Lawrence posits that all economic decisions need not be made at the multilateral level. Like the European notion of subsidiarity, he argues that 'some activities may best be carried out on a global level, others on a plurilateral level, and some may best be left to the subnational level' (Lawrence, 1996: 30). Accordingly, if a country or group of countries pursues a regionalist strategy, this does not necessarily preclude pursuing multilateral strategies as well.

Regional trade blocs may thus be useful in two potential ways. First, they may offer states a safe haven from global competition (OECD, 1995). Individual countries can also exploit economies of scale within the bloc (as Customs Union theory suggests) but without having to confront global competitive pressures (Lewis, 1990). Second, regional trade blocs may be useful in prying open other markets around the world thus contributing to a more open global trading system. An example from Latin America of a trading bloc encouraging trade liberation might be the proposed extension of MERCOSUR (Brazil, Argentina, Uruguay, and Paraguay) to Chile and Mexico. Mexico's membership, and Chile's potential membership, in NAFTA suggests a significant opening of trade throughout the Americas (Pilling and Dombey, 1996).[24]

Some have argued that the lesson of the difficulties in completing the Uruguay Round is that multilateral fora are no longer viable paths to global trade liberalization. In general, there are two major difficulties with multilateral-level negotiations. First, trade experts and politicians may end up spending scarce time and informational resources on regional agreements at the cost of multilateral agreements. These costs vary from country to country since they are driven by the domestic capacity of each country. Second, the greater the number of countries, the more difficult it can be to reach consensus. This may be due to the increased diversity of GATT/WTO membership and the different political agendas of an extremely large number of countries. Others disagree, however. Former EU Commissioner Leon Brittan has argued that it is easier to put together package deals in multilateral fora.

Explaining Trade Blocs Formation at Lower Levels of Analysis

The Relevance of Geography to Trade Bloc Formation

Geographic proximity is often viewed as a natural variable relevant to the formation of trading blocs. Nevertheless, there is considerable debate over its importance. When trade bloc analyses consider geography, two different factors are generally highlighted: shipping (or transportation) costs and costs associated with the amount of time it takes to deliver goods. A few note the 'costs of familiarity' (see below) that results from geographic distance. Transportation costs, for example, should be generally lower if the trading partners are right next door. Historical links among countries provide a related factor. Britain, for example, encouraged discriminatory trading arrangements within the British empire. In addition, at the turn of the century, Germany was concerned about being overwhelmed in a world of giant and rapidly growing empires - Russian, British and American (Kahler, 1995c: 19).

Frankel highlights two other aspects of geography. First, geography can lead to agglomeration, that is, the production of goods by many firms in a given region or country. Examples include the Silicon Valley, the auto industry in the Midwest, and the carpet industry in Georgia (Frankel, 1997: 39). Second, geographic distance seems to be one of the key factors in the decisions of firms to situate their operations and marketing on a local (national or intra-regional) level or an inter-bloc level. Frankel enlists the 'gravity model' to describe how trade between two countries is proportional to the product of their GDP and inversely related to *the distance between them* (Frankel, 1997: Chapter 4).[25]

Geopolitical concerns should also be considered important in the establishment and maintenance of trading blocs. In Europe, Germany was brought into the western European fold after World War II by embedding Germany in complex political and economic institutional structures (notably the European Coal and Steel Community and then the European Community). The West German desire to transform Germany into a 'good European' coincided with the American effort to create a strong Germany (and a strong western Europe) that could prevent communist expansion. In Asia, one of the motivating forces for cooperation has been the desire to embed China in a multilateral framework to minimize the potential for China's bilateral bullying and to ease the negative effects of bilateral tensions in general.

The power of geographic variables, however, is problematic. Bhagwati has argued the basic point that although the flag follows trade, 'trade equally follows the flag which, at least in the 19th century European expansion, was not directly across from the European nations' borders' (Balasubramanyam, 1997: 175; see also Gasiorowski, 1986). Also, one might expect that the decline in transportation costs through the advent of air travel and even global telecommunications should render geography less important than 30, 50 or 100 years ago. Gibb (1994) contends that the changing relationship between market and state and the global reach of multinational corporations render geography less and less relevant to the equation.

Table 2.2   Explaining Regional Trade Blocs: Lower Levels of Analysis

1. The Relevance of Geography

2. Functional Explanations

3. Trade Blocs as Tools of Domestic Policy

- Sectoral Demand and Governmental Supply
- The 'Tie the Hands' Hypothesis
- The 'Dirty Work' Hypothesis
- The 'Domino' Hypothesis
- Reducing the Threat of Destabilizing Immigration

4. Cultural Explanations

- Convergence of Attitudes and Values
- The Requirement of a Common Civilization
- Incorporating Cultural and Non-Cultural Variables

5. Secondary Causes of Trade Blocs

- The 'Emulation' Hypothesis
- The 'Miss the Boat' Phenomenon

6. Social Construction

Lawrence argues that neighbors may not trust each other and may have more in common with others outside the region **(Lawrence, 1996: 9)**. In addition, non-geographic determinants of trade and investment may make *distant* countries more suitable partners. It should be noted, for example, that there is more US trade with Malaysia, Singapore, and Thailand than there is with all of South America (Hormats, 1994).[26] De Melo and Panagariya (1993: 9) also note that Africa and South Asia export 95% of their goods outside their own regions. Quan Li in Chapter 4 of this volume uses the gravity model for 63 countries during 1970, 1980, 1990 and 1992 but highlights the importance of integrating an institutional analysis for a richer story about why the blocs may differ in their performance. Thompson and Reuveny (Chapter 3, this volume) add the important point that geographic propensity as conceived by gravity models does not necessarily result in malevolent trade blocs.

Functionalism

One of the hypotheses from the political science literature that has heavily influenced the debate about European integration is the notion that as economic relations become increasingly intertwined, international political institutions will emerge and deepen. Likewise, as trading ties deepen among a group of countries, the member states will become increasingly aware of remaining national policy differences and have a greater common interest in managing and perhaps accelerating that growth in intra-bloc trade through regional institutionalization. If the functional logic were correct, we would see a positive relationship between the growth of intra-regional economic interactions and efforts at regional institutionalization.

Grieco, however, finds that despite increases in intra-regional trade, there has been no consistent corresponding pattern of institutionalization among the world's trade blocs. In addition, there have even been examples of a growth in institutionalization in the absence of increased intra-regional trade (Grieco, 1997: 171-2). Another challenge to the functional explanation is that as economic integration increases, growing numbers of individuals and groups become adversely affected. Greater political cooperation is likely, but so is a backlash from those struggling to cope with economic integration and those who sense a loss of national sovereignty.

Trade Blocs as Tools of Domestic Policy

There are many domestic political arguments for the emergence of trade blocs although not as full-blown theories. This subsection of the chapter will cover several of the more prominent ones. In some cases, international institutions can lead to unexpected spillover effects; in others, such effects may proactively be created in order to influence the domestic political environment. In essence, political individuals can actively seek out international institutions to help achieve preferred domestic policies. Several domestic political hypotheses are relevant in this regard as will be discussed below.

Another explanatory factor that can partially be considered a domestic level variable is that of industry structure.[27] Helen Milner offers a political economy argument heavily influenced by new trade theory assumptions about the behavior of firms and politicians. Her basic claim is that in order to understand the recent drive for regional – as opposed to bilateral or multilateral – cooperation, particular attention should be paid to the structure of certain industries. More precisely, Milner argues that industries that exhibit increasing returns to scale (IRS) have an incentive in seeking regional trading arrangements. The regionally-oriented business interests will put pressure on political leaders who seek to satisfy a variety of constituencies, including these firms. [28] Eventually, if enough firms exhibit IRS, the government reacts to the pressure by seeking support for regional trade agreements. By contrast, firms experiencing *constant* returns to scale will tend to pressure their governments for domestic protection or multilateral liberalization, depending on their ties to the global economy (Milner, 1996: 86). If the demand for regionalism exists, political leaders, as rational, utility maximizers, will supply the regional trade arrangement. Within the regional free trade area, 'countries agree to regional trade barrier reduction because they can trade scale economies across industries (Ibidem: 79).'

Milner's argument offers two important lessons for the study of trade blocs. First, since governments are motivated differently by factors at the international level, we should expect systematic differences in trade liberalization by economic sector (Milner, 1996: 78). By extension, the international level of analysis alone can not unravel the story behind the diversity in regional trading relationships around the world. Second, Milner's model has good predictive capability regarding the future of regional trading blocs. 'As certain types of industrial structures become more prevalent globally, firms in these sectors will increasingly *demand*, and states will be more willing to *supply*, regional trade arrangements'

(Milner, 1996: 79). It should also be mentioned that the sectoral approach can also help explain why certain major exceptions exist to otherwise open regional arrangements e.g. the EU's Common Agricultural Policy.[29] The key challenge for this approach is explaining why multinational corporations prefer regional and not global solutions. While Milner admits her study is incomplete regarding this issue, she does suggest that imperfect competition can lead firms to follow second or third-best solutions – that is, not the best solution of global free trade.

The 'tie the hands' hypothesis posits that domestic politicians wish to undertake important economic reforms *through regional means* which may not be politically popular back home. The strategy of a national politician is to commit his country to an international organization which assists in 'imposing' the politically unpopular economic measures. When faced with opposition at home over austerity or other unpopular measures, the politician can then claim that his *hands are tied* saying 'the regional institutions require that we take these steps.'[30] Another variation of this theme is the idea that regional trading arrangements provide external credibility for unpopular domestic programs. This observation is important because it suggests that political systems that permit effective domestic opposition will be more likely to seek external credibility than authoritarian or single party governments (Kahler, 1995b).[31] Using what he calls the 'dirty work' hypothesis, Roland Vaubel contends that international agencies are willing to take any work they can get, 'however unpleasant or unimportant' it may be. For a variety of reasons, national politicians can benefit from this situation by passing on dirty work (writ unpopular economic reforms) to these task-seeking international agencies. By doing so, politicians may avoid domestic criticism for policies that they actually prefer. In other words, international agencies help 'immunize' national politicians against the negative effects resulting from unpopular measures (Vaubel, 1986).[32]

The proposed NAFTA, for example, was used to alter the perceptions of domestic and foreign investors about the merits of the Mexican economy. NAFTA was sold as a way to get better access to the US market and as a way of 'confirming a break with the past,' less effective Mexican economic policies (Kahler, 1995c: 21). This issues is taken up by Lynch in Chapter 8 of this volume. Presently, in the European Union, one could argue that politicians are using the European single currency issue as a way to impose strict macro-economic policies that will benefit their countries in the long run.[33] Without reference to the regional institutions and the benefits and obligations that come with membership, such controversial policies would not be feasible in a hostile domestic political climate. A similar argument has been made with respect to Columbia and Venezuela's decision in 1991 to reinvigorate the Andean Pact. Eichengreen and Frankel (1995: 101) state that politicians in these countries found the Andean Pact a useful and 'politically easy' was to dismantle protectionist barriers 'to an extent that their domestic legislatures would never have allowed had the policy not been pursued in a regional context.'

There are other implications for the interaction of domestic politics and trade bloc dynamics. It has been argued that in early 1999, Paraguay came under heavy pressure from its neighbors as well as its fellow MERCOSUR member states to avoid a military solution to the political crisis that erupted after the arrest of a former general and the resignation of President Raúl Cubas. Faced with the prospects of a suspension from MERCOSUR, the ruling elite chose to adhere more or less to constitutional procedures (*Financial Times*, 1999).

Another line of thought emphasizes the institutional structures of states. It is not far-fetched to assume that countries with similar institutional frameworks should find it easier to coordinate economic policies. The European Union comes to mind as a primary example, and the absence of greater regionalism in Asia suggests the same point from the opposite angle. There are obviously other factors involved as the case of Mexico in NAFTA illustrates. This overall issue is treated by Quan Li in Chapter 4 of this volume.

Another domestic politics-based argument that rejoins the notion of 'trade bloc politics' mentioned in earlier in this chapter is the 'domino hypothesis'. According to Richard Baldwin, the current wave of regionalism results from two idiosyncratic events in the Americas and in Europe (Baldwin, 1993: 2-4). First, the 1990 FTA between the US and Mexico was an outgrowth of a radical change in Mexico's economic philosophy. When Canada got wind of the growing cooperation between the US and Mexico, it too wanted to take part, and NAFTA was born. The Canada domino could not fall before the Mexican domino, as evidenced by the limited support for the prior US-Canada FTA. Second, the European Union's plans for expansion to include the EFTA countries eclipsed the rationale for the European Economic Area (EEA), as countries wished to join the EU instead.[34] The desire for EU membership now extends to more dominos – the countries of central and eastern Europe, particularly Poland, Hungary and the Czech Republic.

Yet another domestic political reason for forming trade blocs may be to reduce the threat of destabilizing effects from immigration (Ireland, 1991). In order to forestall social unrest and threats to welfare systems, governments in the advanced industrial countries have an interest in encouraging stable regional environments for fear of uncontrollable immigration (Hormats, 1994). It is unlikely, however, that this variable is more important than the others mentioned thus far since there is virtually no supporting evidence.

The primary challenge for each of these variations on a domestic political theme is to be able to explain why a regional institution rather than a global one is selected by politicians. The dynamic expressed by each of the approaches is equally plausible at the multilateral level. National political leaders could just as conceivably say that their hands are tied by IMF or WTO rules, for example.

Explaining Trade Blocs with Cultural Factors

For the most part, trade bloc analyses are strongly grounded in economic and political developments. In a few cases, cultural variables are brought to bear in the causal explanations of trade blocs. In one particular case, the creation of NAFTA can be understood in the context of converging attitudes and values among its member states. Inglehart, Nevitte, and Basañez (1996) argue that the attitudes of American, Canadian, and Mexican societies towards a wide range of issues are converging and that we might even expect to see greater acceptance of further political integration in the future. The authors demonstrate how attitudes have narrowed among the US, Canada, and Mexico toward sexual permissiveness/restrictiveness, respect for authority and individual autonomy, family duty and independence, religiosity/secularity and civil permissiveness/order. Along similar lines – and following this cultural idea to its logical conclusion – Samuel Huntington suggests that economic regionalism may only work where the members of a trade bloc have a common civilization (Huntington, 1995: 181).

Several avenues of research are required in order for such cultural approaches to be accepted by those who study regional trade blocs from a different angle. Where cultural variables are hypothesized to be causal determinants of trade blocs, critics will need to be convinced that cultural convergence is more important than political-economic behavior. In addition, notions such as 'communal identity' and 'common civilization' are very difficult to pin down. Huntington, for instance, fails to account for how significant clashes have occurred *within* civilizations. The literature on trade blocs would be duly enriched by analytical frameworks that successfully account for *both* political-economic and psychological-cultural factors, assuming both categories of variables are significant.

Typically, though, cultural variables are more likely to be assigned secondary importance. Miles Kahler (1995b) among others, has pointed out, for example, that Asian members in APEC are averse to formal institutions and legally binding obligations. Does this explain APEC's extremely low level of institutional development, or are other factors equally or more important? Others have described how some of the trade friction between the US and the EU reflects differing regulatory traditions (Vogel, 1997). A few analysts have tried to model such factors into their otherwise econometric models. Frankel provides a rare example of situating cultural variables among the more 'objective' variables. Borrowing from Hans Linnemann and others, Frankel explores the 'costs of unfamiliarity' of doing business with or in foreign countries. Linnemann characterizes this cost as the 'psychic distance' or the familiarity (or lack thereof) with another country's laws, institutions, habits, and languages as an important part of marketing.[35] The 'gravity model' is a rare example of how cultural factors are systematically incorporated into a statistical model, but again, it does not push the cultural analysis as far as it could go. At this stage of development in the trade bloc literature, just how valuable these factors are remains underexplored. A more developed theoretical basis needs to be established in order to situate the importance of cultural factors among the many others.

Secondary Causes

Most researchers appear to be interested in the factors that create trade blocs initially. A few focus on developments that occur after this initial step. The 'emulation hypothesis', for instance, suggests that some countries are motivated to seek closer regional political-economic ties because of the perceived success of other trade blocs. The success of the EU, for example, encouraged interest in trade blocs in other parts of the world. Likewise, the EU and NAFTA helped spark interests in APEC. Another secondary cause that influences the membership of trade blocs is the 'miss the boat' phenomenon. Countries not already in trade blocs often worry that the benefits of membership will not be granted to outsiders. There is the obvious fear of trade diversion as well as the concern that foreign investors will find 'outsider countries' less attractive.[36]

Social Constructed Trade Blocs

Contrary to political realist or international economic interpretations which assume some sort of objective political or economic existence of trade blocs, social constructivists argue that trade blocs are the subjective creation of human thinking. It is only after the elite and the public assume a sense of communal or regional identity that a trade bloc comes into existence. A sense of communal or bloc identity may be enhanced by a common language and a shared culture which help regional groups cohere and deepen (Kupchan, 1997: 211). In short, a 'region is conceived of, then it comes to exist' (Kupchan, 1997).[37] If, for example, US political and economic leaders socially construct a world in which they *believe* the US must confront Asia and the EU 'head to head', trade blocs will be more likely to emerge. In this sense, thinking about trade blocs becomes a self-fulfilling prophesy. Such an approach renders economic developments secondary to perceptions about, or rather conceptions of, trade blocs.

Most analysts of trade blocs and European politics in particular should recall the fears expressed in the popular media after the passage of the Single European Act in 1987. More than anywhere, it seemed, the media spoke of a Fortress Europe. After the initial discussions of trade cooperation in North America, there were even more warnings about the emergence of belligerent trade blocs even though the most discernible existence of trade blocs was reflected in economic statistics – which, as noted above, are only partial indicators. It did appear that the elite and the public (via the media) had come to conceive of the world as heading in the direction of harmful regionalized trading blocs.[38] It is possible that fear of (writ the conception of) trade blocs *preceded* their more concrete political and economic forms.

Social construction might also be at work in the minds of opponents of trade blocs; this would be a *consequence* of trade blocs. In the case of NAFTA, for example, US public support appears to be waning – but not because of overwhelming economic problems associated with the trade agreement. Whether grounded in actual developments or not, the growing public perception is that NAFTA is hurting the US economy. It is possible that negatively impacted interest groups in the US are propagating – that is, constructing – this perception for the benefit of their own agenda. One possible result is that people's socially constructed expectations about the effects of trade blocs could lead them to underestimate the gains from free trade in general (Knetter, 1998). This example does not address trade bloc formation per se; but it is possible that socially constructed notions could be brought to bear in a national political debate between supporters and opponents of eventual trade bloc membership.

If trade blocs are indeed a form of social construction, and not simply reflecting economic trends, then we need to understand how these perceptions impact on the issue economic policies. For example, was the idea of a Fortress Europe a socially constructed concept or simply a reaction by people to objective developments in European integration in particular and the global economy in general? The jury is still out. Critics will thus need to be convinced that the causal arrow leads from the intangible concept to the more concrete existence of government policies and corporate behavior. At present, there is not much evidence to work with.

Conclusions

This chapter has critiqued and categorized many theoretical approaches to our understanding of trade blocs. This field of study is an emerging one with a bright research future. The insights from several academic disciplines highlight the complexity of the topic as well as the disagreements over basic issues. This chapter has argued that an analysis of economic trends alone will only yield a few clues about the importance of, and explanation for, trade blocs. The inclusion of trade bloc politics is needed to confirm the growing regionalism of contemporary international relations. At the risk of losing parsimony, it is argue that a better understanding of trade blocs can be achieved by integrating a broader variety of approaches and variables.

As this chapter has described, trade blocs can matter in many ways. They may, for example, be relevant to countries or firms on the outside of a bloc, and they may influence the global trading system in positive and negative ways. Contrary to the perception in much of the media, the regionalization of trade need not be a dangerous trend. For example, the OECD has argued that regional integration agreements have gone hand in hand with a globalization of trade and investment (OECD, 1995: 25-26). In addition, in the US-EU relationship, there are indicators that both Europeans and North Americans are working toward establishing more liberal policies between them – on a sectoral basis as well as on a regulatory basis.[39] Based on the many approaches reviewed in this paper, Table 2.3 provides a list of some of the major ways in which trade blocs may be used as instruments of foreign and domestic policy.[40]

Table 2.3   Trade Blocs as Instruments of Foreign and Domestic Policy

Trade blocs may be used for the following reasons:

1. To achieve traditional trade gains.

2. To build permanent or temporary shields from global competition.

3. To gain greater market access in other countries or blocs or to avoid local content requirements imposed by local (regional) governments.

4. To provide insurance in case of a failure of the multilateral trading system.

5. To further national security goals that favor allies and hurt enemies.

6. To increase multilateral bargaining power.

7. To make politically difficult domestic policies more palatable.

A lesson from this literature survey is that the levels of analysis problem weighs heavily on the trade blocs research agenda. Mainstream economists, neo-Marxists, and proponents of different versions of Hegemonic Stability Theory focus on systemic forces and do not generally admit domestic political arguments. The sub-global arguments will, of course, be criticized for not taking into account the supposedly grander forces that determine lower level variables. And neither of these approaches seems to pay much attention to the internal political and institutional dynamics of trade blocs. As with most topics, the starting assumptions made by the authors will drive the direction of the research.

The top-down versus bottom-up distinction between the determinants of trade bloc formation raises a critical obstacle to an overall theory of trade blocs. There may be, as most trade bloc analyses tacitly indicate, important idiosyncratic factors that determine trade bloc formation and, ultimately, maintenance. If this is so, theory building is all the more difficult since such factors are hard to control for or predict. Jeffrey Frankel's fine analysis of the recent interest in trade blocs is highly instructive of—although not unique to—this theoretical challenge.

Frankel presents four *independent* developments in different parts of the world that explain the recent moves towards greater regionalization of trade (Frankel, 1997). The first was the European Union's Single European Act of the late 1980s. A second development was a reversal in US philosophy in favor of a regional approach in the wake of European resistance to multilateralism. Third, business leaders in Canada felt that the Canadian market was too small to exploit economies of scale; they then pressured the Canadian government to enter into talks with the US. The fourth development was the abandonment of import substitution industrialization measures by countries in the developing world. The latter development was a response to the perceived success of the East Asian NICs and the collapse of the Soviet Union. In this retrospect, we may understand these developments, and we may be able to establish their causal links with the emergence of trade blocs. However, we do not as yet have a theory of either economics or politics (domestic or international) that can predict such dynamics in the future. Few predicted, for example, the financial crisis in Asia, and serious researchers must wait until the dust settles before declaring what consequences it will have on the development of an Asian trading bloc. Perhaps the problem of idiosyncratic factors is the greatest challenge facing a general theory of trade bloc formation and maintenance.

Notes

[1] Serra et al. make a similar point (Serra, 1997: 20).
[2] There are many possibilities; small firms on the outside of a bloc will have one perspective, large countries dominating a bloc will have another, etc.
[3] Not all EU countries are enthusiastic about an EU-US FTA. France, for example is concerned that such a bilateral approach will hinder multilateral efforts. More important for France is the threat that such talks would result in unfavorable decisions regarding two very sensitive sectors in France: agriculture and audio-visual services.
[4] See, also, Kahler (1995b), Vogel (1997), and the American Institute for Contemporary German Studies (1997) for more extensive discussions of the US-EU relationship.

[5] The timing of the GATT talks failure and George Bush's 'Enterprise for the Americas' initiative is surefire proof, according to Jagdish Bhagwati, 'that American regionalism is here to stay whether the GATT talks succeed or fail' (Bhagwati, 1990; see also *The Economist*, 1991).

[6] John Whalley also addresses this issue in terms of 'multilateral and regional interplay' (Whalley, 1996: 19-20).

[7] In general, as Robert Z. Lawrence puts it, 'the rules of the game are determined in the United States [not NAFTA] and the EU and do not reflect the needs or wishes of others' (Lawrence, 1996: 3).

[8] Some may wish to focus on smaller countries or small blocs while others focus on the major players who are most likely to affect the multilateral trading system.

[9] It is not always easy to keep the levels of analysis straight. For example, Hegemonic Stability Theory (HST) suggests, on the one hand, that at the global level in an international system with a declining hegemon, regional trading arrangements should become more likely. On the other hand, HST can also be adapted to imply that a *regional* hegemon is required for the emergence of a trading bloc: the US in the case of North America, Japan in Asia, and Germany in Europe. So, in the former case, we use a global level variable; in the latter, we use a regional level variable. Grieco (1997) makes the regional-level HST argument, albeit under the name 'hegemonic leadership theory'.

[10] See also Kahler (1995a: 1-21), Whalley (1996), and the appendices in Lawrence (1996).

[11] According to Bhagwati, for example, 'the enthusiasm for regional free trade areas is dressed up as a great   free trade move. But it is evident that the main motivation is protectionist: Mexico becomes America's preferential market, with Japan and the EC at a disadvantage. Surely the relatively lukewarm enthusiasm among most American business groups for the Uruguay Round – as compared to passionate support for the North American Free Trade Agreement – can be attributed in large part to the fact that any advantages America gains under GATT are equally doled out to rivals in the EC and Japan, while under NAFTA they flow asymmetrically to the United States' (Bhagwati, 1993).

[12] See, for example, Gowa (1994) and Mansfield and Bronson (1997).

[13] In the case of NAFTA, an exception is acknowledged because of Mexico's original suggestion about forming NAFTA.

[14] Kahler, for example, argues that in the 1950s Third World countries showed interest in regionalism because of its perceived ability to improve market size for import substituting industrialization (Kahler, 1995). Such an argument would not, of course, be relevant for the advanced industrial societies.

[15] Of course, 'robust trade' is also a relative expression.

[16] MERCOSUR consists of Brazil, Argentina, Paraguay, and Uruguay.

[17] Caricom, the Caribbean Community, consists of over 15 countries – islands for the most part – including Jamaica, Antigua, Guyana, and St. Lucia.

[18] 'Hegemony' is a Greek word meaning political leadership (Gilpin, 1987: 66).

[19] With respect to a new WTO round, the Commission's chief trade spokesman, Leon Brittan, argued that the US was abandoning its international free trade leadership role (de Jonquières, 1996).

[20] The hub and spoke notion sometimes refers specifically to a series of *bilateral* arrangements negotiated between the hub country and smaller states.

[21] For discussions of Japan's role in Asia, see many of the individual chapters in Frankel and Kahler (1997).

[22] For an extended discussion of Germany as the potential regional hegemon in Europe, see Grieco (1997: 179-183.)

[23] See also Lipsey and Lancaster (1956). The deterioration of the GATT system, alluded to by Cooper, is debatable. With the completion of the Uruguay Round, it appears that the WTO agenda makes the former-GATT system quite robust as it lowers more trade barriers and addresses many new areas.

[24] Another example, albeit a dead one, is the Transatlantic Free Trade Area (TAFTA) first proposed by Klaus Kinkel in 1995. In theory, TAFTA was also to be used as a lever to open up markets globally and would be open to all who wanted to join it (Norman, 1996).

[25] Mansfield and Bronson (1997) also make use of the gravity model.

[26] Hormats goes on to point out that geography plays a role in subregional trade links across national borders. Examples include: Saxony, Bohemia and Silesia, Hong Kong, South Korea, and the coastal Chinese provinces, the Pacific Northwest and British Columbia, Singapore and Indonesia's Riau archipelago and Malaysia's southern state of Johore.

[27] This variable highlights the value in breaking the commonly held assumption of trade blocs as unitary actors.

[28] Political leaders are assumed to be utility-maximizers, and utility comes from remaining in office, not from pursuing a particular trade policy. Politicians are also motivated by tariff revenues, and consumer surplus which is ultimately felt at the ballot box (Milner, 1996: 86-7).

[29] Indeed, Malcolm Rifkind, UK foreign secretary in 1996, argued that the 'politics of bedlam, the politics of Fortress Europe' were leading to tough curbs on Eastern European farm exports to the EU (Clark, 1996).

[30] This hypothesis is not restricted to international organizations. Although it is still too early to make judgments about the Asian crisis, there is preliminary evidence that national political leaders have 'used' foreign investors to make politically unpopular decisions back home e.g. making companies that borrow money say so publicly. Foreigners who previously could only take out a 26% stake in a Korean company can now buy companies outright. As the *New York Times* put it, Korean President Kim Dae Jung 'declared war on the Korean social structuring and is using foreign financiers as his howitzer (Lewis, 1998: 41).'

[31] The type of political system involved may be important. For example, German Chancellor Helmut Kohl remarked after the Socialist victory in the 1997 French election that it had 'shown how difficult it is to introduce the necessary reforms in a country through the democratic process.' (Owen and Jack, 1997).

[32] According to this Rational Choice approach, the relationship between member states and regional institutions is a division of labor between international agencies and national politicians. For Vaubel, this division of labor is a function of the *demand* for powers from the international agencies and the *supply* of powers from national governments. Support for the European Monetary System (EMS) by the German government can be explained as the attempt to get around the powerful Bundesbank. The international agency (the EU's EMS) allowed national (German) politicians to achieve preferred policies that would have otherwise been politically costly back home. Pedro Schwartz argued, for example, that an

early completion of monetary union in the EU 'would force Spain to control public spending and get rid of its inflationary habits' (Schwartz, 1996).
[33] With respect to the EMU, Wayne Sandholtz (1993) argues that one reason many EU governments supported EMU was to impose strict monetary policies that couldn't be imposed domestically. If voters grow unhappy with monetary decisions, national politicians can claim that their hands are tied by the regional EMU system.
[34] This is not true for all countries, however. For example, the Norwegian government under Gro Harlmem Brundlandt, opted for EU membership, but the Norwegian population rejected it in a referendum in 1994.
[35] See Frankel (1997), Chapter 3, especially pp. 45-6.
[36] This is sometimes referred to as the 'snowball effect' since a relatively small movement toward regional integration builds momentum and size encompassing more and more countries.
[37] Charles A. Kupchan makes this argument in a discussion of European regional security arrangements. Although Jagdish Bhagwati does not explicitly make this argument, the following quote may be interpreted as a demonstration of the effects of social construction. 'As long as the talk of 'head to head' confrontation with the EC and Japan drives U.S. policy – with its zero-sum implication that their success means America's failure – Washington will move toward preferential trading arrangements' (Bhagwati, 1993).
[38] I know of no study that has tracked the thoughts (writ concerns) of the public and public officials over time, but it is my sense that academics took up the idea *afterwards*.
[39] It is too early, however, to assess the real impact of this nascent transatlantic political and business 'dialogue'.
[40] See also Whalley (1996) who looks specifically (albeit briefly) at why countries seek regional trade agreements, and the OECD (1995).

References

American Institute for Contemporary German Studies (1997), *The Limits of Liberalization: Regulatory Cooperation and the New Transatlantic Agenda*, Johns Hopkins University Press, Washington, DC.

Anderson, K., and Blackhurst, R. (eds) (1993), *Regional Integration and the Global Trading System*, St. Martin's Press, New York.

Anderson, K. and Norheim, H. (1993), 'Is world trade becoming more regionalized?', *Review of International Economics*, vol. 1, pp. 91-109.

Axline, W.A. (ed) (1994), *The Political Economy of Regional Cooperation*, Pinter Publishers, London.

Balasubramanyam, V.N. (1997), *Jagdish Bhagwati: Writings on International Economics*, Oxford University Press, Oxford.

Balasubramanyam, V.N. and Greenaway, D. (1992), 'Economic Integration and Foreign Direct Investment: Japanese Investment in the EC', *Journal of Common Market Studies*, vol. 30, no. 2, pp. 175-193.

Baldwin, R. (1993), 'A Domino Theory of Regionalism', *Working Paper* No. 4465, National Bureau of Economic Development, Inc., Cambridge, MA.

Bhagwati, J. (1990), 'Regional Accords Be-Gatt Trouble for Free Trade', *Wall Street Journal*, 5 December.

Bhagwati, J. (1993), 'The Diminished Giant Syndrome: How Declinism Drives Trade Policy', *Foreign Affairs*, vol. 72, no. 2, pp. 22-6.

Belous, R. (1990), 'U.S. Economic Policy in a World of Regional Trading Blocs', in J. P. Hardt and Y. C. Kim (eds) *Economic Cooperation in the Asia-Pacific Region*, Westview Press, Boulder.

Bergsten, C.F. (1996), 'Competitive Liberalization and Global Free Trade: A Vision for the Early 21st Century', *APEC Working Paper 96-15*, Institute for International Economics, Washington, DC.

Clark, B. (1996), 'Trade Policies of "Fortress Europe" attacked', *Financial Times*, 12 June.

Cooper, R. (1972), 'Economic Interdependence and Foreign Policy in the Seventies', *World Politics*, vol. 24, no. 2, pp. 159-181.

Cooper, V.L., Belous, R. and Hartley, J. (eds) (1990), *The Rise of Regional Trading Blocs in the Global Economy*, National Planning Association, Washington, DC.

Crawford, L. (1998), 'Mexico and EU start talks on free trade accord', *Financial Times*, 15 July.

Dyer, G. (1997), 'US confident over talks for hemisphere free trade area', *Financial Times*, 15 May.

The Economist (1999), 'Reviving the European connection', 26 June.

The Economist (1989), 'Fortress, read trade laboratory' in *Supplemental Survey*, 7 July.

Eichengreen, B. and Frankel, B. (1995), 'Economic Regionalism: Evidence from Two Twentieth-Century Episodes', *North American Journal of Economics and Finance*, Vol. 7, n° 2, pp. 89-106.

Financial Times (1999), 'After Cubas', Editorial, 30 March.

Frankel, J.A. (1991), 'Is a Yen Bloc Forming in Pacific Asia?' in R. O'Brien (ed) *Finance and the International Economy*, Oxford University Press, London, pp. 4-21.

Frankel, J.A. (1997), *Regional Trading Blocs in the World Economic System*, Institute for International Economics, Washington, DC.

Gasiorowski, M. (1986), 'Economic interdependence and international conflict: Some cross-national evidence', *International Studies Quarterly*, November, pp. 23-38.

Gibb, R. (1994), 'Regionalism in the World Economy?' in R. Gibb and W. Michalak (eds) *Continental Trading Blocs*, John Wiley and Sons, Chichester, pp. 1-36.

Gibb, R. and Michalak, W. (eds) (1994), *Continental Trading Blocs*, John Wiley and Sons, Chichester.

Gilpin, R. (1975), *U.S. Power and the Multinational Corporation*, Basic Books, Inc. Publishers, New York.

Gilpin, R. (1987), *The Political Economy of International Relations*, Princeton University Press, Princeton, NJ.

Graham, E.M. and Anzai, N.T. (1994), 'The Myth of a De Facto Asian Economic Bloc: Japan's foreign direct investment in East Asia', *The Columbia Journal of World Business,* vol. 29, no. 3, pp. 6-20.

Grieco, J.M. (1996), 'Systemic Sources of Variation in Regional Institutionalization in Western Europe, East Asia, and the Americas', in *The Political Economy of Regionalism*, Columbia University Press, New York, pp. 164-187.

Gowa, J. (1994), *Allies, Adversaries, and International Trade*, Princeton University Press, Princeton, NJ.

Graham, R. and M. Smith, M. (1998), 'France and US initial air pact', *Financial Times*, 9 April.

Grant, R. (1993), 'Trading blocs or trading blows: The macro-economic geography of U.S. and Japanese trade policies', *Environment and Planning.* vol. 25, pp. 273-91.

Hine, R. (1992), 'Regionalism and the Integration of the World Economy', *Journal of Common Market Studies,* vol. 30, no. 2, pp. 115-123.

Hormats, R. (1994), 'Making Regionalism Safe', *Foreign Affairs*, vol. 10, March/April.

Huntington, S.P. (1995), 'The Clash of Civilizations . Or, the West against the Rest', in Charles W. Kegley, Jr. and Eugene R. Wittkopf (eds), *The Global Agenda: Issues and Perspectives 4th ed*, McGraw-Hill, Inc., New York, pp. 179-182.

Inglehart, R., Nevitte, N., and Basañez, M. (1996), *The North American Trajectory: Cultural, Economic, and Political Ties among the United States, Canada and Mexico*, Aldine de Gruyter Press, New York.

Ireland, P. (1991), 'Facing the True "Fortress Europe": Immigrants and Politics in the EC', *Journal of Common Market Studies*, vol. 29, no. 5, pp. 457-480.

de Jonquières, G. 1996), 'EU embraces the cause of free trade', *Financial Times*, 6 August.

de Jonquières, G. (1998), 'European Commission's transatlantic trade initiative clears first political hurdle', *Financial Times*, 12 March.

Kahler, M. (1995a), *International Institutions and the Political Economy of Integration*, The Brookings Institution, Washington, DC.

Kahler, M. (1995b), *Regional Futures and Transatlantic Economic Relations*, European Community Studies Association, New York.

Kahler, M. (1995c), 'A World of Blocs: Facts and Factoids', *World Policy Journal*, vol. 12, no. 1, pp. 19-27.

Keohane, R. (1984), *After Hegemony: Cooperation and Discord in the World Political Economy*, Princeton University Press, Princeton, NJ.

Kotkin, J. (1990), 'With U.S. Looking other Way, Asia Goes Its Own Way', *Los Angeles Times*, 17 February.

Knetter, M. (1998), 'Free trade: why the public is unconvinced', Mastering Global Business supplement, *Financial Times*, 3 April.

Krasner, S. (1976), 'State Power and the Structure of International Trade', *World Politics*, vol. 28, no. 3, pp. 317-348.

Kupchan, C.A. (1996), 'Regionalizing Europe's Security: The Case for a New Mitteleuropa', in *The Political Economy of Regionalism*, Columbia University Press, New York, pp. 209-238.

Lapper, R. and Warn, K. (1999), 'Brazilian currency turmoil buffets Mercosur', *Financial Times*, 12 February.

Lawrence, R.Z. (1996), *Regionalism, Multilateralism and Deeper Integration*, Brookings Institution, Washington, DC.

Lewis, W.H. (1990), 'European Community: A Looming Challenge', in J. P. Hardt and Y.C. Kim (eds) *Economic Cooperation in the Asia-Pacific Region*, Westview Press, Boulder.

Lipsey, R.G. and Lancaster, K. (1956), 'The General Theory of Second Best', *Review of Economic Studies* vol. 24, pp. 11-32.

Mason, M. (1994) 'Elements of Consensus: Europe's Response to the Japanese Automotive Challenge', *Journal of Common Market Studies* , vol. 32, no. 4, pp. 433-453.

Mansfield, E., Bronson, R. (1996), 'The Political Economy of Major Power Trade Flows', in E. Mansfield and H. Milner (eds), *The Political Economy of Regionalism*, Columbia University Press, New York, pp. 188-208.

Mansfield, E. and Milner, H. (eds) (1996), *The Political Economy of Regionalism*, Columbia University Press, New York.

Mansfield, E. and Milner, H. (1999), 'The New Wave of Regionalism', *International Organization*, vol. 53, no. 3, Summer 1999, pp. 589-627.

de Melo, J. and Panagariya, A. (1993), 'Introduction', in J. de Melo and A. Panagariya (eds) *New Dimensions in Regional Integration*, Cambridge University Press, Cambridge, pp. 1-21.

Michalak, W. (1994), 'The political economy of trading blocs', in R. Gibb W. Michalak (eds) *Continental Trading Blocs*, John Wiley and Sons, Chichester, pp. 37-72.

Milner, H. (1996), 'Industries, Governments, and the Creation of Regional Trade Blocs', in *The Political Economy of Regionalism*, Columbia University Press, New York, pp. 77-106.

Norman, P. (1996), 'Perils of a transatlantic alliance', *Financial Times*, 14 October.

OECD (1995), *Regional Integration and the Multilateral Trading System: Synergy and Divergence*, Organization for Economic Cooperation and Development, Paris.

O'Loughlin, J. and Anselin, L. (1996), 'Geo-economic competition and trade bloc formation: United States, German, and Japanese exports, 1968-1992', *Economic Geography*, vol. 72, no. 2, pp. 131-161.

Owen, D. and Andrew, J. (1997), 'Jospin cool on Maastricht', *Financial Times*, 3 June.

Piening, C. (1997), *Global Europe: The European Union in World Affairs*, Lynne Rienner Publishers, Boulder.

Pilling, D. and Dombey, D. (1996), 'Mexico enters talks with Mercosur group', *Financial Times*, 25 October.

Preeg, E. (1974), *Economic Blocs and U.S. Foreign Policy*, National Planning Association, Washington, DC.

Preeg, E. (1992), 'U.S. leadership in world trade: Past, present, future', *Washington Quarterly*, vol. 15, pp. 81-91.

Revzin, P. (1990), 'Japanese Systematically Invest in Europe Prior to 1992 Changes', *Wall Street Journal*, 10 December.

Rohter, L. (1997), 'Backlash from Nafta Batters Economies of the Caribbean', *New York Times*, 30 January.

Sandholtz, W. (1993), 'Choosing Union: Monetary Politics and Maastricht', *International Organization*, vol. 47, no. 1, pp. 1-39.

Schwarts, N. (1996), 'Emu as quack remedy', *Financial Times*, 23 October.

Serra, J. et al. (1997), *Reflections on Regionalism*, Carnegie Endowment for International Peace, Washington, DC.

Smith, M. (1998), 'Mercosur pact would cost EU $15 billion', *Financial Times*, 17, July.

Smith, M. and Buckley, M. (1998), 'France to oppose EU-Mercosur pact', *Financial Times*, 16 July.

Southey, C. (1997), 'EU under fire for trade pact proliferation', *Financial Times*, 16 February.

U.S. General Accounting Office (1990), *European Single Market: Issues of Concern to U.S. Exporters*, Washington, DC.

Vaubel, R. (1986), 'A public choice approach to international organization', *Public Choice* vol. 51, pp. 39-57.

Viner, J. (1961), *The Customs Union Issue*, Garland Press, Inc., New York.

Vogel, D. (1997), *Barriers or Benefits? Regulation in Transatlantic Trade*, Brookings Institutions Press, Washington, DC.

Whalley, J. (1996), 'Why Do Countries Seek Regional Trade Agreements?' *Working Paper No. 5552*, National Bureau of Economic Research, Inc., Cambridge, MA.

Wolffe, R. (1998), 'EU-US antitrust pact will cut market access disputes', *Financial Times*, 9 June.

Yue, C.S. (1997), 'Regionalism and Subregionalism in ASEAN: The Free Trade Area and Growth Triangle Models', in T. Ito and A. Krueger (eds), *Regionalism versus Multilateral Trade Arrangements*, University of Chicago Press, Chicago, pp. 275-312.

3 Trade, Regionalization, and Tariffs: The Correlates of Openness in the American Long Run

RAFAEL REUVENY AND WILLIAM R. THOMPSON

It is often assumed that regional trading blocs and protectionism go hand in hand. When you encounter regional trading blocs, you should also expect to find increased protectionism. We think this assumption is at the very least highly dubious. Regionalism in trade need not always imply increased protectionism. By focusing on NAFTA within the longer-term context of US trading patterns, we evaluate some of the nascent domestic implications of the ongoing North American experiment. Our conclusion squares with those of others in the sense that the domestic impacts, especially in terms of its potential for trade diversion, have been less than great. Next, we turn to the longer-term empirical relationships among tariff levels, trade regionalization, and trade openness. We find that in the US historical case, these variables are less inter-correlated than is frequently imagined. In general, then, the emerging North American regional trading bloc has not led to a noticeable increase in protectionism or a decrease in trade openness. That need not be the case forever, but, in the interim, we need to reexamine some of our instinctive assumptions about international political economy processes. The unqualified equation of greater trade regionalization and less trade openness does not appear to be particularly valid.

Some Preliminary Expectations About Trade Regionalization and NAFTA

The formation of regional trade blocs – or the tendency to trade more within a specific geographical region – may be thought to be a relatively new phenomenon. In the late 1980s and 1990s, seemingly in emulation of the formerly, relatively unique, European common market, regional free trade areas (FTAs) proliferated around the world. In 1994, the agreement creating the North American Free Trade Area (NAFTA) was signed by Canada, Mexico, and the United States (US). Yet it was only one of several new arrangements, joining others in South America (Mercosur), the Pacific Rim (APEC), and anticipating the creation of other arrangements in the Caribbean, Central America, Africa, and the Middle East.[1]

The potentially alarming aspect of these regional trade pacts is the potential that they have for recreating a world economy divided into exclusive trading zones, with each dominated by one of the major economies (i.e., Germany, the US, and Japan). We have seen such arrangements before. Mercantilistic policy preferences led to the development of exclusive colonial zones as early, if not long before, as the putative division of the world between Spain and Portugal in the late fifteenth century. Breaking into Spain's Latin American preserve, or ensuring that the French did not inherit it, became one of the enduring frictions of European international relations for several centuries. Exclusive colonial trading privileges remained characteristic of the world economy in the early nineteenth century. Some overall movement toward freer trade was realized gradually even though various states continued to harbor preferences for restrictions on trading openness, especially in times of political and economic crisis. Napoleon's Continental bloc scheme to preclude British economic domination in Europe, German plans for Mitteleuropa, and the Japanese idea of an east Asian coprosperity sphere come readily to mind as examples.

Related to these older propensities is the idea that free trade has been championed by the leading economic power in the system (for the past few centuries, at least) as long as that power had little to fear in the way of production and trading competition. Once seriously challenged, though, Britain, the nineteenth century leader, eventually retreated to a reliance on its advantages in serving its own imperial markets – another example of reversion to regional trading exclusiveness. The US has been the leading economic power and the leading champion for free trade in the second half of the twentieth century. NAFTA, as well as the strong possibility of further expansion of FTAs throughout the Americas by the first decade of the twenty-first century, could be suggestive of a new retreat away from free trade principles on the part of a declining system leader.

Nevertheless, as discussed in Chapter 2, several questions need to be raised about these fears. Scholars have tended to focus on why and when trade blocs form, what form their general effects on regional and world trade take, and, more specifically, how blocs affect the overall welfare of members and non-members. Less likely to be addressed are the implications for domestic political economies. Who wins and loses at home once a state joins an FTA? Whatever the overall welfare shift, there is likely to be some unevenness in the domestic distribution of costs and benefits that may have some impact on whether these arrangements endure. At the same time, we also need to assess the assumption that trade regionalization tendencies can be equated with the closure of the world trading system. Underlying this correlation is another assumption that all regional trading blocs at all times constitute relatively similar phenomena. A number of scholars believe that regionalization can be either benign or malign.[2] There is no reason to assume that it is always a manifestation of a deteriorating international trade order. Ironically perhaps, the new regionalization may even prove to be a substitute for a faltering multilateralism.[3]

This chapter examines the long-term movement toward regionalism in the important case of US trade. The US case has special significance because of the US historical record as both system leader and free trade champion. On the one hand, if the US trade is becoming more encapsulated regionally, it may be taken as a leading indicator of a deteriorating trade regime established in the aftermath of World War II. On the other hand, if NAFTA represents something other than increasing regional trade encapsulation, we have a useful warning that the proliferation of FTAs need not mean an automatic return to beggar-thy-regional-neighbor policies.

We begin by examining the possible domestic consequences of NAFTA. NAFTA is still very young, but we may still develop some sense of whether its impact is likely to be great or small. For various theoretical reasons, we do not anticipate that it will have a great impact in the near future, and this is basically what the empirical record suggests to date. We then turn to the related, longer run question of whether US trade regionalization necessarily implies a movement toward trade closure and protectionism. The catechism of international political economy portrays tariffs, trade proportions, and the regionalization of trade as an interdependent trinity. When tariffs and/or regionalization increase, trade openness must decrease (implying that the tariffs -> trade openness and regionalization -> trade openness causal relationships are negative). When trade proportions (i.e., trade openness) increase, tariff levels and regionalization propensities must have declined. We are not so sure about the appropriate form of these relationships. Rather than assume their automaticity, we prefer to examine them more closely, over time, and with a highly selected country focus.

The point is not that every country is likely to be associated with a differently signed trinity. There are, after all, only so many possibilities given three variables. Rather, we suspect that, at the very least, some major cases – and the US appears to be a good case in point – deviate from the usual assumptions made about these relationships. If we can develop empirical evidence pertaining to perceived exceptions, that may be all we have accomplished. That is, what we are doing may simply amount to highlighting exceptions to the rule. Yet drawing attention to likely exceptions emphasizes the need to be wary of adopting assumptions about protectionist behavior – especially, when the rule itself has yet to be established empirically in any fashion. Moreover, we are dubious about any generalizations linking tariffs, trade openness, and trade regionalization that portray them moving in lock-step unison, either positively or negatively, with one another.

Our focus rests solely on the US, some dimensions of its trading behavior over the last two centuries and the North American trading region (Canada, Mexico, and the US). We first explore the trade diverting-trade creating impacts of NAFTA and then examine the historical relationships characterizing US tariffs, US trade regionalization in North America, and US trade proportions. Our specific expectations are that the overall net trade creation/diversion will not be great. We expect that both trade regionalization and the proportion of GNP constituted by trade are growing. We also expect a marked tendency for US tariffs to decline at some point in accordance with expectations about the emergence of new political-economic system leaders. In the last two centuries, in any event, the ascendancies of Britain and the United States have been closely associated (and credited) with ushering new eras of freer trade. Whether that decline in protectionism leads to significantly higher trade proportions on the part of the system leader depends on the nature of the system leader's economy. In the US case, one in which trade was not as major an economic factor as in the cases of earlier leaders, we doubt that there is or has been a close relationship. We also suspect that trade regional encapsulation tendencies in North America have increased across time, regardless of trade proportions and perhaps even tariffs.

The Impact of Trade Regionalization

Beginning in the late 1940s, the US support for multilateral trade agreements was reflected clearly by its initiation and stimulation of eight rounds of world trade and tariff reform within the context of the General Agreement on Tariff and Trade (GATT). The relatively recent US embrace of first NAFTA and then the Asian-Pacific Economic Cooperation (APEC) group has polarized scholars into two groups. Some believe that these regional groups facilitate a transition stage toward global free trade. Others worry that such arrangements distort trade patterns, complicate the regulation of trade, impose new trade barriers against non-members, lead to inter-regional trade wars, and, in all, slow down the movement toward freer trade on a world-wide basis.

In this section, we examine the theoretical economic effects of trade blocs on member countries. The literature on trade blocs is quite large and it is not our intent to review it comprehensively. Rather, our present goal is to summarize the main insights offered by political economists and then apply them in our discussion of NAFTA in a following section. As discussed in Chapter 1, there are several types of trade blocs (preferential trade agreements or PTAs, free trade areas or FTAs, customs unions, economic unions). The following discussion applies, in principle, to all of these possible arrangements since they all involve lowered trade barriers among members while at least maintaining higher barriers toward non-members. The economics literature distinguishes between short run and long run effects of such arrangements. Short run effects are based on a static economic analysis (that is, a cost-benefit analysis at one particular time). Long run analysis permits gains and losses to accumulate over time and, therefore, is harder to conduct in a more formal fashion.

The short run effects of trade blocs were first studied by Viner (1950) and then elaborated by Meade (1955) and Lipsey and Lancaster (1956).[4] The theory was formulated for a customs union – an area which prohibits trade barriers among members and harmonizes members' trade barriers toward the outside world. Nevertheless, Viner's insights also apply to other forms of trade blocs such as FTAs - arrangements which also prohibit trade barriers among members but stop short of harmonizing external trade policies.

Jacob Viner's static analysis emphasized the forces of trade creation and diversion. *Trade creation* occurs when the elimination (or reduction) of trade barriers among the trade bloc's members leads to more trade among them, thereby replacing domestic production. Viner and others have shown that trade creation increases the partners' welfare because it leads to greater specialization in production based on comparative advantage. Trade creation may create losses for some regional firms or industries but the overall cumulative gains are believed to outweigh individual losses.

A trade bloc can also have a welfare reducing effect. *Trade diversion* occurs when goods produced by less efficient producers inside the bloc replace the import of goods produced by more efficient producers from outside the bloc. This may happen if trade barriers are lowered among members but remain high toward nonmembers. Bloc consumers may then find it cheaper to buy goods produced inside the region. Yet the price of foreign goods is higher only because of trade barriers. This sort of trade diversion reduces welfare in that it entails a move away from the optimal production resource allocation of open markets. In principle, this effect is similar to other trade barriers. It distorts domestic consumption and production patterns and implies a move away from one's comparative advantage.

A trade bloc can exhibit both trade creation and diversion. Whether trade blocs are welfare reducing or not thus depends on the relative size of trade creation versus trade diversion. We should note that Viner's analysis is but one example of the economic theory of 'the second best.' The first best policy in this respect is world-wide free trade. In the absence of the first best, a trade bloc can be a move in the correct direction, or a second best policy. Nevertheless, the second best policy may not increase members' welfare as long as there remain distortions which prevent market forces from arriving at optimal allocation of production resources.

The second best theory has at least one important implication for the political economy of trade regionalism. The theory implies that only those trade blocs which generate a positive net benefit to members are likely to be either activated or reasonably stable. Otherwise, the losses associated with bloc formation are likely to motivate forces that will object to formation and continued membership. Of course, the political economy of bloc formation is more complicated than this simple model suggests. Such variables as winners' and losers' mobilization, organization, and access to power and other domestic factors are sure to make some difference as well. Periods of world depression and intense conflict are also notorious for encouraging exclusive trading blocs. Still, from a unitary state actor perspective, one can generalize that only trade blocs that entail a net gain will tend to be concluded and/or sustained.

Several scholars have investigated the theoretical conditions under which a trade bloc is more likely to create positive net gains.[5] One is that the higher the trade barriers between members prior to the bloc formation, the larger will be the size of trade creation once the barriers are removed. A second generalization is that the smaller is the trade of the bloc with the outside world prior to group formation, the less likely trade diversion is. A related consideration pertains to the size of the bloc's external trade barriers. The lower are these barriers, the less trade diversion is likely. Moreover, the more countries choose to join the bloc (and the larger the size of their economies), the more likely trade creation is. This outcome is predicated on the assumption that the larger the bloc, the more probable it is that specialization and low cost production of some goods will be located within the bloc. A fifth expectation is that trade creation will be greater for countries that are geographically proximate due to the reductions in transportation costs. Finally, competitive economies that also enjoyed great degree of pre-bloc economic interaction are more likely to create trade than to divert it. In such situations, there are more possibilities for intra-trade industry and production of differentiated goods. This implies that trade creation is more likely between two integrating competitive industrialized economies than between an agricultural nation and a complementary industrial nation.

The second best theory implies that country A, if given a choice between a preferential trade agreements with country B and free trade with country C, should go with C as long as the A-C trade creation effects are larger, and the A-C trade diversion effects are smaller than in the A-B case. Yet country A might still choose to join in a bloc with country B if there is some promise of dynamic gains from their integration (i.e., gains which accumulate over time). This type of economic gain is normally not included in the trade creation/diversion static discussion.

Trade blocs can develop dynamic gains from several sources. First, trade blocs can increase the level of competition. Protected firms, in contrast, typically become less efficient over time. When trade barriers are removed, the previously protected sectors become exposed to new competition which, in turn, should facilitate incentives to become more efficient. A second source of dynamic gain is that larger markets may encourage economies of scale. Facing expanding markets, firms may invest in new plants and equipments to serve their growing markets. Another possibility is that firms external to the bloc may establish production facilities inside the bloc in order to evade the external trade barriers. The ensuing increase in production facilities should further stimulate economic growth within the bloc.[6]

Bloc-joining considerations also include political motivations. As noted earlier, the literature on the politics of bloc formation is large and we can only mention some of the ideas. One argument often invoked in the context of the European Union is that a substantial increase in economic interdependence can reduce the probability of future warfare. Several of the EU founding fathers, such as Robert Schumann, the French foreign minister, and Jean Monnet, the French advocate of functionalist integration, held this view.[7] An alternative approach involves emphasizing the unification incentives stimulated by common external threat. This type of argument is quite compatible with realist perspectives and is exemplified by Mearsheimer's (1990) work.[8] A third view is that trade blocs are formed in reaction to political pressure from various domestic and international groups. For instance, the Generalized System of Preference between developed and less developed countries (LDCs) which gives special trade preferences to LDCs was put in place in the 1970s under pressure from LDCs. A related argument is that trade blocs are a reaction to successful lobbying of exporters – an issue we turn to next.

The main beneficiaries of free trade, consumers, are harder to mobilize than firms. This helps to explain why firms are able in many cases to lobby successfully for protection that is paid for in terms of higher prices by consumers. Exporters typically support free trade since it implies cheaper imported production inputs, frees up inputs for exporting sectors, and can lead to lower trade barriers abroad when a trading partner reciprocates reductions in protectionist policies. As noted by Lawrence (1996), among others, these processes are not widely appreciated by the public. Unilateral trade liberalization as a consequence is difficult politically. Liberalization through multilateral agreements may not be as attractive as bilateral arrangements to exporters who see, as in GATT and the WTO, all members receiving most favored nation benefits automatically. Multilateral agreements may also reflect compromises which do not always match the specific needs or goals of a single country's economy. Bhagwati and Krueger (1995) argue that these types of objections are less likely to apply to trade blocs since the benefits are more visible, less diffused, and thus more apt to stimulate strong support from exporters.

The NAFTA Debate

The NAFTA case provides a useful empirical focus for some of the theoretical arguments and generalizations outlined in the previous section. The formation of NAFTA was controversial from its outset in large part because observers projected varying expectations concerning the likely adverse impact of its formation on the US economy.[9] While NAFTA has not been around long enough to say much that is conclusive about its impact, the circumstances surrounding its formation are especially revealing for our interest in assessing the trade regionalization phenomena in the US case.

In January 1, 1994, the US, Canada, and Mexico began the implementation of NAFTA. The agreement requires the three members to remove all tariffs on trade among the three states over a period of 15 years. Some restrictions on farm products and the flow of foreign direct investment (FDI) are exempted. The agreement also imposes strict rules on the use of non-tariff barriers, spells out regional anti-trust and intellectual property right rules, and provides dispute settlement mechanisms. Each country can upgrade its own environmental standards as long as they can claim a scientific basis for changing standards. Attracting FDI is not regarded as an appropriate reason for lowering environmental standards.[10]

NAFTA is unique because it joins two developed countries with a less developed country. Other trade blocs tend to be more homogeneous in the economic sense and, therefore, more likely to generate higher gains. Indeed, much of the debate over NAFTA has been about the desirability of close and free links between the US (and to a lesser extent, Canada) and Mexico. As we have pointed out, trade blocs are second best and, therefore, may reduce bloc members' welfare. But they are also capable of generating gains 'down the road.' Hence, the resultant political game is often one in which short run losers mobilize to thwart the bloc formation, while potential, long run, winners promote the agreement. Since future gains usually are less visible than current losses, short run losers tend to be quite vocal.

While many US policy makers supported NAFTA in 1993, there was (and continues to be) considerable objection to the bloc arrangement, stemming mainly from three groups: 1) organized labor and owners of industries facing competition from cheaper LDC (i.e., Mexican) labor; 2) environmentalists; and 3) some consumer groups. NAFTA was only approved in the House of Representatives by a narrow margin (234 to 200) and remains contentious, as was demonstrated in the late 1997 debate over granting presidential fast-track authority to expand NAFTA to encompass additional states in South America.[11]

The objection to NAFTA, predicated on the US-Mexico economic development differences, can be summarized in the following way.[12] It has been claimed that NAFTA would result in the loss of American jobs because Mexican labor is less expensive and its workplace standards are more lax, and therefore less costly.[13] The implication was that labor intensive goods from Mexico would outsell US labor intensive goods. It was also claimed that whatever trade diversion is created could generate other economic losses and might also contribute to the deterioration of major trading partners of the US, such as Japan and members of the EU.

Another assertion was that American firms would relocate to Mexico in order to avoid the higher costs of doing business in the US Polluting industries, in particular, might be encouraged to move south, thereby contributing to the degradation of the Mexican environment. All of these shifts would not only reduce US leverage on Mexico to tighten its environmental regulations, it would also increase global pollution. Firms in the US might also reduce their production standards and product quality in order to compete with less costly Mexican goods and firms producing in Mexico. To the more general extent that NAFTA bolstered Mexican elites and their positions within the Mexican polity, one might also expect slower movement toward economic and political reforms unless those same reforms encouraged the countervailing formation of new elite-mass groups that benefited from the changes and were in a position to work towards expanding the reforms. Yet given universal tendencies toward some degree of societal inertia, one might expect a healthy lag between the successful impact of new group demands and the drag of established elite clout.

NAFTA supporters largely followed the logic normally associated with an emphasis on trade creation and free trade. According to one view, NAFTA would increase competition and lower prices. The potential dynamic gains have also been emphasized. Hufbauer and Schott (1992), for instance, estimated that NAFTA would lead to a decline of 150,000 unskilled US jobs and an increase of 325,000 skilled jobs. Low wage zones in the US might suffer, then, but other areas would benefit. Another argument was that NAFTA would allow US industries to import labor intensive goods from Mexico while keeping their main plant operations within the US. Contrary to the criticism of jobs migrating south, NAFTA could provide an alternative for the relocation of American firms to low wage countries. The attractions of low wages in Mexico should be offset by the equally low productivity or real output per Mexican worker.[14] In any event, the issue of trade diversion was thought to be exaggerated in as much as the US already possesses very low trade barriers toward the outside world. Finally, supporters argue that any negative environmental impacts should be regulated within NAFTA-negotiated guidelines.

The Impacts of NAFTA

The relatively short time since its 1994 inception makes it a bit too early to assess fully the NAFTA outcome. Nevertheless, some interim observations are feasible. For our purposes, NAFTA effects can be grouped into two categories: economic and political.

In the summer of 1997, the Clinton Administration issued a report on the economic impact of NAFTA (as was called for by the original legislation).[15] In general, the US and Canadian impacts of the trade bloc agreement are modest, but it does seem to have made more of an impression on the Mexican economy. The small Canadian impact is due mainly to the earlier US-Canadian free trade agreement (1989) and the fact that even before 1989 their bilateral tariffs were low. Moreover, the potential Canadian gains from free Mexican-Canadian trade are likely to be quite small.

US exports to Mexico rose from $40 billion in 1993 to $57 billion in 1996. US imports from Mexico rose from $39 billion to $73 billion over the same period. Just what proportion of these increases should be attributed to NAFTA trade creation is harder to estimate. The evaluation is further complicated by the sharp devaluation of the Mexican peso in 1994-1995 and the recession it induced in Mexico. The peso devaluation alone must have worked toward boosting Mexico's exports and suppressing its imports. Recession might also be expected to have an import suppressing effect.[16] More clearly, the effect on US employment is not great. Ojeda, Dowds, McCleery, Robinson, Runsten, Wolff and Wolff (1996) estimate that the net employment impact of NAFTA on US employment amounted to a gain of 10,000 workers (within a pool of 120 million workers). US FDI in Mexico since 1994 averaged less than $3 billion which, again, is a rather small number.[17]

NAFTA's trade diversion effects are less than clear. Despite Hufbauer and Schott's (1993) prediction of little trade diversion, given low US trade barriers, some trade diversion may be taking place. In the automobile industry, in particular, some of Asia's car exports to the US market have been replaced by Mexican car exports. The combined decline in trade barriers attributable to NAFTA, the relocation of some American auto plants to Mexico, and the sharp decline in the value of the peso in 1994-1995 resulted in almost doubling the number of cars and trucks exported from Mexico to the US from 1994 to mid-1997.[18]

The positive effect of NAFTA on the Mexican economy, therefore, has been noticeable and is expected to grow further in the long term. As estimated by Klein and Salvatore (1995) and Salvatore (1998), the Mexican economy will gain from NAFTA in terms of export-led growth, reduced capital flight, and the encouragement of structural economic (and political) reforms vis-a-vis freer markets. Mexico's average yearly growth rate is forecast to be 5.2% from 1995 to 2005. Without NAFTA, it is estimated that it would have been about 3.8% per annum. NAFTA is also expected to boost FDI to Mexico by $3.2 billion per year over the same period, reduce inflation by 4.8% and boost exports to the US by 2.1% per year. However, the peso crisis dragged down performance (below the forecast) in 1995 and 1996. Only in late 1997 were there signs that the Mexican economy was recovering from its unanticipated recession. Even so, some authors have attributed the relatively quicker recovery, compared to the 1982 debt crisis, to NAFTA.[19]

The relatively small effect of NAFTA on the US economy can be explained in two ways. Since US trade barriers for all goods and states were already low, the trade bloc arrangement bestows little in the way of competitive advantage on Mexican involvement in the US economy. A modest amount of overall trade diversion corresponds with this observation. Perhaps more importantly, the Mexican economy is around 25 times smaller than the US economy. The largest share that Mexican firms had in any US sector does not exceed 10%, and in many cases is smaller than 2% (Leamer, 1993). Mexico's economy could hardly be expected to satisfy US import demands even in sectors that are considered to be within the domain of Mexican comparative advantage (for example, textiles).

Given the history of Mexican authoritarianism, it is not surprising that the political effects of NAFTA are frequently highlighted. Some authors (Poli, 1995; Lopez-Villicana, 1997) assert that NAFTA has locked in Mexico's commitment to liberal reforms. Tornell and Esquivel (1995) emphasize that the Mexican response to the peso/debt crisis of 1994-95 was much different than its response to the 1982 debt crisis. In the 1980s, Mexico reacted by raising its trade barriers sharply. In the mid-1990s, it again raised trade barriers toward the outside world but continued to cut tariffs on US and Canadian trade. Thus, NAFTA has contributed to the credibility of Mexican commitment to liberal economic reforms. It is also possible to argue that NAFTA could be used as a political weapon against protectionist forces within Mexico that can be expected to become stronger in periods of economic crisis (Frankel, Stein and Wei, 1997).[20]

Symbolically, NAFTA obviously underlines closer US-Mexican relations. Mutual foreign policy issues are more likely to be dealt with in an interdependent manner. From one US perspective, a strategy for combating drug smuggling and illegal immigration is to facilitate the success of the Mexican economy. Should NAFTA-induced liberalization accelerate Mexican growth, as anticipated, the 'Gringo-bashing' rhetoric of the past may decline.[21] The American embrace of Mexico was demonstrated in two recent cases. In 1994 and 1995, the US rushed to put together a $50 billion rescue loan to support Mexico in the aftermath of the peso crisis. Two years later, the US renewed Mexico's certification as an ally in fighting drugs even though large quantities of drugs are still smuggled from Mexico to the United States.

Finally, some observers have argued that NAFTA has had some impact on Mexico's domestic political system. Almazan (1997) argues that by transferring authority from state to markets, NAFTA has weakened the formerly highly centralized position of the Mexican government and, as a consequence, also strengthened rebels within the various indigenous communities. In a related fashion, Purcell (1997) suggests that Mexico's relatively low key response to the Chiapas rebellion reflects Mexico's official concern with its image in the US and the fear that a negative reaction to a stronger response might jeopardize NAFTA. Husted and Logsdon (1997) have also concluded that NAFTA encouraged more commitment to Mexican policies aimed at pollution reduction and environmental regulation enforcement.

In sum, NAFTA has had some impact and it is likely to continue to do so. Nonetheless, its primary impact has been focused on the Mexican economy – the smallest member of the NAFTA trio. The net effect of that impact has been to open Mexican markets and not to close North American markets to outside participation. As long as opening works to the benefit of Mexican economic development the general impact should, in principle, be beneficial for freer trade in the world economy. At the same time, the Mexican contribution to the world economy is rather small. Therefore, we assume the net impact of NAFTA on the world economy will not be any larger. But, if NAFTA per se does not constitute a major shift away from freer trade, either in North America or the world at large, we still do not know what the general relationship are, and have been, among trade regionalization tendencies, expanding trade, and protectionism. That is the topic to which we turn in the second half of this chapter.

Trade Regionalization, NAFTA and Openness

An early and highly influential article by Krasner (1976) established the trinity of tariff levels, trade proportions, and regional trade encapsulation as markers for the behavioral and institutional dimensions of trade structure. Krasner's argument revolved around several points. One was that no single indicator would suffice to capture trade structure. Tariff levels, in particular, are awkward in that they are difficult to operationalize, tricky to interpret, and tend to overlook non-tariff barriers to trade. Krasner proposed to supplement tariff levels, an institutional indicator, with two behavioral indicators. One focused on the proportion of trade to national income or gross domestic product as a measure of the importance of external economic activity in comparison to domestic economic activity. The other indicator looked at the tendency for large states to protect their welfare by creating regional blocs through the concentration of their trade with nearby smaller states. The idea here is that political coercion is employed to distort what the trade outcome might have been if only comparative advantage was at stake.

A trade structure becomes more open, then, as tariffs fall, trade proportions rise, and regional encapsulation propensities decline. Krasner's reference point is clearly aimed at systemic structure. Since we are primarily interested in the US case at this point, we are not necessarily challenging the accuracy of his aggregate structural generalization. In general, we accept the notion that falling tariffs, rising trade proportions, and declining regional encapsulation have been historical hallmarks of an opening trade structure. What we are curious about, though, is whether these relationships hold at less aggregated levels of analysis? Should we expect all states to be characterized by the same relationships? For that matter, should we expect the leader of the system to adhere to the aggregate pattern? There is also the question of novelty. Trade regionalization in the past has been equated with protectionist tendencies. That does not guarantee that the contemporary movement toward regionalization is equally protectionist in nature. Things change in international political economy as in other spheres of activity.

Krasner's (1976) historical evidence was at best ambiguous. In Europe, the 1820-1879 period was described as one of decreasing tariff levels. In the years immediately leading up to World War I, European tariff levels, in most cases, rose and then increased again after World War I, and most dramatically after 1930. After 1945, European tariffs decreased at least through the mid-to-late 1960s. In contrast, the US was described as remaining highly protectionist throughout the nineteenth century and especially between the American Civil War and World War I, and then again in the early Depression years. Only in the mid-1930s did the US take the lead in promoting lower tariff levels.

European trade proportions were described as paralleling tariff movements for the most part. Trade proportions in Europe increased in the nineteenth century through 1880, decreased between 1880 and 1900, increased 1900 to 1913, decreased in the 1920s and 1930s, before increasing again after 1945. The US pattern is described and depicted as roughly holding constant at a low ratio throughout most of this same time period.

Regional encapsulation information is less easy to obtain. However, Krasner's data suggested some tendencies toward generally declining regionalization between 1890 and 1928, increasing encapsulation after 1928, and slowly decreasing regionalization after 1954. The data most pertinent to the US case consist of the percentage of Latin American exports to the US and the percentage of US imports from Latin America (where Latin America is defined as Argentina, Bolivia, Brazil, Chile, Colombia, Ecuador, Mexico, and Paraguay). These data show increasing regionalization between 1890 and the 1950s and then declining percentages in the 1960s through 1967 or 1968.

There are of course some conceptual and empirical problems here. Krasner's tariff generalizations were not data based and the regional encapsulation data were limited in the number of observations that were examined. The encapsulation data are asymmetrical in that they look at 'Latin American' flows to the US but not US flows to Latin America. One could also note that in the US case, the question of regional encapsulation calls for an examination of trade flows to and from Canada as well as with more southern neighbors. It is also awkward to evaluate movement in a few years in the 1960s as to whether a new trend line has been established. Mansfield (1994) notes, too, that after all is said and done, we end up with rather crude, dichotomous characterizations of periods of relative openness and closure.

Yet, index quibbling aside, the picture described by Krasner in 1976 has the US beginning to lower its tariffs in the 1930s, not altering its trade proportion all that much, and retaining its regional trade biases well into the late 1950s. Such a picture suggests a rather uneven movement toward greater trade openness, with tariff decreases preceding deregionalization by several decades which in turn precedes the relative absence of change in trade proportion or significance. This history does not necessarily violate the interdependence of the trinity but it does suggest that the relationships among these three variables may be more complicated than is sometimes thought. Yet we are also left with something of an implied puzzle. If US trade became less regional in scope only in the late 1950s, how should we regard the more recent interest in NAFTA? Does NAFTA represent still another reversal in regional encapsulation fluctuations? Is the US hedging its openness bet as the post-World War II system leader by developing a regional enclave in its backyard much as the British did in the late nineteenth century with its more geographically extensive Commonwealth/ Empire?

However we answer these questions, there are reasons to be cautious about interpreting NAFTA. On the one hand, it is an unfinished product (Weintraub, 1997) that has yet to take full shape. At the same time, none of the members appear to have been motivated by a desire to reduce trade with nations outside the bloc. To the contrary, most accounts stress various types of trade liberalizing motivations and not straight forward protectionist urges, especially on the part of Mexico (see Haggard, 1997; Weintraub, 1997; Milner, 1998).[22] Moreover, not only are there restrictions on what NAFTA covers, all NAFTA members are also members of APEC, the trans-Pacific arrangement. It has been noted that if NAFTA should expand to encompass the Americas, the APEC membership is retained and strengthened, and some new trans-Atlantic arrangement were to be concluded, most of the world's trade would be encompassed in three overlapping 'blocs' that would hardly represent blocs at all. The bottom line, already anticipated in earlier sections of this chapter, seems to be that we need not equate NAFTA, as a matter of assumption, with a retreat from free trade principles.

Long Run US Trade and Protectionism Data

One way to address some of these questions about the meaning of NAFTA is to develop a set of longer time series for the US case. We may then 'eyeball' their patterns of fluctuations over time and also correlate the extent to which they covary. Figure 1 presents a long run view of US tariff levels, trade proportion, and regional encapsulation. The measure of US tariff levels is nominal tariff rate averages (Reuveny and Thompson, 1997). Trade proportion is the ratio of imports and exports to gross domestic product. Regional encapsulation is captured crudely by the size of trade with Canada and Mexico as a percentage of total US trade.[23]

Figure 3.1   A Long Run View of US Tariff Levels, Trade Proportion, and Regional Encapsulation

Although subject to some year-to-year extreme fluctuations due to wars and depressions, the general patterns are reasonably clear. Tariff levels are shown as increasing to about 1835, decreasing to the Civil War, remaining mostly constant to the period just before World War I, then rising once again in the 1920s until they peaked prior to World War II. After 1940, they plummeted and remained low through the next 50 or more years. Keep in mind, however, that this series does not measure non-tariff barriers (NTBs). If we had serial data on NTBs, the 50 plus years of decreased protectionism may look a bit different and less free trade oriented. At the same time, since the use of NTBs only intensified since the mid to late

1970s (or, the last few years of our series), we may assume that their effect on our analysis is rather small.

Trade proportions were fairly high in the first few decades of US history but also quickly began to decline. They continued to decline until the late 1960s and have more recently climbed back to levels not sustained since well before the American Civil War. Regional encapsulation, at least as we are measuring it (with an emphasis on North America) has been steadily trending upward for the last 170 years or so. Nevertheless, we do observe some short-term but recent decline in this propensity in the early 1970s that is not maintained after 1980, and which is presumably related to oil pricing problems.[24] This departure from the trend line, though, does not appear to be the same shift captured in Krasner's Latin American series for the 1960s.

Data Analysis

We do not propose a definitive examination of the relationships among trade proportions, regional encapsulation, or tariff levels because, at this point, we do not have strong theoretical expectations about how they might be related, or what other variables might be critical. Our focus is also American-centric. A more definitive examination, minimally, would require a less selective country sample. Thus, our examination is preliminary and exploratory. There is some reason to anticipate a less than perfect correlation among these variables and we are curious just how much deviation from high correlations are observed. Yet our interest is not simply casual. The US case has more than average significance. While NAFTA may not be representative of other FTAs, it is certainly one of the more important regional trade arrangements – if only because it is centered on the system's lead economy of the twentieth century.

Our operationalizations of the three variables are straightforward and represent the same data discussed descriptively earlier in this paper. Trade proportion is measured as the ratio of US exports and imports to gross domestic product (denoted in Tables 3.1 and 3.2 as trade/GDP). Regional encapsulation is the proportion of US trade with Canada and Mexico in terms of total US trade (denoted in Tables 3.1 and 3.2 as regionalization). Tariffs are measured as average tariff rates. The correlations among these three variables are based on the 1854-1990 period.[25]

Table 3.1 summarizes the correlational outcomes for two interpretations of the data. The first matrix is based on levels of the

variables in question and without lagging (i.e., the contemporaneous relationship at t_0). The second matrix reports the unlagged correlations among
the year to year change scores since the level data are characterized by
discernible trends that might influence unduly the correlational outcomes.
Given our sample size, correlations higher than +0.171 or lower than -0.171
are significant at the 0.05 level.[26]

Table 3.1   Correlation Matrix for Regionalization, Trade/GDP, and Tariffs

Level Scores

	Regionalization	Trade/GDP	Tariffs
Regionalization	==	-.392*	-.785*
Trade/GNP	==	==	-.103
Tariffs	==	==	==

Change Scores

	Regionalization	Trade/GDP	Tariffs
Regionalization	==	-.547*	0.198*
Trade/GNP	==	==	-.311
Tariffs	==	==	==

Note: Entries are correlation scores between a variable whose name is
written in a column with a variable whose name is written in a line. == for
diagonal elements means N/A and for non diagonal elements means as a
result already written in the correlation matrix.

The level outcomes certainly support the idea that these three variables
have not moved in unison across time in the North American case. Trade
proportion and regional encapsulation are negatively related, which is what
we would expect if both variables measured trade openness/closure in
similar ways. Note, however, that the correlation is only in the moderate
range (-0.392). In marked contrast, however, the other two relationships are
different from what might otherwise be expected. Trade proportion and
tariff levels are not correlated in a statistically significant way (the
association is -0.103). Tariff levels and regional encapsulation are highly
and significantly correlated, but the relationship is negative (-0.785): lower
US average tariffs are associated with more US regional encapsulation, or
less US trade with the world, a result which may seem a bit odd.
Nevertheless, this last finding is not very mysterious. As we noted earlier,

US average tariff levels have been mostly decreasing in the post-1945 period, while US regional trade has been increasing.

Yet the change scores (the second matrix in Table 1) suggest something different. Changes in trade proportion and regionalization remain negatively related as in the levels case, albeit at a higher level of correlation (-0.547). Changes in average tariff levels and trade proportion are now negatively and significantly related at a moderate level (-0.311) which is a result to be expected based on short run oriented trade theory. Changes in average tariff levels and regionalization are now positively and significantly related (0.198). This means that, historically, a rise in average tariffs is positively associated with a rise in US regionalization, all other things being equal. Theoretically, one would not expect changes in either one of these two variables to lead to positive changes in the other.

One possibility is that we are not working with the appropriate lag structure. If these variables are not perfectly correlated at t_0 and changes in at least some of them do lead to changes in other values of the trio, we should look for lagged relationships, rather than t_0 relationships. Table 3.2 summarizes the outcome when one looks systematically at the six possible pairs of relationships subject to one to five year lags. The overall pattern that emerges suggests that these variables are even less inter-related than Table 3.1's correlations might suggest.

Table 3.2 Cross-correlations for Regionalization, Trade/GDP, and Tariffs

Level Data

t-5	t-4	t-3	t-2	t-1	t$_0$	t-1	t-2	t-3	t-4	t-5
Regionalization -> trade/GDP						*Trade/GDP -> regionalization*				
-.224	-.265	-.295	-.319	-.350	-.392	-.389	-.391	-.402	-.392	-.392
Tariffs -> trade/GDP						*Trade/GDP -> tariffs*				
-.035	-.049	-.067	-.083	-.096	-.103	-.074	-.032	-.020	-.080	-.144
Tariffs -> regionalization						*Regionalization -> tariffs*				
-.723	-.739	-.753	-.761	-.776	-.785	-.782	-.781	-.784	-.787	-.791

Change Score Data

t-5	t-4	t-3	t-2	t-1	t$_0$	t-1	t-2	t-3	t-4	t-5
Regionalization -> trade/GDP						*Trade/GDP -> regionalization*				
.132	-.105	-.003	0.20	.074	-.547	-.056	.171	-.157	.080	.196
Tariffs -> trade/GDP						*Trade/GDP -> tariffs*				
.187	.099	.019	-.045	-.149	-.311	-.218	-.119	-.190	-.111	.075
Tariffs -> regionalization						*Regionalization -> tariffs*				
-.231	-.048	-.012	-.026	0.26	.198	.145	.009	.003	-.012	-.100

Note: Correlations higher than +0.171 or lower than –0.171 are significant at the 0.05 level.

The negative relationship between the US trade proportion and regional encapsulation is most consistent for level scores (in all lags), and is concentrated at t$_0$ for the change scores. The US trade proportion and regional encapsulation have moderately discouraged one another. But the lagged, change score correlations and the size of the level correlations suggest caution in assuming that these processes necessarily have much of a causal relationship. The levels of trade proportion are not particularly related to tariff levels at any lag. Their moderate and negative relationship in the change scores is strongest in t$_0$ and generally supports the view that a rise in trade proportion drives a decline in tariffs (as reflected by the significant -0.218 and -0.190 scores).[27] Finally, regionalization and average tariff levels are negatively related at the highest levels reported in the table at all lags. But the change scores again suggest caution. They are much weaker, primarily insignificant, with the two significant scores having an opposite sign (0.198 and -0.231). If there is a causal relationship between these variables, based on our results it is not clear what it might be.

Concluding Remarks

Overall, we can find long run empirical relationships among US regional encapsulation, trade proportions, and tariffs. However, the correlations are much less than unity and, in some instances, the relationships are either statistically insignificant (levels of tariffs and trade proportions) or signed differently than might have been expected (changes in regional encapsulation and tariffs). Only the correlation between average tariffs and regional encapsulation levels approximates the high, negative relationship that might be anticipated if the three variables were measuring processes that operated in parallel directions. Most of the other correlations we obtained here suggest weaker, more moderate relationships.

As we have emphasized earlier, our analysis is not definitive and should be considered exploratory because, in part, the number of our country cases are so few and clearly a two by two correlation analysis falls short of a fully specified econometric model which links our variables. Yet the statistical outcome certainly supports the notion that trade regionalization, trade proportions and protectionism do not necessarily go hand in hand. That is, trade regionalization does not necessarily mean an increase in protectionism. A considerable proportion of trade regionalization tendencies, no doubt, reflect the lower transportation costs associated with proximate economies and possibly political considerations of the bloc's members as suggested by several authors in the cases of the European Union and NAFTA.[28]

Other things being equal, we might expect neighboring economies to trade more with neighbors than with non-neighbors. This result is confirmed in numerous trade studies which have relied upon the bilateral trade gravity research design.[29] We might also expect, as reflected by our theoretical and empirical analysis, some tendency for trade diversion due to the formation of trade blocs. Yet this does not make trade bloc behavior necessarily malign as some observers have contended. The important question is at what point does trade regionalization take on an exclusive flavor in which trade within the region and trade outside the region start assuming a zero sum nature.

From what we find in our review of the NAFTA case, the trade diversion tendency of this trade bloc is not strong. That is, NAFTA per se has not constituted a major shift away from freer trade, either in North America or the world at large. This US tendency is also evident in our longer run data analysis. Of course, trade blocs can become malign. But, a zero sum movement toward trade regionalization would seem to require explicit political interventions. Intra-regional activities would have to be given priority over extra-regional activities by either prohibiting extra-regional trade or by making it relatively too expensive to compete. Politically sanctioned regional trade encapsulation has certainly occurred before. But, in the US case at least (and we suspect elsewhere as well), regional trade encapsulation can coexist with declining tariffs and expanding trade proportions. Increasing propensities toward regional trade cannot be interpreted automatically as a movement away from (or toward) freer trade order.

Notes

[1] Grilli (1997), however, reminds us that the more recent spate of regional arrangements actually represents a second, post-World War II wave. The first wave occurred between 1957 and 1975, generating the EC in western Europe, LAFTA and CACM in Latin America and the Caribbean, ACM in the Middle East, UDEAC, SACU, CEAO, and ECOWAS in sub-Saharan Africa. Most of these arrangements were intra-southern affairs and were less than successful (see Deutsch, 1977; Langhammer and Hiemenz, 1990; and Salvatore, 1998). The second wave has tended to be more north-south in orientation.

[2] Analysts disagree on the likely outcome of trade regionalization. Analysts who emphasize negative consequences include Gilpin (1987), Bhagwati (1991, 1993), Krugman (1991a), and Garten (1992). Oye (1992) and McDonald (1998) are among those who argue for positive consequences. In between are scholars such as Viner (1950), Lawrence (1996), Grilli (1997), and Haggard (1997).

[3] Analysts also disagree about whether the new or reinvigorated regional arrangements constitute movement toward trade exclusivity. Pomfret (1988) argues that regionalism is not increasing. Grieco (1997: 172) suggests that there is considerable variation among different groups on this question. Mansfield and Branson (1997) demonstrate that one must control for other influences such as major power alliances in assessing the effects of trade blocs on the flow of trade. Faini (1997) argues that inter-bloc trade actually increased in the 1980s. El-Agraa (1997: 370) agrees and notes that both intra- and inter-bloc trade was able to increase thanks to overall growth in gross domestic product.

[4] For a survey and more detailed development of these ideas, see Lipsey (1968), Pomfret (1986), and Bhagwati and Pangariya (1996).

[5] This discussion summarizes ideas from Krugman (1991b), Frankel, Stein and Wei (1993), Deardorff and Stern (1991), Lawrence (1996), and Salvatore (1998).

[6] For instance, US firms made massive investments in Europe following the 1957 formation of the European Common Market and then again after 1986 when the union membership grew to 15 nations.

[7] See Keohane and Hoffmann (1990).

[8] As of 1999, Mearsheimer's prediction concerning European political instability following the end of the Cold War has not materialized outside of the Balkans. Nevertheless, it is clear that an emphasis on external threat does not help to explain cases, such as NAFTA, in which there is no overt perception of threat.

[9] On the NAFTA debate and its expected impact on the US economy, see, for example, Brown, Deardorff and Stern (1992), US International Trade Commission (1993), Fatemi and Salvatore (1994), Garber (1993), and Hufbauer and Schott (1993). For critical views of the NAFTA impact on the Mexican economy, see, for example, the papers contained in Appendini and Bislev (1999).

[10] For details on the agreement, see Bannister (1997). Some protection from FDI will continue for Mexico's energy and railway sectors, the US airline and communication sectors, and Canada's cultural sectors.

[11] Ross Perot, the one time presidential candidate, has been a leading opponent of NAFTA. See, for instance, Perot and Choate (1993).

[12] It is interesting to note that the US-Canadian 1989 FTA did not meet strong opposition. On the NAFTA debate, see, for example, Garber (1993). *The Economist* (November 13, 1993) provides a survey and summary of the opposing views.

[13] For example, manufacturing wages in Mexico are roughly 10 percent of US wages (Reyes, 1999: 175, ftn 24).

[14] In 1995, for example, Mexico's GDP per capita was about one-tenth that of the US According to the world bank, Mexico's labor productivity is roughly one-fourth of the US level (see Husted and Melvin, 1997).

[15] For a summary of the US Administration's report, see the *Washington Post* (July 11, 1997) as well as reports issued by the Office of the US Trade Representative and Related Entities at www.sice.oas.org/forum/p_sector/govt/nafta_repe. On the 1989 US-Canada free trade agreement and the Canadian gains from NAFTA see Lawrence (1996) and Salvatore (1998).

[16] *The Economist* (July 5, 1997), the *New York Times* (December 19, 1996), the *Washington Post* (July 11, 1997), Husted and Melvin (1997), Sweeney (1997), and Bannister (1997) provide discussions of NAFTA's trade effects. In a 1997 study cited in *Washington Post*, July 11, 1997 and www.sice.oas.org/forum/p_sector/nafta_repe/chap1_1.stm) McGraw-Hill's DRI (a private consulting group) estimates that in 1996, NAFTA raised US exports to Mexico by $12 billion and imports from Mexico by $5 billion dollars.

[17] On NAFTA's small effect on US employment see also *Wall Street Journal* (November 17, 1993). Moreover, this small labor effect is reflected by the fact that by mid-1997, only 117,000 US workers have signed on to receive government benefits offered to workers displaced by NAFTA. This number is quite small compared to the 2.8 million jobs created in the US from 1994 to 1997 and the 1.5 million workers that lost jobs due to non-NAFTA related factory closures, corporate restructuring and low demand. The FDI number is less than 0.5 percent of total US firms' investments in new plants and equipment (*The Economist*, July 5, 1997).

[18] On the trade diversion interpretation of these Mexican car exports data, see *The Economist* (July 5, 1997). While less important due to its small size, Central American and Caribbean countries have also seen some of their trade diverted to Mexico following the agreement.

[19] See www.sice.oas.org/forum/p_sector/govt/nafta_repe/chap1_1.sum.

[20] Pangariya (1995) and others have argued that commitment to trade liberalization through the WTO (and GATT) may work better than through the formation of a trade bloc.
[21] This suggestion was advanced by former Clinton adviser Richard Feinberg: 'We bought ourselves an ally with NAFTA.' (as cited in *The Economist*, July 5, 1997: 22). For a related argument, see Purcell (1997).
[22] NAFTA non-protectionist motivations do not appear to be all that unique in the latest wave of regional trading arrangements. See, among others, Lawrence (1996), Haggard (1997) Higgott (1998), Milner (1998), and Tussie (1998).
[23] Mitchell (1993) represents the primary source for data on trade and gross domestic product. The sources for the tariff data are reported in Reuveny and Thompson (1997).
[24] Regional encapsulations are computed from ratios of trade values. As the price of oil rose sharply in the 1970s and early 1980s, the value of US oil imports rose. Since US oil is coming mostly from outside of NAFTA, the rise in oil price implied a decline in US regional trade encapsulations during that period.
[25] The 1854-1990 period stems solely from the authors' interest in paralleling other and earlier analyses of ours that involve other major economic powers and are restricted to 1854 starting points due to non-US missing data problems.
[26] A correlation of, say, 0.2, is not problematic in anyway. However, while this correlation is statistically significant at the level of 5 percent in this sample, it probably means that the two variables are probably not the only determinants of each other.
[27] Thompson and Reuveny (1998) find, contrary to what one might expect, that in the long run trade volume Granger causes tariffs but that the reciprocal relationship did not hold. We take this to mean that the main driving force is prosperity/depression. In a depressed era, trade volumes decline and tariffs are likely to rise but the causal emphasis needs to be placed on the negative economic growth -> trade volume relationship rather than the more celebrated, tariff -> trade volume relationship.
[28] As noted, some observers argue that the move to form the EU is also aimed to reduce the likelihood of warfare in Europe. Similarly, it is argued that the move to form the NAFTA is also aimed to accelerate Mexico's democratic and free market reforms and strengthen the US-Mexico political relations.
[29] See Li (this volume) for a summary or Frankel, Stein and Wei (1997) for a more complete review of the extensive trade gravity literature.

References

Almazan, M.A. (1997), 'NAFTA and the [Mexico] Mesoamerican States System', in *American Academy of Political and Social Science*, vol. 550, pp. 42-50.

Appendini, K. and Bislev, S. (eds) (1999), *Economic Integration in NAFTA and the EU*, St. Martin's Press, New York.

Bannister, R.R. (1997), *The NAFTA Success Story: More Than Just Trade*, D.C.: Progressive Policy Institute, Washington DC.

Bhagwati, J. (1991), *The World Treaty System at Risk*, Princeton University Press, Princeton, NJ.

Bhagwati, J. (1993), 'Regionalism and Multilateralism: An Overview', in J. de Melo and A. Pangariya (eds), *New Dimensions in Regional Integration*, Cambridge University Press, New York, pp. 22-51.

Bhagwati, J. and Pangariya, A. (eds) (1996), *Free Trade Areas of Free Trade? The Economic of Preferential Trading*, AEI Press, Washington DC.

Bhagwati, J. and Krueger, A.O. (1995), *The Dangerous Drift to Preferential Trade Agreements*, American Enterprise Institute for Public Policy Research, Washington DC.

Brown, D.K., Deardorff, A.V., and Stern, R.M. (1992), 'North American Integration'. In *Economic Journal*, vol. 102, pp. 1507-1518.

Deardorff, A.V. and Stern, R.M. (1991), 'Multilateral Trade Negotiations and Preferential Trading Arrangements', in A.V. Deardorff and R.M. Stern (eds), *Analytical and Negotiating Issues in the Global Trading System*, University of Michigan Press, Ann Arbor, pp. 27-85.

Deutsch, K.W. (1977) 'National Integration: Some Concepts and Research Approaches'. In *Jerusalem Journal of International Relations*, vol. 2, pp. 1-29.

El-Agraa, A.M. (1997), "Fortresses' and Three Trading Blocs?', in A.M. El-Agraa (ed), *Economic Integration Worldwide*, St. Martin's Press, New York, pp. 368-378.

Faini, R. (1997), 'Integration or Polarization? Regionalism in World Trade during the 1980s', in R. Faini and E. Grilli (eds), *Multilateralism and Regionalism After the Uruguay Round*, St. Martin's Press, New York, pp. 144-160.

Fatemi, K. and Salvatore, D. (1994), *The North American Free Trade Agreement*, Pergamon Press, New York.

Frankel, J.A., Stein, E., and Wei, S.J. (1993) 'Trading Blocs and the Americas: The Natural, the Unnatural, and the Supernatural', in *Journal of Development Economics*, vol. 47, pp. 61-96.

Frankel, J.A. with Stein, E. and Wei, S.J. (1997), *Regional Trading Blocs in the World Economic System*, Institute for International Economics, Washington DC.

Garber, P.M. (ed) (1993), *The Mexico-US Free Trade Agreement*, MIT Press, Cambridge.

Garten, J.E. (1992), *A Cold Peace: America, Germany and the Struggle for Supremacy*, Times Books, New York.

Gilpin, R. (1987), *The Political Economy of International Relations*, Princeton University Press, Princeton NJ.

Grieco, J.M. (1997), 'Systemic Sources of Variation in Regional Institutionalization in Western Europe, East Asia, and the Americas', in E.D. Mansfield and H.V. Milner, (eds),

The Political Economy of Regionalism, Columbia University Press, New York, pp. 164-187.

Grilli, E (1997), 'Multilateralism and Regionalism: A Still Difficult Coexistence', in R. Faini and E. Grilli, (eds), *Multilateralism and Regionalism After the Uruguay Round*, St. Martin's Press, New York, pp. 194-233.

Haggard, S. (1997), 'Regionalism in Asia and the Americas', in E.D. Mansfield and H.V. Milner (eds), *The Political Economy of Regionalism*, Columbia University Press, New York, pp. 20-49.

Higgott, R. (1998), 'The International Political Economy of Regionalism: The Asia-Pacific and Europe Compared', in W.D. Coleman and G.R.D. Underhill (eds), *Regionalism and Global Economic Integration: Europe, Asia and the Americas*, Routledge, London, pp. 42-67.

Hufbauer, G.C. and Schott, J.J. (1992), *North American Free Trade: Issues and Recommendations*, Institute for International Economics, Washington, DC.

Hufbauer, G.C. and Schott, J.J. (eds) (1993), *NAFTA: An Assessment*, Institute for International Economics, Washington, DC.

Husted, B.W. and Logsdon, J.M. (1997), 'The Impact of NAFTA on Mexico's Environmental Policy', in *Growth and Change*, vol. 28, pp. 24-48.

Husted, S. and Melvin, M. (1997), *International Economics*, Addison-Wesley, Reading, MA.

Keohane, R.O. and Hoffmann, S. (1990), 'Conclusions: Community Politics and Institutional Change', in Wallace, W. (ed), *The Dynamics of European Integration*, Pinter, London.

Klein, L. and Salvatore, D. (1995) 'Welfare Effects of the North American Free Trade Agreement', in *Journal of Policy Modeling*, vol. 17, pp. 163-176.

Krasner, S. (1976), 'State Power and the Structure of International Trade', *World Politics*, vol. 28, pp. 317-348.

Krugman, P. (1991a), 'Is Bilateralism Bad?', in Helpman, E. and Razin, A., eds., *International Trade and Trade Policy*, MIT Press, Cambridge, pp. 9-23.

Krugman, P. (1991b), 'The Move Toward Free Trade Zones', in *Policy Implications of Trade and Currency Zones*, Federal Reserve Bank of Kansas City, Kansas City, MO.

Langhammer, R.J. and Hiemenz, U. (1990), *Regional Integration Among Developing Countries: Opportunities, Obstacles and Options*, J.C.B. Moher, Tübingen.

Lawrence, R.Z. (1996) *Regionalism, Multilateralism, and Deeper Integration*, The Brookings Institution, Washington DC.

Leamer, E. (1993), 'Wage Effects of a US- Mexican Free Trade Agreement', in P. Garber (ed), *The Mexican-US Free Trade Agreement*, MIT Press, Cambridge, MA, pp. 57-125.

Lipsey, R.G. (1968), 'The Theory of Customs Unions: A General Survey', in R.E. Caves and Johnson, H.G. (eds), *Readings in International Economics*, Irwin, Homewood, IL.

Lipsey, R.G. and Lancaster, K. (1956), 'The General Theory of the Second Best', in K. Lancaster, Collective Volume, *Trade, Markets and Welfare*, 1996, Elgar, Cheltenham, pp. 193-220.

Lopez-Villicana, R. (1997), 'Mexico and NAFTA: The Case of Ministers of Foreign Affairs', in *Annals of the American Academy of Political and Social Science*, vol. 550, pp. 122-129.

Mansfield, E.D. (1994), *Power, Trade and War*, Princeton University Press, Princeton, NJ.

Mansfield, E.D. and Bronson, R. (1997), 'The Political Economy of Major-Power Trade Flows', in E.D. Mansfield and H.V. Milner (eds), *The Political Economy of Regionalism*, Columbia University Press, New York, pp. 188-208.

Meade, J. (1955), *The Theory of Customs Unions*, North Holland, Amsterdam.

Mearsheimer, J.J. (1990), 'Back to the Future: Instability in Europe After the Cold War'. In *International Security*, vol. 15, pp. 5-56.

Milner, H.V. (1998), 'Regional Economic Cooperation, Global Markets and Domestic Politics: A Comparison of NAFTA and the Maastricht Treaty', in W.D. Coleman and G.R.D. Underhill (eds), *Regionalism and Global Economic Integration: Europe, Asia and the Americas*, Routledge, London, pp. 19-41.

McDonald, B. (1998), *The World Trading System: The Uruguay Round and Beyond*, St. Martin's Press, New York.

McKeown, T.J. (1991), 'A Liberal Trade Order? The Long-Run Pattern of Imports to the Advanced Capitalist States', in *International Studies Quarterly*, vol. 35, pp. 151-171.

Mitchell, B. (1993), *Historical Statistics of the Americas, 1750-1988*, Stockton Press, New York.

Ojeda, R.H., Dowds, C., McCleery, R., Robinson, S., Runsten, D., Wolff, C. and Wolff, G. (1996), 'North American Integration Three years After NAFTA', in *NAID Working Paper*, UCLA North American Integration Development Center, Los Angeles, CA (http://naid.sppser.ucla.edu/nafta96/).

Oye, K.A. (1992), *Economic Discrimination and Political Exchange: World Political Economy in the 1930s and 1980s*, Princeton University Press, Princeton, NJ.

Panagariya, A. (1995), *The Free Trade Area of the Americas: Good for Latin America?*, University of Maryland Center of International Economics, College Park, MD.

Perot, H. R. and Choate, P. (1993), *Save Your Job, Save Our Country: Why NAFTA Must Be Stopped-Now!*, Hyperion Press, New York.

Poli, E. (1995), 'NAFTA and Mexico: An Example of Cooperation Between Developed and Developing Countries', in *Economia-Internazionale*, vol. 48, pp. 569-597.

Pomfret, R. (1986), 'Preferential Trading Agreements', in *Weltwirtschafliches Archive*, vol. 122, pp. 439-465.

Pomfret, R. (1988), *Unequal Trade: The Economics of Discriminatory International Trade Policies*, Blackwell, Oxford.

Purcell, S.K. (1997), 'The Changing Nature of US-Mexican Relations', in *Journal of Interamerican Studies and World Affairs*, vol. 39, pp. 137-152.

Reuveny, R. and Thompson, W.R. (1997), 'The Timing of Protectionism', in *Review of International Political Economy*, vol. 4, pp. 179-213.

Reyes, E.D. (1999), 'Regionalism: The Case of North America', in K. Appendini and S. Bislev (eds), *Economic Integration in NAFTA and the EU*, St. Martin's Press, New York, pp. 161-177.

Salvatore, D. (1998), *International Economics*, Prentice-Hall, Upper Saddle River, NJ.

Sweeney, J. (1997), *NAFTA's Positive Impact on the US: A State-by-State Breakdown*, The Heritage Foundation, Washington, DC.

Thompson, W.R. and Reuveny, R. (1998), 'Does Protectionism Matter as Much as We Think?', in *International Organization*, vol. 52, pp. 421-440.

Tornell, A. and Esquivel, G. (1995), 'The Political Economy of Mexico's Entry to NAFTA', in *NBER Working Paper 5322*, National Bureau of Economic Research, Cambridge, MA.

Tussie, D. (1998), 'In the Whirlwind of Globalization and Multilateralism: The Case of Emerging Regionalism in Latin America', in W.D. Coleman and G.R.D. Underhill (eds), *Regionalism and Global Economic Integration: Europe, Asia and the Americas*, Routledge, London, pp. 81-96.

US Trade Commission (1993), *Potential Impact on the US Economy and Selected Industries of the North American Free Trade Agreement*, US Government Printing Office, Washington DC.

Viner, J. (1950), *The Customs Union Issue*, Carnegie Endowment for International Peace, New York.

Weintraub, S. (1997), 'The North American Free Trade Agreement', in A.M. El-Agraa (ed), *Economic Integration Worldwide*, St. Martin's Press, New York, pp. 203-229.

4 Institutional Rules of Regional Trade Blocs and their Impact on Trade

QUAN LI

The number of trade blocs notified to GATT/WTO is over 30 by 1994 and according to various data sources, has exceeded 50 by now. GATT article 24 permits the formation of customs union, free trade area or some interim agreement. Trade blocs have been analyzed from legalistic, institutional, economic, historical, and comparative perspectives. These different perspectives are not mutually exclusive, but they do emphasize different aspects of the process of regionalization in world trade. This paper seeks to link the rich institutional analysis of various trade blocs with the quantitative assessment of their consequences on bilateral trade.

A long-standing issue in the liberalization of world trade concerns the effects of regional trade blocs. Numerous theoretical and empirical studies have been published to gauge their effects upon world, regional, or bilateral trade. Often theoretical explorations of the effects of institutions are rich and interesting and yet remain detached from empirical testing. Rarely one would find in the quantitative studies how differences in institutional arrangements among trade blocs affect their trade. The quantitative results are either specific to each trade bloc or a general category of such blocs such as free trade area or customs union. Put simply, these analyses fail to exploit the causal link between institutional arrangements within blocs and their trade performance and hence fail to make full use of the available information about trade blocs to evaluate accurately how institutions are related to the performance of trade blocs. This paper makes a preliminary effort in that direction.

The rest of the chapter is organized as follows. First, an overview of the issues are presented. Second, an argument is made for why institutional rules of trade blocs should matter and how. Third, a research design is

85

discussed for how to carry out a quantitative analysis incorporating information regarding various institutional arrangements within trade blocs. Fourth, the findings are presented and discussed. Fifth, an explanation is provided for why the EC presents a unique case among various trade blocs. Finally, a short conclusion ends the chapter.

Overview

Ever since Viner (1950) raised the issue of trade creation or diversion, regional trade blocs have been associated with the second best solution (Meade, 1955; Krugman, 1991). It is argued that statically, regional trade blocs including customs union are trade diverting. A dynamic view is also presented (Bhagwati, 1993), which suggests that over the temporal path, trade blocs may be stumbling blocs or building blocs to liberal world trade.

In the past decade, some scholars suggest that it may be meaningful to examine the issue by differentiating between trade blocs. Some blocs are natural whereas others unnatural (Krugman, 1991b). Natural trade blocs include members who are trading partners anyway in the absence of a formal trade bloc because the transportation cost between them is naturally low. They are welfare improving. Unnatural blocs include members who are far apart, which may be welfare reducing. Wei and Frankel (1997) and Frankel (1998) follow up this idea with empirical testing and show that some blocs are more open than others. The intra-bloc trade bias is greater for some than others.[1]

Meanwhile, many studies compare and contrast trade blocs from an institutional perspective. Krueger (1997) shows how differences in the rules of origin between the customs union and free trade area can have different effects over trade. Enders (1993) compares the dispute settlement procedures for EFTA and CUSFTA. Hoekman and Leidy (1993) insightfully pinpoints the loopholes (both legal and institutional) in GATT and some regional agreements. Kahler (1995) and Lawrence (1996) provide broad institutional analysis of regional trade agreements and their relationship with GATT. Torre and Kelly (1992) present a schematic comparison of the different institutional arrangements of trade blocs by the developing countries, which include bloc coverage, the manner of liberalization occurrence (negative list or positive list approach), rules of origin and liberalization timetable. Despite these efforts, however, Whalley (1998) points the weakness of the simplistic typology of various trade blocs into free trade area, customs union, and preferential trade arrangements in their discussion of trade blocs. He emphasizes the need to examine the effects of institutional differences among blocs. The motivation of the chapter is to take advantage of these institutional analyses and offer an institutional explanation for why some trade blocs have greater intra-bloc trade bias than others.

How Do Institutional Rules of Trade Blocs Matter?

The legalistic and institutional studies of the trade blocs remain largely descriptive, and they discuss how institutional differences might affect trade without controlling for other related factors. On the other hand, the quantitative assessment of the welfare effects of trade blocs usually subsumes the institutional variations across different blocs into dummy variables (1 or 0). Coding blocs into dummy variables has the advantage of separating their partial effects. But the method fails to capture the effects of institutional variations fully as the bloc variables coded as 1 or 0 do not reflect the institutional differences. Such an information loss may be quite important. Trade blocs provide exclusive club benefits to members and by definition discriminate against nonmembers. Both the exclusive benefits and the discriminatory consequences derive from the associated institutional arrangements. Thus, the institutional variations across blocs may be causally related to the degree of inclusiveness for members and exclusiveness for nonmembers, which affects both intra-bloc trade (between members) and extra-bloc trade (between members and nonmembers). Instead of treating bloc effects as being distinctive from each other, I look at their similarities in institutional arrangements for a causal explanation.

   The Table 4.1 in annex compares variations of the rules across seven trade blocs regarding the bloc coverage (tariff and nontariff measures, goods and services movement, factor movement), the implementation strategy and the dispute resolution mechanism. The comparison focuses on dimensions that may be reasonably regarded as comparable across blocs.[2] Comparisons of the institutional variations suggest two things. First, it is deceiving to take the difference in bloc typology as the only major difference between trade blocs. Conventional typology, which classifies blocs into preferential trading arrangements, free trade areas, customs unions, and common market, is less useful in this regard. Noticeably, the Andean Pact and the European Community are both customs unions (or at least they claim to be the same), and yet their bloc coverage and implementation strategies are extremely different.   Another similar example is the comparison of CUSFTA and EFTA. Both belong to the free trade areas (FTA), but their institutional variations are in fact enormous. One is quite comprehensive and refined whereas the other is narrow and flexible.

Second, the trade performance of a trade bloc is causally related to the rules in its coverage, implementation and dispute resolution. The broader the bloc coverage, the lower the transaction cost to trade among the bloc members, and the greater the incentive to engage in intra-bloc trade. The more specific and institutionalized the implementation strategies, the more credible the bloc is among its members, the less likely its members renege on the rules. Likewise, the institutionalization of a dispute resolution mechanism enhances the credibility and continuity of a bloc and reduces the transaction costs for the intra-bloc trade. On the other hand, the more favorable the bloc's institutional design is for the intra-bloc trade, the more suppressive it may be for its trade with nonmembers. A trade bloc is by definition exclusive and discriminatory against nonmembers. Rules that are favorable to the intra-bloc trade become barriers to entry for nonmembers.

Table 4.2 (see annex) presents the ratios of the intra-bloc trade over the bloc trade with nonmembers for seven trade blocs during four different years. EC and CUSFTA have the highest and the second highest ratios of intra-bloc trade over the bloc's external trade, followed by EFTA, ASEAN, LAFTA, ANZCERTA and ANDEAN. Interestingly, this pattern appears to correspond to the level of institutional sophistication for intra-bloc trade liberalization. Of course, one may argue that the evidence is too preliminary. The high or low ratios may be correlated with other factors, such as geographical proximity or contiguity or the level of development, etc. The argument is reasonable, and therefore a convincing test of the hypothesis that the institutional variations of the trade blocs affect the intra-bloc trade bias should control for other relevant factors. Such a multivariate analysis is carried out in the next section to test this hypothesis.

Research Design

This section empirically assesses the effect of institutional variations over intra-bloc trade controlling for other possible causal variables. The basic framework for this purpose is the gravity model, but the key is to come up with a measure of the institutional variations that is amenable to statistical analysis. The gravity model has been the working horse of quantitative analysis of bilateral trade. Recent scholarship has found that the gravity model is theoretically consistent with both the Heckscher-Ohlin theory and the theory of imperfect substitutes (Deardorff, 1997; for a review of the empirical use of the gravity model, see Frankel, 1998). The model asserts that bilateral trade is positively related to the two trading countries' incomes and negatively related to the distance between them. Geographic contiguity, common language and per capita income are the other three factors that are frequently added to the gravity model.

The basic gravity model is specified as the following. The dependent variable is the log of the bilateral volume of total trade (exports plus imports). Some typical independent variables include the log of the product of the two countries' GNP ($LGNP_{ij}$), the log of the product of the two countries' GNP per capita ($LPCGNP_{ij}$), the log of the distance between the capitals or major port cities of the two countries ($LDIST_{ij}$), a dummy variable for the dyadic geographical contiguity (ADJ_{ij}), and a dummy variable for the dyadic common language (LIN_{ij}). The size of the economy (GNP), the level of economic development (GNP per capita), factors contributing to lower transaction costs (geographical contiguity and common language) are expected to increase the level of the bilateral trade. Geographical distance, associated with the transport cost, is expected to reduce the bilateral trade.

Most pertinent to my analysis is how to measure institutional variations between blocs. Previous quantitative studies are of limited help in this regard. Different dimensions of the institutional variations between blocs have never been directly incorporated into any quantitative analysis. The closest is the dummy variable method Wei and Frankel (1997) and Frankel (1997) use to examine the effects of a bloc over intra-bloc and extra-bloc trade. They introduce two different dummy variables for each bloc to study the issue of open or closed trade blocs. For a particular bloc, the first variable, the intra-bloc dummy variable ($BLOC\_I$), is coded one if both countries in a pair belong to the same bloc, and zero otherwise. Its coefficient measures the amount of additional trade between the bloc members relative to that the gravity model predicts for an otherwise identical pair of countries. The second variable, the bloc openness dummy variable (BLOC_O), is coded one if either country in a pair belongs to the bloc. Its coefficient measures the extent of additional trade between a bloc member and a nonmember relative to that the gravity model predicts for a random pair of countries that do not belong to any bloc. If the coefficient for the second variable is statistically significant and negative and that for the first variable is statistically significant but positive, it suggests trade diversion vis-à-vis nonmembers and a closed trade bloc. However, if the coefficient for the second variable is statistically significant and positive, it is evidence for an open trade bloc. Wei and Frankel's method has the advantage of separating the effects of intra-bloc trade, bloc member's trade with nonmembers, and trade between countries having no bloc affiliation whatsoever. But the intra-bloc dummy variables for the different blocs do not contain information about the institutional variations among them. Therefore, a better measure needed for examining how inter-bloc institutional differences affect intra-bloc trade bias.

The discussion in the previous section suggests that the trade performance of a bloc is causally influenced by its rules in coverage, implementation and dispute. Such between-bloc differences in rules are then captured by an institutional variations index for each bloc. The index consists of information about the bloc coverage (tariff elimination, nontariff elimination, free trade in services, free movement of labor, free movement of capital), the bloc implementation (whether a timetable is specified for liberalization), and the dispute resolution (whether dispute settlement procedures are institutionalized). The index is thus composed of these three dimensions with a total of seven categories. If a bloc agreement specifies a rule for a particular category, then the category takes on a value of one and zero otherwise in the index. The index is a sum of these seven categories, ranging between 1 and 7. Based on this constructed institutional variations index, Figure 4.1 compares the differences between these blocs.

Figure 4.1   Comparison of Institutional Variations

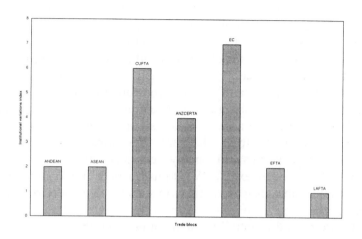

To test how the intra-bloc trade is affected by these institutional rules, I construct a variable INSTVAR. If both countries in a pair belong to the same trade bloc, the variable INSTVAR takes on the value of the institutional variations index for that particular bloc. Otherwise, INSTVAR equals zero. Apparently, the higher the value of INSTVAR, the more liberalized the intra-bloc trade is, the greater the trade volume between two countries of the same bloc. Compared to Wei and Frankel's method of creating an intra-bloc dummy variable for each bloc, INSTVAR combines the information about different blocs with respect to their institutional arrangements.

The measure has some weaknesses. First, it fails to capture the between-bloc differences in the same category if two countries happen to belong to two different blocs that have rather different arrangements in this very category. For example, two blocs may both have dispute resolution procedures, but these procedures are very different in terms of the degree of institutionalization. Yet, both blocs will score the same (a value of one) for this category in the index. Second, it weighs the different categories equally, which implies they are given the same degree of importance. This may be a problem if countries in a bloc prioritize and rank the different types of arrangements. Third, it relies on the assumption that the same category has comparable meanings across different blocs. Fourth, the index has ignored certain institutional arrangements by selecting only those comparable and generally important across blocs.

Despite those weaknesses, the measure INSTVAR allows us to extract much more information about the effects of institutional arrangements than the bloc dummy variables that are conventionally used to distinguish bloc effects. Besides, the assumption of category comparability between blocs is not any stronger than our usual practice of lumping different blocs under the same rubric of free trade area or customs union. On the contrary, by incorporating information from different categories of institutional arrangements that countries commonly consider in the intra-bloc liberalization process, the index INSTVAR pushes much further in terms of distinguishing trade blocs than a general term such as 'free trade area'. Last but not least, it allows us to assess empirically how those institutional arrangements are related to intra-bloc trade, a question that remains to be addressed in the current literature.

The estimation uses the data of Wei and Frankel (1997). The dataset has 1953 country pairs, covering 63 countries or regions and four different years (1970, 1980, 1990, 1992). The data sources are the UN trade matrix and the IMF Direction of Trade Statistics. One advantage of the dataset is its inclusion of a large number of developed and developing countries that enables the analysis of seven different trade blocs (EC, EFTA, CUSFTA, ANDEAN, ANZCERTA, ASEAN, LAFTA/LAIA) in the sample.[3]

Several issues about estimation deserve some additional explanation. I first estimate a model that is similar to the Wei and Frankel (1997) model specification for the pooled data (a time series cross sectional design) and the four different cross sections (1970, 1980, 1990, and 1992 respectively). The model includes the gravity model variables plus the BLOC_I and BLOC_O variables. Given that there are seven trade blocs, there are seven BLOC_I variables and seven BLOC_O variables. This model provides a benchmark for comparing models using intra-bloc dummy variables and models using the institutional variation index.

Next, I estimate the same model specification with six of BLOC_I variables (except EC_I) replaced by the institutional variations index INSTVAR. There are two reasons why INSTVAR should replace the

BLOC_I variables. The first reason is that the institutional variations index should capture the bloc related institutional influences over bilateral trade and is generally applicable to different blocs. BLOC_I variables simply reflect such influences in a cruder manner. The second reason is that the way INSTVAR is constructed lends itself to be a linear combination of the BLOC_I variables. But INSTVAR contains more information about the different blocs than the set of BLOC_I variables. I include the EC_I variable in the estimation to control for the unique EC effect because as will be discussed later, the unique EC intra-bloc trade effect confounds the effect of INSTVAR over the bilateral trade.

Finally, year dummy variables are included in each of the pooled models to control for effects unique to particular years (note that one year is excluded as the reference to avoid perfect multicollinearity).

Findings

Table 4.3 (see annex) presents the results for the gravity model with the intra-bloc dummy variables (BLOC_I) and the bloc openness dummy variables (BLOC_O). First, the gravity model variables are all statistically significant and have the expected signs for both the panel data and the four cross sections. In the first column, $LGNP_{ij}$ (the log of the product of two countries' GNPs) has a parameter estimate 0.847, indicating a positive but less than proportional relationship between economic size and bilateral trade. The parameter estimate on $LPCGNP_{ij}$ is 0.211, showing a positive relationship between economic development and the bilateral trade. $LDIST_{ij}$ shows that as the distance between two countries increases by one percent, their bilateral trade drops by 0.716 percent. ADJ_{ij} has a parameter estimate 0.534, indicating that if two countries share common border, their bilateral trade is higher by about 70% (computed from [exp(0.534)-1]), compared to those that do not. The coefficient on LIN_{ij} indicates that if two countries share a common language, their bilateral trade is about 59% higher, compared to those that do not.

The set of BLOC_I variables indicates the amount of intra-bloc trade bias after controlling for the gravity model variables, the bloc's trade with nonmembers and yearly effects. The set of BLOC-O variables shows the degree of the bloc's trade with nonmembers after controlling for the gravity model variables, the intra-bloc trade bias and the yearly effects. Column 1 shows that EC_I, EFTA_I, ANDEAN_I, LAFTA_I, ASEAN_I, ANZCERTA_I are statistically significant. Except for EC_I, the rest have a positive sign, showing that members of these blocs trade between themselves more than that predicted by the model. Instead, the EC members trade less between themselves than the model prediction. For the set of BLOC_O variables, EC_O, EFTA_O, CUSFTA_O, ASEAN_O are statistically significant. EC_O and ASEAN_O have a positive sign, showing that their members trade more with the nonmembers than the gravity model predicts for a random pair of countries. On the other hand, EFTA_O and CUSFTA_O have a negative sign, showing that the two blocs tend to be more closed than the gravity model predicts.

The four cross section model results in Table 4.3 (see annex) show some interesting findings. First, the gravity model variables remain statistically significant and in the same directions, but exhibit some interesting anomalies over time. For example, the size of the economy exhibits an upward trend in its effect, from 0.7 in 1970 to 0.9 in 1992. Second, ANDEAN_O, LAFTA_O, EC_O and EFTA_O show some flip-flop of the signs or changes in statistical significance for different years. The results remain the same for CUSFTA_O, ASEAN_O, ANZ_O as in the pooled model. Third, the intra-EFTA bias is positive for all years, but only statistically significant for 1970 and 1980. ANDEAN_I and LAFTA_I are positive and statistically significant except for 1970. ASEAN_I are positive and statistically significant for all years, with a temporal decline in the size of the bias. ANZ_I remains statistically insignificant for the two individual years 1990 and 1992. Most noticeably, the intra-EC bias is negative for three years and statistically significant for 1990 and 1992. Together with the results for the pooled model, EC_I is the only intra-bloc bias variable that has a statistically significant but negative sign. This implies that there exists some EC specific effect that weakens the intra-EC bias for trade, a question left to be addressed in a later section. Such bloc-unique effect should be controlled for in estimation when I test for the effect of INSTVAR because INSTVAR is intended to capture some generally applicable institutional influences rather than the bloc unique effect. Besides, the bloc unique effect may very well confound testing the effect of INSTVAR.

Table 4.4 presents the model estimation with the INSTVAR variable. I skip discussion of the gravity model variables as they appear to be extremely robust regardless the model specification. The first column is results of the pooled model with six of the BLOC_I variables replaced by INSTVAR. EC_I is statistically significant and negative, suggesting that there exist some unique EC effect, which should be controlled for to avoid the omitted variable bias. Besides, results for the set of BLOC_O variables remain the same as in the pooled model of Table 4.3 in terms of their signs and statistical significance.   Even their parameter estimates are quite similar in size to those in Table 4.3. Between the two pooled models, both have reasonably good overall model fit and they have the same adjusted R^2s (in fact, their R^2s are also the same).   Even though the pooled model has five more variables in Table 4.3, the pooled model in Table 4.4 explains the same amount of variations in the bilateral trade with the INSTVAR variable. (One may argue from the point of model selection that even if the Table 4.4 model is not necessarily better, it is at least more parsimonious and elegant.).

I am particularly interested in whether the rather crude measure of institutional variations (INSTVAR) is able to explain some pattern that is generalizable across the different trade blocs. INSTVAR is statistically significant at 0.01 level and has a positive sign as expected. The coefficient suggests that that bilateral trade for a pair of countries of the same bloc increases by about 0.4% with a unit increase in INSTVAR (that is a one-category increase). Alternatively, the bilateral trade for a pair of countries of the same bloc is 0.36% higher (INSTVAR has a value of one), compared to another pair of two countries that are otherwise identical according to the model but do not share the bloc membership (INSTVAR has a value of zero).

The cross sectional models have some interesting results about INSTVAR. First, it is statistically significant for each of the four years (1970, 1980, 1990, 1992) at the 0.01 level and consistently in the expected direction. Second, the parameter estimate declines in size over time, from 0.444 in 1970 to 0.211 in 1992. The intra-bloc institutional arrangements have decreased in their trade creation effect within the bloc or the intra-bloc bias. This suggests an interesting contrast against the trend of growing regionalization of world trade. In the past two decades, the number of countries that joined or formed regional trade blocs has increased dramatically. They intended to reap the gains in trade from preferential intra-bloc arrangements. The finding here, however, shows that they are getting decreasing returns in trade from such arrangements over time.

Why is the EC unique?

The results in Table 4.3 (see annex) show that the intra-EC trade is significantly lower relative to that the model predicts for any pair of countries, which is a EC specific effect. For the other six blocs, intra-bloc trade is significantly higher relative to that predicted by the model with the exception of CUSFTA (note that in the case of CUSFTA, intra-bloc trade is not statistically different from zero, which is not the same as the EC effect). Table 4.4 (see annex) also shows EC_I is statistically significant and negative for the pooled model as well as all the cross sectional models. Besides, the parameter estimate remains approximately the same in these models. These results raise the question: why is there the unique EC effect? The institutional variations index is supposed to capture the inter-bloc disparities. What then is missing from this index that makes the EC different from the other blocs?

Table 4.5 (see annex) presents the two dimensions along which Winters (1993) argues that make the EC rather unique among the various trade blocs. First, the EC has been on a path of active enlargement since its inception. Despite its 'take it or leave it' strategy for accession, the EC expands over time, much faster than the other blocs. The EC expansion outshines those of CUSFTA, LAFTA or EFTA in speed and scale. Second, the EC has numerous preferential trading agreements with various African, Caribbean, Pacific, Mediterranean and most recently, East European countries. It also has association agreements with the EFTA countries. As the third column of table 4.5 shows, these trade preferences share one similarity, that is, the free movement of industrial goods and they vary in terms of services and factors. Its expansion in membership and extension of various trade preferences render the EC much less discriminatory against nonmembers, compared to other trade blocs.

Conclusion

This chapter argues that the degree of intra-bloc trade bias is causally related to the institutional arrangements of a trade bloc. Rules regarding the bloc coverage, implementation and dispute resolution reduce transaction costs for trade among bloc members and increase the credibility of these international agreements. The causal argument is tested within the framework of the gravity model for 63 countries during 1970, 1980, 1990 and 1992. The statistical evidence provides empirical support although the analysis may be weakened by its data limitation. Future research is desirable in extending the empirical domain to more countries and a longer time span.

The chapter also illustrates that the rich institutional analysis of regional trade blocs may be integrated into the quantitative assessment of the effects of blocs over bilateral trade. The conventional bloc dummy variable approach that is widely used in econometric analysis is good for showing the inter-bloc differences, but falls short in delineating the commonality in and impact of their institutional rules and arrangements. Integrating the institutional analysis provides a richer story about why the blocs may differ in their performance. Therefore, it pushes one step further than the conventional typology of free trade area, customs union, preferential trade arrangements, and common market.

Notes

[1] For a review of other efforts in quantitative analysis of trade blocs, see Srinivasan, Whalley and Wooton (1993).

[2] Dimensions that are considered as unique to particular blocs are excluded. For example, one feature with trade blocs by many developing countries is the specification of some goal in industrialization. This, however, does not apply to the developed countries and hence my focus on the comparable dimensions.

[3] The Wei and Frankel analysis studies a different set of trade blocs, and for each, they use the same set of countries for different years. Their purpose is to look for evidence of explicit as well as implicit bloc effects resulting from opaque institutions, cultures, or implicit policies. The practice is not appropriate for the purpose of this chapter. The institutional arrangements should affect the countries that did not join the bloc differently from those that were already part of the bloc. An accurate assessment of how institutional variations affect the intra-bloc trade requires a careful tally of when a country becomes a member of a bloc.

Thus, the model estimation presented here includes only those blocs that already existed during the period under study and excludes informal or later ones (such as the East Asia bloc, Nafta, and Mercosur). The bloc related variables (BLOC_I and BLOC_O) use the actual bloc membership starting years for all relevant countries.

References

Bhalla, A.S., and P. Bhalla, P. (1997), *Regional Blocs: Building blocs or Stumbling Blocs?* St. Martin's Press, New York.

Balasubramanyam, V.N. (1989), 'ASEAN and Regional Trade Cooperation in Southeast Asia', in D. Greenaway, T. Hyclak, and R. J. Thornton (eds), *Economic Aspects Of Regional Trading Arrangements*, New York University Press, New York, pp. 167-188.

Bhagwati, J. (1993), 'Regionalism and Multilateralism: An overview', in J. de Melo and A. Panagariya (eds), *New Dimensions In Regional Integration*, Cambridge University Press, New York.

Deardorff, A.V. (1998), 'Determinants of Bilateral Trade: Does Gravity Work in a Neoclassical World?', in J.A. Frankel (ed), *The Regionalization of The World Economy*, University of Chicago Press, Chicago, pp. 7-32.

Edwards, S. and Savastano, M. (1989), 'Latin America's Intra-Regional Trade: Evolution and Future Prospects', in D. Greenaway, T. Hyclak, and R. J. Thornton (eds), *Economic Aspects Of Regional Trading Arrangements*, New York University Press, New York, pp. 189-234.

Enders, A. (1993), 'Dispute Settlement In Regional And Multilateral Trade Agreements', in K. Anderson, and R. Blackhurst (eds), *Regional Integration and the Global Trading System*, St Martin's Press, New York, pp. 344-357.

Frankel, J.A. (1997), *Regional Trading Blocs in the World Economic System*, Institute of International Economics, Washington DC.

Frankel, J.A. and Wei, S. (1998), 'Regionalization of World Trade And Currencies: Economics and Politics', in J.A. Frankel (ed), *The Regionalization of The World Economy*, Chicago, University of Chicago Press, Chicago, pp. 189-226.

Hoekman, B. and Leidy, M. (1993), 'Holes and Loopholes in integration agreements: History and Prospects', in K. Anderson, and R. Blackhurst (eds), *Regional Integration and the Global Trading System*, St Martin's Press, New York, pp. 218-245.

Jovanovic, Miroslav (1998), *International Economic Integration*, Routledge, London.

Kahler, Miles (1995), *International Institutions and the Political Economy of Integration*, The Brookings Institution, Washington DC.

Krueger, A.O. (1997), 'Problems with Overlapping Free Trade Areas', in T.Ito, and A.O. Krueger (eds), *Regionalism versus Multilateral Trade Arrangements*, University of Chicago Press, Chicago, pp. 9-23.

Krugman, P.R. (1991), 'Is Bilateralism Bad?', in E. Helpman and A. Razin (eds), *International Trade and Trade Policy*, MIT Press, Cambridge, MA.

Krugman, P.R. (1991b), *The Move Toward Free Trade Zones. Policy Implications of Trade and Currency Zones*, Federal Reserve Bank of Kansas City, Jackson Hole, WY.

Lawrence, R.Z. (1996), *Regionalism, Multilateralism, and Deeper Integration*, The Brookings Institution, Washington DC.

Mace, G. (1994), 'Consensus Building in the ANDEAN Integration System: 1968-1985', in W. Andrew Axline (ed), *The Political Economy of Regional Cooperation: Comparative Case Studies*, Pinter publishers and Associated University Presses, London, pp. 34-71.

Meade, J. (1955), *The Theory of Customs Unions*, North-Holland, Amsterdam.

Morici, P. (1989), 'The Canadian-US free trade agreement: Origins, Contents and Prospects', in D. Greenaway, T. Hyclak, and R. J. Thornton (eds), *Economic Aspects of Regional Trading Arrangements*, New York University Press, pp. 43-68.

Srinivasan, T.N., Whalley, J., and Wooton, I.. (1993), 'Measuring the Effects of Regionalism on Trade And Welfare', in K. Anderson and R. Blackhurst (ed), *Regional Integration and the Global Trading System*, St Martin's Press, New York, pp. 52-80.

De la Torre, A. and Kelly, M.R. (1992). *Regional Trade Arrangements*, International Monetary Fund, Washington DC.

Viner, J. (1950), *The Customs Union Issue*, Carnegie Endowment For International Peace, New York.

Wei, S. and Frankel, J.A. (1997), 'Open versus Closed Trade Blocs', in T. Ito, and A.O. Krueger (eds), *Regionalism versus Multilateral Trade Arrangements*, University of Chicago Press, Chicago, pp. 119-139.

Whalley, J. (1998), 'Why do Countries Seek Regional Trade Agreements?', in J.A. Frankel (ed), The Regionalization of The World Economy, University of Chicago Press, Chicago, pp. 63-91.

Winters, A. (1993), 'Expanding EC Membership And Association Accords: recent experience and future prospects', in K. Anderson and R. Blackhurst (ed), Regional Integration and the Global Trading System, St Martin's Press, New York.

Table 4.1 **Institutional Variations across Seven Trade Blocs**

	Australia-New Zealand Closer Economic Relations Trade Agreement (ANZCERTA)	European Community (EC)	European Free Trade Association (EFTA)	Latin American Free Trade Association (LAFTA); Latin American Integration Association (LAIA)
Effective Date	1/1/83	7/6/67	5/3/60	6/2/61; 8/12/80
Members	Australia, New Zealand	France, Germany, Belgium, Italy, Netherlands, Luxembourg; UK (1973), Ireland (1973), and Denmark (1973); Greece (1981); Spain and Portugal (1986); Austria, Sweden and Finland (1995)	Austria (left 1995), Denmark (left 1972), Norway, Portugal (left 1986), Sweden (left 1995), Switzerland, UK (left 1972), Finland (associated, 1961; full membership 1986; left 1995), Iceland (1970), Liechtenstein (1991)	Argentina, Brazil, Bolivia (1966), Chile, Colombia, Ecuador, Mexico, Paraguay, Peru, Uruguay, Venezuela (1967)
Type	Free trade area	Customs union	Free trade area	Free trade area
Tariff Elimination	Remove all tariffs (by 1988) and quantitative restrictions (by 1995)	Free movement of goods	Removal of tariffs and quantitative restrictions in the trade of industrial goods	Preferences in specific sectors; national lists of goods for which each country agreed to reduce nominal tariffs by at least 8% percent annually; the common lists for goods that all countries agreed to have zero tariffs and no quantitative restrictions;

	Australia-New Zealand Closer Economic Relations Trade Agreement (ANZCERTA)	European Community (EC)	European Free Trade Association (EFTA)	Latin American Free Trade Association (LAFTA); Latin American Integration Association (LAIA)
Nontariff Elimination	Eliminate all direct export subsidies and antidumping; harmonize business laws, customs procedures, government purchasing and technical standards	Free movement of goods	NA	NA

	Australia-New Zealand Closer Economic Relations Trade Agreement (ANZCERTA)	European Community (EC)	European Free Trade Association (EFTA)	Latin American Free Trade Association (LAFTA); Latin American Integration Association (LAIA)
Free Trade in Services	Negative list approach for services (liberalized unless otherwise indicated)	Free movement of services	NA	NA
Free Movement of Labor	NA	Free movement of capital	NA	NA
Free Movement of Capital	NA	Free movement of labor	NA	NA
Specified Timetable for Liberalization	Annual steps till 1995	Economic and monetary union by 1999	NA	NA
Dispute Settlement Procedures	NA	Establish community law and supranational institutions for common decision making and enforcement (the Commission, the Council and the Court of Justice)	Formal complaints can be submitted to the Council (the oversight body) for arbitration under a majority rule; unilateral actions are allowed in the absence of commonly acceptable solutions	NA

	Andean Pact	Association Of South East Asian Nations (ASEAN)	Canada-United States Free Trade Agreement (CUSFTA)
Effective Date	10/16/69	8/8/67	1/1/89
Continent	South America	Asia	North America
Members	Bolivia, Chile (left 1976), Colombia, Ecuador, Peru, Venezuela (1973)	Indonesia, Malaysia, Philippines, Singapore, and Thailand, Brunei (1984), Vietnam (1995), Laos, Myanmar (1997)	Canada, US
Type	Customs union	Preferential tariff arrangements (PTA, 1976); Asean Free Trade Area (AFTA 1992)	Free trade area
Tariff Elimination	Automatic yearly reduction of the average tariff level for about 7% of the initial tariff structure (except for Bolivia and Ecuador); exceptions for some sectoral programs and those on the negative list	PTA to promote intra-ASEAN trade; a negative list for sensitive items to be excluded; integration through regulation	Tariff liberalization for trade in goods
Nontariff Elimination	NA	Liberalization of non-tariff measures on a preferential basis	Prohibit import quota, export control, dual pricing of exports, and export taxes, harmonize product standards and technical regulations

	Andean Pact	Association Of South East Asian Nations (ASEAN)	Canada-United States Free Trade Agreement (CUSFTA)
Free Trade in Services	NA	NA	To eliminate barriers to bilateral trade in services; accord national treatment to each other's providers of trade in services
Free Movement of Labor	NA	NA	Limited liberalization in professional labor services
Free Movement of Capital	NA	NA	Accord national treatment to each other's businesses; limited liberalization in financial services

	Andean Pact	Association Of South East Asian Nations (ASEAN)	Canada-United States Free Trade Agreement (CUSFTA)
Specified Timetable for Liberalization	A complete trade liberalization with common external tariff by 1980, then a free trade area with a common external tariff set for 1992; customs union to be achieved by 1995	NA; AFTA to be fully implemented till 2003	Tariff elimination for 3 phases (immediate, 5 year and 10 year)
Dispute Settlement Procedures	NA	NA	Disputes about anti-dumping and countervailing duty law are dealt with in Ch.19; other disputes for trade in goods are under Ch.18. Bilateral consultations as the first step; if they fail, then the Commission may settle for safeguard actions by arbitration, and for others, a panel may be set up or a binding arbitration be given. The panel is of five members, two selected by each party and unaffiliated with the governments and the fifth by the Commission. Panel findings are published, then the Commission decides on a resolution. In the absence of resolution, unilateral suspension of benefits is allowed.

Table 4.2   Ration of IntraBloc Trade over Bloc Trade with Nonmembers

Year	EC	CUSFTA	EFTA	ASEAN	LAFTA	ANZCERTA	ANDEAN
1970	0.36		0.15	0.08	0.06		0.02
1980	0.40		0.06	0.07	0.06		0.02
1990	0.46	0.20	0.07	0.09	0.05	0.04	0.03
1992	0.47	0.20	0.07	0.10	0.07	0.04	0.04

Table 4.3   Parameter Estimates of the Gravity Model with Bloc Dummy Variables

Model	Panel		1970		1980	
Variable	Parameter Estimate	Standard Error	Parameter Estimate	Standard Error	Parameter Estimate	Standard Error
INTERCEP	-10.124***	0.268	-11.302***	0.532	-12.940***	0.0552
LGNP	0.847***	0.009	0.731***	0.019	0.823***	0.018
LPCGNP	0.211***	0.012	0.338***	0.027	0.273***	0.023
LDIST	-0.716***	0.025	-0.544***	0.050	-0.592***	0.046
ADJ1	0.534***	0.090	0.523***	0.184	0.563***	0.172
LIN	0.462***	0.045	0.476***	0.090	0.464***	0.088
EC_1	-0.238***	0.106	0.114	0.371	-0.128	0.235
EFTA_1	0.512***	0.140	0.769***	0.222	0.625	0.299
CUSFAT_1	-0.229	0.809				
ANDEAN_1	0.819***	0.200	0.539	0.416	0.647*	0.379
LAFTA_1	0.530***	0.138	0.291	0.262	0.470*	0.267

Model	Panel		1970		1980	
	Parameter Estimate	Standard Error	Parameter Estimate	Standard Error	Parameter Estimate	Standard Error
ASEAN_I	1.311***	0.198	1.718***	0.382	1.692***	0.388
ANZ_I	1.872***	0.806				
EC_O	0.183***	0.041	0.591***	0.091	0.282***	0.075
EFTA_O	-0.298***	0.046	0.115	0.083	-0.180*	0.086
CUSFTA_O	-0.203***	0.084				
ANDEAN_O	-0.011	0.050	0.340***	0.110	0.110	0.099
LAFTA_O	-0.045	0.044	-0.349***	0.093	-0.140*	0.086
ASEAN_O	0.653***	0.047	0.509***	0.105	0.546***	0.092
ANZ_O	-0.090	0.085				
N	5575		1131		1389	
Adjusted R^2	0.80		0.76		0.76	

Note: ***, **, and * denote 1%, 5%, and 10% level statistical significance respectively for two tailed tests.

Model	Panel		1970		1980	
Variable	Parameter Estimate	Standard Error	Parameter Estimate	Standard Error	Parameter Estimate	Standard Error
INTERCEP	-10.124***	0.268	-10.076***	0.597	-12.700***	0.553
LGNP	0.847***	0.009	0.887***	0.019	0.908***	0.017
LPCGNP	0.211***	0.012	0.134***	0.024	0.231***	0.021
LDIST	-0.716***	0.025	-0.897***	0.052	-0.814***	0.047
ADJ1	0.534***	0.090	0.494***	0.176	0.543***	0.172
LIN	0.462***	0.045	0.310***	0.090	0.612***	0.082
EC_1	-0.238***	0.106	-0.362***	0.183	-0.509***	0.170
EFTA_1	0.512***	0.140	0.147	0.316	-0.118	0.292
CUSFAT_1	-0.229	0.809	-0.484	1.169	-0.836	1.085
ANDEAN_1	0.819***	0.200	0.947**	0.389	1.185***	0.378
LAFTA_1	0.530***	0.138	0.839***	0.280	0.583**	0.272

Model	Panel		1990		1992	
Variable	Parameter Estimate	Standard Error	Parameter Estimate	Standard Error	Parameter Estimate	Standard Error
ASEAN_I	1.311***	0.198	1.076***	0.400	0.958***	0.371
ANZ_I	1.872***	0.806	1.707	1.160	1.476	1.077
EC_O	0.183***	0.041	0.131	0.085	-0.186**	0.076
EFTA_O	-0.298***	0.046	-0.468***	0.102	-0.739***	0.090
CUSFTA_O	-0.203***	0.084	-0.101	0.136	-0.543***	0.121
ANDEAN_O	-0.011	0.050	-0.109	0.095	-0.169*	0.089
LAFTA_O	-0.045	0.044	0.438***	0.088	-0.272***	0.078
ASEAN_O	0.653***	0.047	0.885***	0.092	0.619***	0.084
ANZ_O	-0.090	0.085	0.161	0.139	-0.165	0.122
1980	-1.238***					
1990	-1.814***					
1992	-1.985***					
N	5575				1543	
Adjusted R^2	0.80				0.82	

Note: ***, **, and * denote 1%, 5%, and 10% level statistical significance respectively for two tailed tests.

Table 4.4   Parameter Estimates for Testing Effects of Institutional Variations among Trade Blocs
(63 countries, 1970–1992)

Model	Panel		1970		1980	
Variable	Parameter Estimate	Standard Error	Parameter Estimate	Standard Error	Parameter Estimate	Standard Error
INTERCEP	-9.968***	0.266	-11.212***	0.529	-12.860***	0.549
LGNP	0.847***	0.009	0.732***	0.019	0.825***	0.018
LPCGNP	0.207***	0.012	0.331***	0.027	0.269***	0.023
LDIST	-0.728***	0.025	-0.547***	0.050	-0.598***	0.046
ADJI	0.534***	0.089	0.509***	0.180	0.569***	0.171
LIN	0.468***	0.044	0.456***	0.088	0.454***	0.086
EC_I	-2.766***	0.326	-2.989***	0.674	-3.342***	0.710
EC_O	0.183***	0.041	0.590***	0.091	0.283***	0.075
EFTA_O	-0.310***	0.046	0.108	0.083	-0.194***	0.086
CUSFTA_O	-0.216***	0.084				
ANDEAN_O	-0.003	0.049	0.319***	0.108	0.097	0.098
LAFTA_O	-0.027	0.042	-0.367***	0.090	-0.137*	0.083
ASEAN_O	0.681***	0.046	0.557***	0.103	0.582***	0.091
ANZ_O	-0.072	0.085				
INSTVAR	0.360***	0.046	0.444***	0.086	0.458***	0.099

Model	Panel		1970		1980	
Variable	Parameter Estimate	Standard Error	Parameter Estimate	Standard Error	Parameter Estimate	Standard Error
1980	-1.229***	0.054				
1990	-1.804***	0.056				
1992	-1.972***	0.058				
N	5575		1131		1389	
Adjusted R^2	0.80		0.76		0.76	

Note: ***, **, * and * denote 1%, 5%, and 10% level statistical significance respectively for two tailed tests.

Model	Panel		1990		1992	
	Parameter Estimate	Standard Error	Parameter Estimate	Standard Error	Parameter Estimate	Standard Error
INTERCEP	-9.968***	0.266	-9.753***	0.590	-12.386***	0.548
LGNP	0.847***	0.009	0.887***	0.019	0.0908***	0.017
LPCGNP	0.207***	0.012	0.126***	0.023	0.223***	0.021
LDIST	-0.728***	0.025	-0.921***	0.052	-0.835***	0.047
ADJ1	0.534***	0.089	0.497***	0.175	0.530***	0.171
LIN	0.468***	0.044	0.337***	0.089	0.642***	0.082
EC_I	-2.766***	0.326	-2.337***	0.633	-1.992***	0.591
EC_O	0.183***	0.041	0.136*	0.085	-0.181***	0.076
EFTA_O	-0.310***	0.046	-0.478***	0.102	-0.756***	0.090
CUSFTA_O	-0.216***	0.084	-0.103	0.136	-0.549***	0.121
ANDEAN_O	-0.003	0.049	-0.087	0.094	-0.131	0.088
LAFTA_O	-0.027	0.042	0.490***	0.085	-0.234***	0.077
ASEAN_O	0.681***	0.046	0.910***	0.091	0.642***	0.083
ANZ_O	-0.072	0.085	0.195	0.138	-0.138	0.121
INSTVAR	0.360***	0.046	0.281***	0.090	0.211***	0.084

Model	Panel		1990		1992	
	Parameter Estimate	Standard Error	Parameter Estimate	Standard Error	Parameter Estimate	Standard Error
1980	-1.229***	0.054				
1990	-1.804***	0.056				
1992	-1.972***	0.058				
N	5575		1512		1543	
Adjusted R^2	0.80		0.79		0.82	

Note: ***, **, and * denote 1%, 5%, and 10% level statistical significance respectively for two tailed tests

Table 4.5   Efforts of EC Enlargement and Trade Preferences

EC Enlargement	EC's Preferential Trading Agreements (PTA) and Association Agreements (AA)	Content of EC PTA and AA
First enlargement (1961-2) Denmark, Ireland, Norway, UK (first rejected, then admitted in 1973)	General system of preferences (GSP)	Limited tariff free access for most industrial goods; few agricultural concessions; active safeguards
The southern enlargement: Greece, Portugal and Spain (political gains for new democracies, economic transfers for regional development)	EFTA (pre-1993)	Free trade in industrial goods; many cooperation agreements
The EFTA countries: Austria, Finland, Sweden, Switzerland	Africa, Caribbean and Pacific (ASP) countries (Lome Convention)	Free access to EC in industrial goods, some preferences for agricultural goods; exemption for MFA restrictions on textiles and clothing
The Mediterranean candidates: Turkey, Cyprus and Malta (all have preferential trading agreements with the EC)	Mediterranean countries	Duty free access for industrial goods, but several non-tariff import barriers; a few agricultural preferences; most subject to ceilings
The Central European candidates: Czechoslovakia, Hungary, and Poland	Eastern European countries (European Agreements of 1992)	Free access for industrial goods to be phased in over six years; agricultural preferences; considerable harmonization of laws; rights of establishment

Appendix   List of 63 Countries and Cities

#	Country	City	#	Country	City
1	Algeria	Algiers	17	France	Paris
2	Argentina	Buenos Aires	18	Ghana	Accra
3	Australia	Sydney	19	Greece	Athens
4	Austria	Vienna	20	Hong Kong	Hong Kong
5	Belgium	Brussels	21	Hungary	Budapest
6	Bolivia	La Paz	22	Iceland	Reykjavik
7	Brazil	Sao Paulo	23	India	New Delhi
8	Canada	Ottawa	24	Indonesia	Jakarta
9	Chile	Santiago	25	Iran	Tehran
10	China	Shanghai	26	Ireland	Dublin
11	Colombia	Bogota	27	Israel	Jerusalem
12	Denmark	Copenhagen	28	Italy	Rome
13	Ecuador	Quito	29	Japan	Tokyo
14	Egypt	Cairo	30	Kenya	Nairobi
15	Ethiopia	Addis Abeba	31	Kuwait	Kuwait
16	Finland	Helsinki	32	Libya	Tripoli

#	Country	City	#	Country	City
33	Malaysia	Kuala Lumpur	49	South Korea	Seoul
34	Mexico	Mexico City	50	Spain	Madrid
35	Morocco	Casablanca	51	Sudan	Khartoum
36	Netherlands	Amsterdam	52	Sweden	Stockholm
37	New Zealand	Wellington	53	Switzerland	Geneva
38	Nigeria	Lagos	54	Taiwan	Taipei
39	Norway	Oslo	55	Thailand	Bangkok
40	Pakistan	Karachi	56	Tunisia	Tunis
41	Paraguay	Asuncion	57	Turkey	Ankara
42	Peru	Lima	58	UK	London
43	Philippines	Manila	59	Uruguay	Montevideo
44	Poland	Warsaw	60	US	Chicago
45	Portugal	Lisbon	61	Venezuela	Caracas
46	Saudi Arabia	Riyadh	62	West Germany	Bonn
47	Singapore	Singapore	63	Yugoslavia	Belgrade
48	South Africa	Pretoria			

5 The Links between Domestic Political Forces, Inter-Bloc Dynamics and the Multilateral Trading System

BART KERREMANS

Introduction

The emergence of regional trade agreements and their effect in the multilateral trading system is currently one of the hot issues in international political economy (cf. Sekwat and Lynch, 1995; Bergsten, 1997; Baldwin, 1997). In most of the cases, the questions that surround this issue refer to the way in which regional trade agreements or trading blocs affect the multilateral trading system. Are they detrimental to or beneficial for it?

In this chapter we will try to answer this question from the domestic side of trade policy-making. To what extent and why does the pursuit of regional trade policies by states or customs territories affect their openness towards multilateral trade liberalization? The answer to this question will be provided by looking into the policies of the United States and the European Union towards regionalism and multilateralism and the way in which the choice for either of these options has affected the openness towards the other one.

Why the EU and the US? The answer to this question is twofold. First, these two entities form the two largest trading blocs in the World Trade Organization. Consequently, their policies have potentially a serious effect on the WTO and the multilateral trading system. Domestically, this means that policymakers in the two entities have to take into account the effects of their policy choices on the WTO. Second, both the EU and the US have both played a pro-active role in the development of the GATT/WTO, and developed a policy of regionalism. In the case of the US, such regionalism has been developed more recently than in the EU, but has quickly achieved a prominent place on the American foreign trade policy agenda. At the same time, as we will see, the European Union seems to have entered a stage in which it is becoming increasingly careful about concluding new regional trade agreements (RTAs). This is remarkable as the EU/EC has traditionally been a strong initiator of such agreements.

This chapter is structured as follows. First, EU policies towards regionalism and multilateralism will be analyzed. Questions that will be dealt with are the factors behind the conduct of an EU policy in favor of RTAs, and the way in which the choice for regionalism has affected the EU approach towards multilateralism. Second, the same kind of questions will be dealt with for the United States. In a final part of this chapter, we will try to extrapolate from these two case studies towards the question whether multilateralism and regionalism are mutually exclusive in the domestic realm of states and customs territories.

The European Union, Regional Trade Agreements, and Multilateralism

The Sheer Number of EU RTAs

Compared with the United States and most other countries in the world, the European Union has been the most active in developing regional trade agreements. In its external trade policy such agreements have always occupied a prominent place, and this from the inception of the EU/EC on. Already in the negotiations for the EEC Treaty, the question of the trade relations between the EEC and a number of colonies and former colonies of the member states was resolved in a way that became the precursor of a wide range of preferential trade relations between the EU and what is now known as the ACP-states. Equally, EU enlargements have spilled over into trade relations of a preferential nature with an expanding group of third countries. This EU practice was so widespread that one could almost say that the EU for years had the monopoly of regional trade agreements in the multilateral trading system of the GATT/WTO. It was only with the emergence of an American regional trade policy at the end of the eighties and with the proliferation of RTAs on all continents of the globe, that this EU monopoly could be dethroned. This doesn't mean that the EU - during this period - had become less active in the field of RTAs. On the contrary, since the end of the Cold War, the European Union has showed a renewed

'RTA Dynamism' by concluding free trade agreements with numerous third countries.[1] Some of these RTAs have improved and intensified the trade relations between the EU and countries with whom it already had concluded trade agreements in the past.[2] Others have created trade relations with countries with which the EU hadn't concluded any trade agreement before. The end of the Cold War itself forms part of the explanation as it opened the perspective of trade relations with countries that until then had been relatively insulated from the multilateral trading system to which the EU belongs. Equally, the dissolution of the Soviet Union provided the EU the opportunity to establish trade relations with the former Soviet republics.

But also outside Europe's former Eastern Bloc, new opportunities emerged. The end of Apartheid in South Africa opened the door for negotiations on a free trade agreement. The end of the military regime in Chile, and the change in trade policies of many Latin-American countries made the Western Hemisphere more attractive for the development of preferential trade relations. As Mexico became part of the North American Free Trade Agreement, the interest of the Europeans for its market increased. This stems from its greater attractiveness for European investors and traders on the one hand, and the relatively strict rules of origin in NAFTA on the other (cf. Pomfret, 1997: 161). The latter has engendered a certain European fear for trade diversion.

In the same vein, South America became much more attractive for the EU. This largely stems from four reasons. The first consists of the rising economic growth of most of these countries, which brought many of them into the group of the so-called emerging economies. A second factor consists of the formation of the Mercosur customs union and to a lesser extent of the customs union of the Andean Community in 1995. The third one consists of the increasing interest of the United States for the Western Hemisphere (cf. the FTAA). Fourthly, the EU membership of Spain and Portugal (since 1986) formed an additional impetus to pay more attention to this subcontinent.

Also in Asia, the European Union started to show more interest, partly in response to the creation of APEC in 1994. The European reaction to this has been the creation of ASEM (Asia-Europe Meetings) and the adoption of the Trade Facilitation Action Plan (TFAP), both in 1996.[3] Also in the EU's backyard, the Mediterranean basin, a new impetus to improved trade relations has been given by the start of the so-called Barcelona Process in 1995.

As already has been indicated, the EU is not the only one however in shaping and concluding RTAs. Other countries and groups of countries have showed an increasing dynamism in this field as well.[4] As the next graph indicates, although the EC/EU has traditionally been the most active on RTAs (the EC was involved in more than 60% of the RTAs reported to the GATT/WTO), the number of RTAs without the EU reported to the GATT/WTO has steadily increased since the end of the Cold War.

Figure 5.1   Share of EC-Initiated RTAs in the RTAs Reported to the WTO (1957-97)[5]

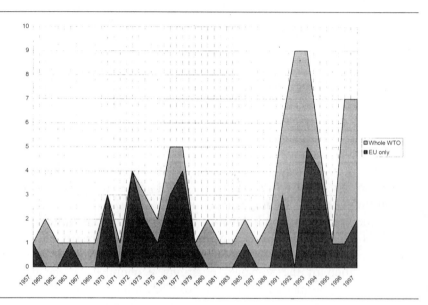

The EU's Dual External Trade Policy

The prominent place of RTAs in the EC/EU from its inception on, has resulted in the simultaneous development of the current multilateral trading system built on the GATT/WTO, and the EU's system of regionalized trade preferences. For that reason, one could say that the EU's has been conducting a dual trade policy in which the two components - EU-initiated RTAs, and market opening through multilateral commitments - have been relatively insulated from each other. This has resulted in a structure of market access preferences that has been compared with a pyramid. In this pyramid, the countries with the highest preferential access to the EU form the top. Those with the lowest preferences are at the bottom. In addition, it is understood that the lowest levels of market access have been granted to those countries that are members of the GATT/WTO but with which the EU has not established preferential trade relations through RTAs.

The Potential collision between EU regionalism and the WTO-rules In legal terms, the gap due to the relative insulation of the two parts of the EU's external trade policy has been bridged by article XXIV GATT. But the obscurity of this provision has given the EC serious leeway in the extension and the deepening of its network of RTAs, without making the GATT compatibility of such arrangements a prior or major concern. After the Uruguay Round this has changed somewhat as the Understanding on GATT Article XXIV has allowed for a more rigorous interpretation and application of this article and as the new dispute settlement procedure has opened the door to a more strict enforcement. Indeed, with the new provisions and procedures, the Fourth Lomé Convention concluded between the EU and the ACP-countries in December 1989, was one of the first RTAs to be declared incompatible with the WTO-obligations of the EU. The temporary solution to this problem - the granting of a WTO waiver - has forced the EU to consider in which way its RTA-policies and its WTO commitments can be integrated. One of the consequences of this is that the ACP-EU relations will have to be revamped substantially.

But the European Union has not been waiting for a WTO decision on one of its RTAs before starting to pay more attention to its WTO-compatibility. Already in 1995, largely as a consequence of the entering into force of the Uruguay Round Agreements, the Commission submitted a communication to the EU Council of Ministers on this issue.[6] Upon request by the European Council of Firenze (June 1996), the Council ordered the Commission in October 1996 to conduct further research on the issue, namely by concentrating on the 'evolution of trade policies and the preferential agreements of the Community.'[7] Equally, the EU asked for a clarification of Article XXIV GATT at the first Ministerial Conference of the WTO in December 1996 in Singapore.

This attention for preferential agreements and their compatibility with article XXIV of the GATT 1994, was a consequence of the new dynamism in concluding RTAs as mentioned above and was raised as part of the discussions to start negotiations on free trade agreements (FTAs) with Mexico and with South Africa. Especially on the demand of France, the Commission issued a new Communication to the Council in 1997. The French demand stemmed from the fear that the EU would have to extend the benefits of the concerned RTAs to all WTO-members, in case these would violate article XXIV of the GATT. The French were supported in this by Germany and the Netherlands, and by several southern member states. The support of the first stemmed from their concern that FTAs, if ill conceived, could be detrimental to the objectives of multilateral trade liberalization. This could ultimately lead to retaliation from the other WTO-members in case such violations were indeed determined through the WTO dispute settlement procedure.

The support of the second group of member states and France was due to the question whether RTAs – in order to be compatible with article XXIV GATT – had to contain provisions on liberalization of trade in agricultural goods.

RTAs are by definition incompatible with the principles of MFN-treatment and non-discrimination as enshrined in the GATT. As a result GATT only allows exceptions if they fulfill a number of conditions. This is equally the case for the General Agreement on Trade in Services (GATS) where RTAs are considered to be exceptions to the principles of non-discrimination and national treatment. In both cases, the GATT and the GATS, specific provisions have been provided that outline the conditions under which RTAs can be allowed for. We will only deal with these provisions briefly, as the purpose is to outline their relevance for the discussions inside the EU on its policy concerning RTAs.

The basic assumption of article XXIV – which is often neglected in much of the criticisms on RTAs – is that RTAs can indeed be and often are vehicles that promote international trade liberalization. Indeed, as the first sentence of article XXIV: 4 says:

> The Contracting Parties recognize the desirability of increasing freedom of trade by the development, through voluntary agreements, of closer integration between the economies of the countries parties to such agreements.[8]

The second sentence, however, directly points at the risks of such agreements, despite their potential benefits for the multilateral trading system:

> They [the Contracting Parties] also recognize that the purpose of a customs union or of a free-trade area should be to facilitate trade between the constituent territories and not to raise barriers to the trade of other contracting parties with such territories.

It is because of these risks that a number of conditions exist before a RTA can be considered to be compatible with the GATT Agreement. There are two kinds of conditions. The first conditions are related to the trade barriers between the countries belonging to a RTA on the one hand, and those outside the RTA on the other, before and after the RTA is concluded (Article XXIV: 5 (b)). The second conditions are related to the shape of a regional agreement itself. Article XXIV only recognizes customs unions and free trade areas. Therefore, in order to be compatible with the GATT, a RTA has to be at least a free trade area as defined in Article XXIV: 8 (b):

> A free-trade area shall be understood to mean a group of two or more customs territories in which the duties and other restrictive regulations of commerce (except, where necessary, those permitted under Articles XI, XII, XIII, XIV, XV, and XX) are eliminated on substantially all the trade between the constituent territories in products originating in such territories.

The big issue in the EU concerned the 'substantially all the trade' requirement. Already during the discussions on the compatibility of the European Economic Community itself with Article XXIV GATT, the question was raised. The six EEC member states of that time proposed a specific criterion whereby 'a free-trade area should be considered as having been achieved for substantially all the trade when the volume of liberalized trade reached 80% of total trade' (WTO, 1995: 824). The Contracting Parties of the GATT have never accepted that.[9] Instead, a negative criterion (i.e. a criterion that defines when the condition of 'substantially all the trade' has not been met) has been adopted. This criterion, as adopted by several GATT Working Parties on Agreements Presented Under Article XXIV, stated that (WTO, 1995: 825):

> Article XXIV: 8(b) had to be interpreted to mean free trade in all products and not carved out by sectors; the exclusion of a whole sector, no matter what percentage of current trade it constituted was contrary to the spirit of both Article XXIV and the General Agreement.

This reasoning has been included in the Understanding on Article XXIV, which is part of the Uruguay Round Agreements. In the preamble of this Understanding, after having recognized the contribution to the expansion of world trade that customs unions and free-trade areas *may* make, the Members of the WTO recognize:

> (..) that such contribution is increased if the elimination between the constituent territories of duties and other restrictive regulations of commerce extends to all trade, and diminished if any major sector of trade is excluded.[10]

According to Grossman and Helpman (1995: 681-682) this means that 'substantially all trade' can be interpreted '(..) to place a limit on the number of industries that can be excluded from an agreement, on the fraction of bilateral trade excluded, on the fraction of total trade excluded, or perhaps on something else' (see also Senti, 1994: 145).

The obscurity of the 'substantially all the trade' requirement has not been eradicated, however, at least not according to the European Commission.[11] As it stated in its own analysis of Article XXIV (European Commission, 1996a, p. 7):

> There are indications that the operation of GATT Article XXIV (already marked by uncertainty) is coming under more strain than before. There are long-standing concerns about the difficulty of interpreting elements of GATT Article XXIV, including the definition of 'substantially all trade', the definition of a major sector and related questions of coverage in terms of non-traded goods.[12]

It is obvious, as is made clear in the Commission report itself, that the main concern about a sectoral approach to the 'substantially all the trade' requirement is due to the possible requirement that agriculture has to be included in RTAs before they can be considered to respect Article XXIV. An expert group convened by the Commission Directorate-General for Agriculture (DG VI) has defended this opinion.[13] In its report[14] on the EU's common agricultural policy (Expert Group, 1997, par. 4.2), the group recognized that:

> The inclusion of agriculture in the Uruguay Round has had an important effect for the operation of Customs Unions and Free Trade Areas. Previously, it has been possible for groups of countries to create zones of free trade but effectively to exclude agriculture. Now that agriculture is part of the WTO, this may no longer be acceptable. Article 24 paragraph 8 of the GATT requires that Free Trade Areas should cover 'substantially all the trade between the constituent territories'. Excluding agricultural products can hardly be interpreted as consistent with this requirement.[15]

In its own assessment of the EU-initiated RTAs, the Commission (1996a: 8) has particularly paid attention to the position of agriculture in these:

> Agriculture is included in most of our existing free trade agreements. Sectoral exclusion is not a feature of any recent agreement but total liberalisation of agriculture has never been possible because of the need, which has been

explicitly recognised in some negotiating mandates and implicit in them all, to avoid conflict with the common agricultural policy. The problem of conflict with the common agricultural policy would be most acute if unrestricted free access were to be granted under a free trade agreement for products where the CAP provides for limits on production, high level of external protection and high support prices.

And the Commission concludes (1996: 9):

(..) it remains the case that a more restrictive regime in agriculture remains possible in a manner consistent with Article XXIV provided the sector itself is covered and provided there is real liberalisation within that sector over the transitional period.

The reference to agriculture as a specific item for which careful attention is required, indicates that this sector can be considered as a 'fly in the ointment' of a general EU trade policy based on the assumption that RTAs should, and that the EU-initiated RTAs indeed do, promote multilateral trade liberalization.[16] The 'fly in the ointment' sometimes becomes very disturbing however, as is shown by the role of agriculture in impeding the establishment of a free trade area between the European Union and South Africa or the start of negotiations on a trade pact between the US and the EU.

The impact of non-European RTA proliferation on the EU The interest of the European Union in clarifying the rules concerning RTAs is not only due to its fear of violating Article XXIV GATT, or to its belief in the possible contribution of such agreements to promoting trade liberalization – which could be expected as the EU is by far the most active of all WTO members in concluding such agreements – but also to the rising use of RTAs in other parts of the world. The lack of discipline or the risk created by the obscurity of Article XXIV is considered to be potentially detrimental to the global trade interests of the Union. A clear, probably the most, visible example of this has been the North American Free Trade Agreement (NAFTA). As NAFTA reduced the tariff barriers among the United States, Canada, and Mexico,[17] and as Mexico continues to maintain high tariff barriers in its trade with other countries, NAFTA resulted in a serious case of trade diversion between the European Union and Mexico.[18] This not only triggered an increased interest from the EU in concluding a free trade agreement with Mexico, but also in stricter rules concerning RTAs in general.

The Council, when it considered the Commission's report on RTAs,[19] clearly took into account its belief in the potential benefits of RTAs, its fears for a proliferation of EU-initiated RTAs that would violate the GATT, and its concern to 'discipline' the RTAs concluded by other WTO-members. The Council's conclusions, as later confirmed by the Amsterdam European Council, consisted of four parts.

First, the Council recognized the need for a clarification of the provisions of Article XXIV GATT and its Understanding. Second, the Council pointed to the potential benefits of RTAs for multilateral trade liberalization as long as such agreements fulfilled certain requirements. Third, the Council considered that the European Union 'has an interest in further reinforcing the position of its own agreements in the WTO.' The clarification of the WTO rules as mentioned above would help to ensure 'that EU agreements conform.' Fourth, the Council decided that in the future, proposals for new preferential agreements should be the subject to 'close scrutiny' before negotiations on such agreements could start.

Especially the last conclusion will have serious consequences for the initiation by the European Union of new preferential trade agreements with third countries. Indeed, the Council has decided that the 'close scrutiny' of any proposal on a new preferential agreements implies that 'priority should be given to the development of trading agreements with those partners where a commitment to preferential negotiations already exist.' The Council indicated that this means that 'the fundamental architecture of the EU's policy on preferential agreements has been put in place and should be preserved.' This means that the Council decided not to extend the scope of countries or groups of countries with which the EU already has concluded RTAs. As the Secretariat of the WTO (WTO, 1997a: 24) concluded in its 1997 Trade Policy Review of the EU: 'The Council implicitly left little scope for further expansion of the current network of agreements.' Changes in the EU's trade policy related to Article XXIV GATT can be expected therefore, to involve a deepening of its trade relations with countries with which it has already concluded RTAs, rather than the conclusion of such RTAs with countries with which no such agreements have been concluded yet. This will reduce the probability that EU-initiated RTAs violate the provisions of Article XXIV GATT. Indeed, such RTAs will focus more on an extension of their coverage and on the additional reduction or removal of trade barriers at a rate faster than the one applied in the different WTO agreements.[20] That is not to say that the risk of trade diversion as a consequence of such agreements will disappear. But the chances that the effects on trade creation and trade liberalization will outweigh such diversion will increase[21] this for three reasons. First, because new EU-initiated RTAs will – more than in the past – focus on the creation of free trade areas with the EU. Second, because the increased number of such areas will increase the probability that the EU will accumulate the rules of origin between many or most of these. Third, because the emphasis on the WTO-compatibility of these areas will entail a stronger awareness by the EU that the free trade agreements that it concludes cannot and will not raise the barriers between the EU or its partners in such FTAs on the one hand, and the other WTO-members on the other.

Explaining for the Relationship between RTAs and Multilateralism in the European Union

There are a number of factors that explain the prominent place that RTAs have been taken and continue to take in the EU's external trade policy. There is, however, an equal number of factors that explain why the EU is becoming much more careful in using RTAs as a tool for achieving better market access. Let's first focus on the first group of factors, then on the second group, and finally on the interaction between the two.

Factors behind the EU's regionalism   A first factor that can be distinguished in explaining the zeal of the EU towards RTAs consists of what one could call the jigsaw puzzle effect. EU membership can be compared with a jigsaw puzzle in which the different pieces are formed the member states or groups of member states. The colors of these pieces are different from each other and from pieces outside the jigsaw puzzle. Almost each member state has a color, however, that is similar to the one of a country or a group of countries outside the EU. The only difference is then in the darkness of the colors. The similarity in colors is due to historic reasons in the larger sense or to the intensity of current trade and investment flows. Historic reasons can consist of colonial ties in the past, or of preferential relations - either political or commercial - before the member state had joined the EC/EU. The benefit of the metaphor of the jigsaw puzzle is that it clarifies in a graphical way the fact that a large group of third countries has succeeded - either actively or passively – in getting a group of member states inside the EU that 'sponsors' their cause. France can be considered, for instance, the defender of special relations with a large number of its former African colonies. In the same vein, France has more recently become the sponsor of better relations with the

South-East Asian region to which a number of its former Indochinese colonies belong.

In a sense the jigsaw puzzle effect highlights the fact that as soon as a country becomes a member of the European Union, it has to substitute its bilateral preferential relations with third countries by EU preferential relations with these countries. In a sense, this is not only necessary for political reasons (such as maintaining some influence in ones former colonies) but also for reasons directly related to trade (i.e. trade diversion). Whereas the EU-ACP relations are an example of the first, the relations between the EU and the EFTA-countries can be considered as an example of the second.

Attention for the jigsaw puzzle effect equally highlights the fact that in order to explain the expanding scope of EU-initiated RTAs, focussing on the possible role of a regional hegemon inside the EU (see chapter 2)[22] is just not sufficient. The country that is mostly claimed to fulfil this role is Germany. Rather than one member state, it is the role of many member states and the interaction among them that explains the dynamics of the EU-initiated RTAs and thus, of the expansion of the EU trade bloc.

By looking at the pyramid of EU preferences, one can see how the jigsaw puzzle effect has been an important - albeit not the only - factor in its emergence. The European Economic Area (EEA), which is on top of it, is not exactly a good example of this effect but its precursors, the free trade agreements between the EU and the different EFTA members, were. When the UK, together with two other EFTA-countries, namely Denmark, and Ireland, joined the EC in 1973, the relations with the remaining EFTA-countries were affected in two ways. First, as these countries had established a free trade area (in terms of the removal of tariff barriers and quantitative trade restrictions) among themselves, the accession of the United Kingdom, Denmark, and Ireland entailed a serious risk of trade diversion for them. This led to an EFTA-triggered demand for the establishment of preferential trade relations with the EC.

Second, the accession of the three new EC members created a strong constituency of states inside the EU in favor of preferential relations with EFTA,[23] as the EFTA-countries were important trading partners for them (especially for Denmark, and the UK). As a consequence, the 1973 enlargement of the EC went hand in hand with the establishment of preferential trade relations with the remaining EFTA-countries. In 1972 and 1973 Free Trade Agreements were concluded with Austria, Finland, Iceland, Norway, Sweden, and Switzerland.[24] These agreements provided for free trade in industrial products (agricultural products were excluded, there were no provisions on services). Since then countries like the UK, Denmark, and Germany, have been strong supporters in favor of the intensification of the preferential trade relations with the EFTA countries. Since 1995, the effect of this has been more limited as most of the EFTA-members have become members of the EU itself and as EFTA has become a small organization.

More than any other agreement concluded by the European Union, the Europe Agreements are the best and most obvious expression of the radical new political situation in Europe after the end of the Cold War. They have been concluded either with countries that even didn't recognize the EC until 1988 (Maresceau, 1989: 4), or with countries that didn't exist as *de facto* independent states before 1992-93.[25] In addition, they were meant to support the democratic reforms and the economic transitions of the countries concerned. Finally, and related to this, the Europe Agreements were meant to prepare them ultimately for EU-membership.

Until today the European Union has concluded Europe Agreements with ten Central and Eastern European countries. These agreements have been concluded in four waves. The first wave consisted of Poland, Hungary, the Czech Republic, and Slovakia.[26] The second one involved Romania, and Bulgaria. The third one included Estonia, Latvia, and Lithuania, whereas the last one consisted of Slovenia, until now the only former Yugoslav republic with which such an agreement has been concluded.[27] All these agreements fitted into attempts by the European Union to stabilize the economic and political reforms in the Central and Eastern European countries (CEEC's), to anchor them into the west, to promote trade among them, and eventually to prevent ethnically related conflicts among them from escalating.[28] Market access,[29] political dialogue, but especially the long-term perspective of EU-membership were provided as a carrot to achieve these objectives.

The Europe Agreements – which are Association Agreements based on article 238 of the EC Treaty – provide for a free trade area between the EU and each of the CEEC's. During a period of transition, in principal ten years,[30] these agreements are non-reciprocal as the EU has to dismantle its trade barriers sooner than the CEEC's. The general framework – largely common to all the Europe Agreements – looks as follows.

The Europe Agreements provide for free access of industrial goods from the associated countries to the EU and vice versa. The associated countries have to open their markets after a period of transition (Kennedy and Webb, 1993; Peers, 1995). The EU immediately opened its markets, except for a number of sensitive products.[31] These last concern products for which employment in the EU is important but for which the EU competitiveness is weak or threatened. These include steel, coal, textiles, clothing, and agriculture. For these products the EU has been less eager to open its markets to the east.[32] This is most obvious for agriculture where the EU market is protected and supported by trade barriers, export subsidies, and internal support mechanisms.

Nonetheless, during the negotiations on the Europe Agreements the EU agreed to open its markets for sensitive products after long periods of transition. These periods were the shortest for steel and coal (four years[33]) and a little bit longer for textiles and clothing (five years[34]). For agricultural products however, the agreements remained vague. Many of the possible concessions still had to be negotiated by the Association Council (consisting of the EU, and for each of the Agreements, the country concerned[35]) and were defined in additional protocols.[36] Besides that, some of the quantitative restrictions that have been abolished by the Agreements are subject to special safeguard clauses. This makes it possible for the EU to reintroduce such restrictions in case of an increase of agricultural imports above certain predetermined thresholds,[37] as it has done on a regular basis during the last few years.[38]

As for most Europe Agreements (except those with the Baltic States and with Slovenia), the periods of transition are over now. This means that no quotas on steel and coal, and textiles and clothing are applied anymore. In the case of the Baltic States and of Slovenia, such would have to be the case in 2001.

As has been indicated, the Europe Agreements have been perceived as a tool to promote stability and economic growth in Central and Eastern Europe. That doesn't mean that negotiations on them have always been easy. Especially the first three of them—the ones with Poland, Hungary, and Czechoslovakia—proved very difficult to negotiate. It was basically the failed coup of August 21, 1991 in the Soviet Union, which contributed to a major breakthrough. Because of this coup, the EC member states realized that closer links with Central Europe were central to preventing that once again they would become part of a Soviet bloc in case the old communists would succeed in a second coup. The then Polish president, Lech Walesa made a clear appeal to this, right after this coup.[39]

A number of EC member states promoted the idea of the Europe Agreements, and the one of the eastern enlargements, and they therefore played an important role in the conclusion of these RTAs with the European Union. Germany has played a central role in this, as far as the Visegrad countries are concerned. This is not surprising, as the German government perceived better relations to be in the interest of Germany this for reasons of trade, investment, and stability.

As far as trade is concerned, even before the entry into force of the Europe Agreements, Germany became the most important western partner of the Central European countries as these started to turn away from their traditional markets: those of the member states of the CMEA.[40] It was almost natural that Germany – because of its economic size, its geographic proximity, and its historical ties – would become the focus of the CEECs who wanted to get access to the market of the European Union. The same was true for Austria, as far as EFTA was concerned. With the Europe Agreements, this tendency was tremendously reinforced. According to a number of economic studies (cf. Schumacher, 1996: 5; Black, 1995: 6). Germany, together with Austria, was the first country to reach its trade potential with the Visegrad countries, followed by Greece, and Italy. This was largely due to exports from and imports to the western side of Germany.[41] The perspectives were that in case of intensified trade relations of the EU with Central and Eastern Europe, many member states, but especially Germany and Austria, would reap the benefits, especially as market opening in the CEECs would entail economic growth and new export opportunities for the EU. In addition, as Schumacher has stressed, with the 'catching up' of the eastern part of Germany in the longer run an 'additional boost' may be given to trade between Germany and Central and Eastern Europe (Schumacher, 1996: 9).[42] From that perspective, it was almost logical that Germany became a strong proponent of the Europe Agreements inside the EU.

Besides trade, investment equally played an important role in explaining Germany's role in intensifying trade and economic relations with the CEECs and in creating a strong German and Austrian constituency in favor of the CEECs inside the EU. Both Germany and Austria were the first to invest on a large scale after the opening of the economic systems in Central Europe. As Donges and Wieners (1994: 169) have put it, the factors explaining this were 'links of geography and culture, combined with the desire to gain a foothold in untapped markets of countries that happened to be traditional trading partners (..) and could become so again as the reform process makes headway (..).'

The investments in the CEECs were clearly aimed at producing products at a lower relative cost,[43] aimed at export to the markets of Western Europe.[44] This means that the investments themselves created a strong business constituency inside Germany and Austria in favor of a dismantling of both tariff barriers (which happened by way of the Europe

Agreements) and non-tariff barriers (which still has to be completed through the pre-accession and the accession process).

Last but not least, security and stability played an important role in explaining Germany's interests in intensive trade relations between the European Union and the CEECs and ultimately in their accession to EU-membership.

From the earliest days of the European Community the issue of its relations with a number of African countries was put on the table. Already during the negotiations on the EEC-Treaty France raised the question. France wanted to maintain its preferential trade relations with its colonies and made a precondition of it for its adoption of the EEC Treaty.[45] Between 1958 (the entry into force of the EEC Treaty) and 1960 (the year that most French colonies in Africa gained independence), these special relations were determined by Part IV of the EEC Treaty on the Association with the Dependent Overseas Countries and Territories. These countries and territories were enumerated in annex IV to the Treaty.

The implementation of the association as provided by Part IV of the Treaty required an Implementation Convention.[46] When most of these countries became independent, the establishment of preferential trade relations became important, especially for the former motherlands, Belgium and France. Between 1963 and 1975 the new agreements became known as the Yaoundé Conventions, based on article 238 of the EEC Treaty. These conventions not only applied to former French and Belgian colonies but also to territories with similar economic structures. This enlarged geographical scope had been a precondition for the Netherlands to approve the first Yaoundé Convention (1964-1971) (Faber, 1982: 8).[47] Although this expanded the geographical scope of the Conventions, most of the associated states were former French colonies.[48] The British EC accession in 1973 reopened the question of the association agreements again. This time, both the geographical scope and the substance of the association were drastically changed. A large number of Caribbean and South Pacific countries joined the new conventions whereas the reciprocal nature of the preferences as provided by the Yaoundé Conventions was replaced by unilateral preferences granted by the EC. In exchange, the EC enjoyed MFN status in its access to the markets of the countries concerned.[49] Despite the fact that the relative number of former French colonies was reduced because of this enlargement, France remained by far the most ardent supporter of the relations between these countries and the EC/EU. Proof of this can be provided by the fact that the French were prepared in both 1989 and 1994 to pay a disproportionate amount of money in order to fulfill the demands by the ACP countries for more financial support as part of the negotiations for the Fourth Lomé Convention in 1989 and of the Second Financial Protocol of the Fourth Lomé Convention in 1994 (cf. Kerremans, 1996). This French generosity strongly contrasted with the declining preparedness of the other member states to pay more to the European Development Fund.[50]

The history of the relations between the EU and the Mediterranean countries is largely similar to the one between the EU and the ACP countries. Once again, France has played the role of a strong and powerful constituency inside the EU in favor of establishing better relations between the EC/EU and these countries, especially as far as the Northern African states are concerned. Once again historic reasons partly explain for this interest. As Morocco, Algeria, and Tunisia have been French colonies in one way or the other, France has tried to keep a certain political influence over there by establishing and maintaining preferential trade relations through the EU. Since the end of the Cold War, the establishment of preferential relations with the CEEC's through the Europe Agreements, and the start of the negotiations for the accession of some of them, this French inclination to take the lead in determining the Euro-Mediterranean relations has become more visible. During the Cannes European Council of June 1995 this became quite visible when the German and the French governments reached a kind of compromise on the distribution of the EU's foreign financial aid. Whereas the Germans emphasized the importance of the support for the CEEC's, France defended such aid for its Mediterranean neighbors. With the accession of Spain in 1986 and the increasing political instability combined with serious social problems and emigration pressures in Northern Africa (Roy, 1997: 31; Whitehead, 1992: 148), the Franco-Spanish drive for better Euro-Mediterranean relations has become more pronounced. In 1995, this resulted in the establishment of a Euro-Mediterranean Partnership. This partnership has provided the framework for the replacement of a number of association agreements (concluded in the Seventies) by a second generation of Euro-Mediterranean Association Agreements that aim at establishing a Euro-Mediterranean free trade area against 2010. Agreements have already been concluded with Morocco, Israel, and Tunisia.[51] With Egypt and Jordan negotiations are still going on.

With the accession of Spain and Portugal to the EC/EU in 1986, a new color joined the jigsaw puzzle of EU membership. The two countries - especially Spain - soon developed a leading role inside the EC/EU in favor of the establishment of preferential relations with the countries of the Western Hemisphere. Although this Spanish-Portuguese constituency certainly wasn't the only factor in explaining the intensification of these relations, it was definitely a very important one. This proved to be the case in two ways. First the Spanish attempts during the negotiations for the Fourth Lomé Convention to enlarge the group of ACP countries with the Dominican Republic and Haiti (Kerremans, 1996). Second, by the fact that both Spain and Portugal took the lead in convincing the European Commission in taking new initiatives in more cooperation with the countries of the Western Hemisphere (March Pujol, 1997: 9; Laurent, 1992: 157).[52] This was certainly not an easy task to do as - as Whitehead (1992: 145) wrote in 1992 – 'As far as Latin America is concerned the sub-continent is a low priority and the EC is unlikely to pay too high a price for the application of its distinctive policies in this area of the globe rather than elsewhere.' As a consequence, the EU started to pay much more attention to its relations with Central America and with South America than it had done until then, helped in this by the process of democratization and economic liberalization in most of these countries in the 1980s and 1990s (European Commission, 1995: 3). This clearly engendered a number of results as Laurent (1992: 155) has observed: 'There is no doubt that Central America, let alone the Rio Group and Latin America as a whole, has emerged as a new part of the EC agenda in terms of relations with developing countries.' Indeed, as the Commission (1995) has indicated in its 1995 Report on EU relations with Latin America, the relations with Latin America have been intensified in the political as well as the economic sphere. The first by the institutionalization of the San José Dialogue (since 1984) and of the dialogue with the Rio Group (since 1990). The second by the conclusion of a wide range of a 'third generation' cooperation agreements with the countries concerned.[53] In addition, official development aid from the EU has increased with 47% since 1991. However, as has been indicated in the 1995 Report, the EU has no plans to establish a free trade with the large and diversified subcontinent. Rather, a bilateral (with particular countries) or inter-regional approach (with Mercosur) seems to prevail. But rather than the jigsaw puzzle effect, other factors seem to explain for this, as we will see.

From the above, it has become clear that internal developments of a specific kind have influenced the relations between the EC and its trading partners. EU enlargements not only integrate new states in the EC/EU but also new defenders for preferential relations with specific countries. In this sense, one could say that a process of externalization of enlargement has occurred. Externalization refers to the situation where policy decisions taken within a particular political system entail consequences for other political systems and where these consequences trigger a demand in these other systems towards the system that has taken the decision[54] (cf. Ginsberg, 1989). The demand focuses then on the consequences and on the need for a policy that deals with these.

Externalization not only exists in the case of enlargement (an EU policy with serious consequences for third countries), but also in the case of many other internal EU policies, such as the internal market program, the common agricultural policies or the EU's competition policies. In the case of the EU, but also of the United States, the consequences concerned are difficult to neglect because of their market power and of the trade and investment dependence of other countries from these customs territories. EU enlargements reinforce this effect because they increase the EU's market power on the one hand, and the trade and investment dependence of other countries on the other.

The effect of externalization on the EU's policies towards regional trade agreements is largely due to the combination of externalization with the jigsaw puzzle effect. Internal EU policies create consequences in third countries and these consequences trigger demands from these countries to the EU. This is in the first place the case for those third countries that are largely dependent on exports to the EU market (one could call this the foreign constituencies). It is because these third countries' demands are 'picked up' by particular EU member states, that the effects of externalization are internalized through EU-initiated RTAs or through their deepening or scope expansion.

The jigsaw puzzle effect is of crucial importance here as it affects to a large extent the choice of instruments that the EU will use in order to deal with the external demands. Indeed, nothing forces the EU to meet these demands through regional trade agreements. It is perfectly possible - as has often been the case - that the EU meets these through multilateral negotiations. The choice to do it through the creation, the deepening, or the scope expansion of RTAs is mediated then by member states that play the role of constituencies for preferential relations with particular third countries inside the EU. A typical example of this is the Agreement on the European Economic Area with most of the EFTA-countries. This agreement forms the framework through which the EU grants the most preferential treatment to third countries. It is nothing less than the expansion of the internal market and a number of accompanying (flanking) policies to states that are not EU members. The agreement currently extends the EU's internal market to Norway, Iceland, and Liechtenstein. Originally, it intended to do this to Austria, Sweden, Finland, and

Switzerland as well. Switzerland never joined the EEA however because the majority of its population rejected EEA-accession in a referendum. The other three countries were members of the EEA until 1994, as all three became EU members on January 1, 1995.

The EEA Agreement provides for the free movement of goods, services, and capital among the EU-member states, Norway, Iceland, and Liechtenstein. This free movement covers in principle all goods and services although exceptions exist for agriculture and fisheries. The first due to the relatively higher level of protection for. agriculture in Norway, and the second to conflicts about the access of EU-vessels (especially from Spain) to the fishing resources of Norway and Iceland.

In practice the free movement of goods, services, and capital is created by the integration of the body of EU-rules on the internal market (the *acquis communautaire*) in the legislation of Norway, Iceland, and Liechtenstein. For all those sectors where such integration has been realised, no anti-dumping or countervailing measures can be applied anymore. They are basically replaced by competition rules that are enforced in the EU by the European Commission (as defined in the EC Treaty) and in the EFTA-countries by an EFTA-authority, especially created for that purpose.

The relations between the EFTA and the European Union have to a large extent been determined by internal developments in the EC/EU and by the reactions of the EFTA-countries to these. As a matter of fact, the EFTA itself has been founded as a reaction to the creation of the European Economic Community in 1957-58. It was on the initiative of the United Kingdom, which was looking for economic integration in Europe without the extent of political integration as enshrined in the EEC-Treaty, that the EFTA was founded in 1960.

As the EC became a large market for the EFTA-countries,[55] their interest in market access to the EC grew, especially when the EC countries reacted to the recessions of the 1970s and 1980s with the erection of non-tariff barriers (NTB's). The initiation by the Commission in the first years of the 1980's of proposals to remove the NTB's inside the EC, and the consequent compilation of these in the Internal Market Program in 1985, triggered therefore, an ever stronger demand by the EFTA-countries for new agreements with the EC in which the NTB's against them would be removed. Moreover, the fear for a 'Fortress Europe' in these days, entailed efforts by the EFTA to become part of the Internal Market itself (Magnus Wijkmans, 1990; 1991; Pelkmans, 1990). Once again, inside the EC, the strong constituency in favor of trade with EFTA (the UK, West Germany,

Denmark) supported a move in this direction. As a consequence, in 1984, the EC started to negotiate a whole range of bilateral agreements with the EFTA-countries, as part of a process, which aimed at removing NTB's in trade between them. This process, the so-called Luxembourg Process, wasn't very satisfying. It entailed a proliferation of bilateral agreements on a wide array of issues and was, therefore, incoherent and inconsistent. In addition, it resulted in an overburdening of the Commission services responsible for the negotiations. This led to the announcement by Jacques Delors, then Commission president, in the European Parliament, of the idea of an all-encompassing agreement with the EFTA.[56] This agreement – the European Economic Area[57] - would integrate the EFTA-countries in the Internal Market, without jeopardizing the decision-making autonomy of the EC, and without them becoming EC-members. As a condition, Delors asked for negotiations based on a two-pillar approach. This meant that the EC would negotiate with the EFTA, and not with each of the EFTA-countries separately.

For the EFTA-countries, the idea of the EEA was attractive as it would make them part of the Internal Market, without requiring them to become full EC-members.[58] The negotiations dragged on for years however, because of difficulties with fisheries, the contribution of the EFTA-countries to the structural funds of the EC, and the question of the decision-making autonomy of the EC where a Court ruling required a second round of negotiations after a first version of the EEA-Agreement had been signed and submitted for approval to the European Parliament. Also because of the decision of Switzerland not to join, the EEA-Agreement entered into force on January 1, 1994, one year later than originally hoped for.[59]

Factors impeding EU regionalism   It has already been indicated above. Whereas for a long time, the EC/EU has been the main and major initiator of RTAs within the GATT/WTO, since the fall of the Berlin Wall other initiators have come to the forefront. Two recent tendencies can, therefore, be distinguished. First, there is the increasing number of RTAs in which the EU is not involved. Second, after an initial upsurge in EU-initiated RTAs at the beginning of the 1990s, the share of such RTAs in the total number of RTAs reported to the WTO has dropped dramatically in the last few years. Why is this the case?

A first reason could be that the EU has reached a point of saturation in its RTA-policies. Indeed, there are almost no regions in the world anymore that have not been linked to the EU through a kind of RTA, North America, and East Asia being the exceptions. But this argument is limited in value because the number of RTAs is just one aspect. The deepening of existing RTAs is another one, and here the WTO-figures also indicate a decline.[60] The reason of this decline has to be found elsewhere therefore. And the place to look at it is once again the number of RTAs reported to the WTO.

Until recently, the EU almost had the monopoly of RTAs in the multilateral trading system. Otherwise stated, the EU was almost the only one that used RTAs as a trade policy instrument. That changed in the 1990s when besides the EU, the United States, the EFTA-countries, the CEECs, and the Latin American countries started to use this instrument as well. Before that happened, the EU could to a large extent determine itself to what extent regionalism could affect multilateralism in trade since it had the quasi-monopoly of this regionalism in the GATT. Since the proliferation of RTAs, however, this is not the case anymore. As the largest trading bloc in the WTO, the EU has an interest in the maintenance of a credible and effective rules-governed multilateral trading system. Since it lost its monopoly on RTAs, it now needs a multilateral disciplining of RTAs in order to avoid that RTAs that have been initiated by *others* would negatively affect its multilateral trading interests through for instance, trade diversion. As a consequence, since the 1990s the EU has become a staunch supporter of a stricter formulation and interpretation of the WTO rules on RTAs (cf. Article XXIV GATT & Article V GATS). That has made the EU much more careful on its own RTAs and has diminished its zeal to establish trade relations with third countries through RTAs.

The negative effect of the proliferation of non-EU initiated RTAs on the EU's zeal to establish trade relations with third countries through RTAs has also been influenced by what one could call the bloc size effect. The increasing size of the EU as a trade bloc in the multilateral system increases the effect of violations or neglect of WTO-rules by the EU on the credibility and sustainability of the WTO system. The same holds for the United States. As far as RTAs are concerned and given the fact that the EU has an interest in an open rules-governed WTO system, this means that the EU has to discipline itself on its own RTAs in order to avoid that a lower credibility of the WTO rules on RTAs would negatively affect its own export opportunities to countries that have acceded to or have concluded RTAs that violate the WTO rules. This may sound paradoxical. One would expect that the growth of a trade bloc would entail more control on the WTO and the enforcement of its rules. But rather than on the enforcement of its rules, the WTO system depends on the voluntary compliance with its rules. And this last depends to a large extent on the credibility and the perceived legitimacy of these rules. If the big trading blocs neglect or violate these rules, the smaller customs territories will feel less inclined to abide by them, unless their larger counterparts would be prepared to force them otherwise. That is basically the difference between a rules-governed and a power-based trading system. For the EU this means that in order to sustain the multilateral system it has to respect quite strictly the multilateral rules on regional trade agreements.

The bloc size effect increases the effects of EU policies on the WTO credibility and sustainability while at the same time the proliferation of market power in the multilateral trading system and the expanding WTO membership has made the EU more dependent on WTO rules compliance by a larger and more diverse group of countries.

Indeed, the EU has succeeded in increasing its market power in the multilateral trading system because of the expansion of its internal trade, and of its successive enlargements. At the same time, however, market power has been dispersed by the accession of a large number of countries to the GATT/WTO during and right after the Uruguay Round. As a matter of fact, from a club mainly consisting of the industrialized countries, the GATT/WTO has become a truly universal organization. As a consequence, new market powers have emerged inside the WTO.

It is precisely because the proliferation of market power has been going on hand in hand with the accession to and the emergence of these new market powers inside the WTO that the WTO has become the most effective tool for disciplining these countries by creating, reinforcing, and deepening the level playing field on a global scale. That doesn't mean that it would be impossible for the EU to discipline these market powers through RTAs. It means, however, that a credible and sustainable WTO has become a necessary part of any compliance strategy of the EU towards this level playing field. For that reason, it may be not surprising that for the first time in the history of the GATT/WTO, the European Union has been the one to launch the idea of a new all-encompassing trade negotiating round, the so-called Millenium Round.

The United States, Regional Trade Agreements, and Multilateralism

US Regionalism as a New Approach

Unlike with the European Union, regionalism has only recently acquired a prominent place in American foreign trade policy. Whereas in the EU RTAs have been from the beginning a substantial part of its external trade policies, the breakthrough of RTAs in US trade policy only dates from the late eighties. With CUSFTA and NAFTA, the US started to embark on a trade policy course of which both regionalism and multilateralism are part.

Before 1988 the US did not conclude any RTA except with Israel (1985). But that agreement had a lot to do with the special place of Israel in the US's Middle East policies (Bayard and Elliott, 1994: 17), rather than with new trade policy strategies and was featured by its 'limited coverage. and unambitious approach' (Hart, 1994: 244). From 1988 on, however, that started to change. The agreement with Canada - concluded on insistence of the Canadians - formed the first real, that means all-encompassing, regional trade agreement of the United States since the GATT/WTO system had been created.[61] In 1993 CUSFTA was followed – and basically superseded – by NAFTA – the North American Free Trade Agreement – and its two side agreements, the North American Agreement on Labor Cooperation (NAALC), and the North American Agreement on Environmental Cooperation (NAAEC). From then on, regionalism started to achieve a more prominent place in US external trade policy. In November 1993 the United States played a central role in the organization of the first APEC summit in Seattle. One year later, Bill Clinton, at a summit in Miami, launched the idea of a Free Trade Area of the Americas (FTAA), a proposal that occupies the first place on the trade policy priority list of the second Clinton Administration. Despite Clinton's lack of 'fast track' trade negotiating authority, the April 1998 Summit of the Americas in Santiago de Chile, resulted in the commitment of the countries of the Western Hemisphere to start the talks on a FTAA in September 1998.

In addition, American interest for Africa grew in the course of 1997 leading to the Africa Growth and Opportunity Act proposal in Congress and to a historic visit by president Clinton to Africa in March 1998. However, the Africa Growth and Opportunity Act is not a free trade agreement, nor does it establish preferential relations with African countries on a bilateral or plurilateral basis. The objective is first to promote private investment in the Sub-Sahara African countries through better access to the US market, and to negotiate free trade areas with these countries in the future.[62] Better market access would be realized through a deal in which African countries that move towards free market reforms would enjoy the abolishment of import quotas and tariffs for the export of their textile and apparel to the US. Not all African countries have reacted enthusiastically to the proposal however, especially not South Africa where president Mandela has given a lukewarm receipt to the proposal. He basically rejected the idea of a free trade area.[63]

When one compares these American initiatives and commitments to RTAs or negotiations on them, and compares this with the position of RTAs – or rather, the lack of them – in America's external trade policy before 1988, the conclusion is clearly that regionalism is gaining a prominent place on the US's trade policy agenda. Indeed, one could even say that during the last two years, regionalism has reached a place more prominent than multilateralism on this agenda. It is interesting, therefore, to look deeper into the factors explaining the rise of regionalism in US external trade policy. In doing this we will look first into the objectives that the United States hopes to achieve with this recent Regionalism. Afterwards, we will try to answer the question why the US is trying to pursue those objectives and why regionalism is used as an instrument to do this.

The Objectives of American Trade Regionalism

In order to expound the objectives of the new American trade regionalism, the US approach to NAFTA - and to a lesser extent to APEC – is illuminating. CUSFTA – the precursor of NAFTA - reflected bilateral concerns and trade interests, rather than a new approach in American thinking about trade and trade liberalization. It reflected the interests that the US had in improving access to the market of its largest trading partner, Canada.[64] That partly changed with the North American Free Trade Agreement (NAFTA). Although NAFTA was initiated by Mexico, the Bush Administration soon realized its potential benefits for American interests in the multilateral trading system.[65]

Mexican president Salinas made the proposal first. He was looking for a bilateral free trade agreement between Mexico and the United States. A number of factors explain for this. First, the fact that the United States is by far the largest import/export market of the Mexican economy. Second, the change in Mexican trade policies in the 1980s, following the 1982 financial crisis. Instead of continuing its import substitution policies of the previous decades, the Mexican government started to conduct a policy of trade liberalization, export performance (cf. The *Maquiladores*, see Ganster, 1995: 146-148; Marquez Peres, 1995b), and gradual deregulation (Marquez Peres, 1995a; 1995b: 223; Gerber and Kerr, 1995: 96-97). In 1986, for instance, Mexico - with its previously closed economy - acceded to the GATT. Crucial in the sustainability of these new policies was market access, especially to Mexico's biggest potential outlet, the United States. Such market access would attract foreign direct investment, which became necessary for the sustainability of Mexico's new trade policies (Orne, 1996: xix). In addition, once Mexico concluded a free trade agreement with the US, it would become much more difficult for future governments to overhaul Mexico's new love affair with free trade. Otherwise stated, a free trade agreement would freeze current free trade policies by creating an external (i.e. American) control on it.

George Bush' positive reaction to the idea of an FTA with Mexico— and later to Canada's demand to expand such an agreement to the whole of North America[66]—was due to two groups of factors of which it remains unclear which prevails in terms of importance. The first group consists of bilateral (i.e. Mexican-American) arguments. First, Bush hoped – just like Salinas did – that an FTA or NAFTA would 'freeze' Mexico's new trade policy course. For the US, this meant potential new outlets (although, given the relatively less developed Mexican market and the fact that there was already a certain degree of integration between the American and the Mexican economies,[67] the expected gains in terms of exports were limited).

In addition, and related to the first, Mexico's free trade policies would enhance the competitiveness of the Mexican economy, would reduce consumer prices in Mexico, would create more employment, and would therefore, raise the standard of living. This would not only benefit American exports, but would entail a benefit that was perceived to be even more important. It would weaken the push factor on legal and illegal Mexican immigration in the United States (cf. Ganster, 1995: 145). As such immigration was becoming an increasingly important political subject in large states such as Texas and California, Bush even had an electoral interest in taking a positive stance towards Salinas' proposal for an FTA.

The second group of factors is related to the multilateral system. It consists of the frustration of the Americans with the ongoing Uruguay Round of multilateral trade negotiations. This round had been launched in Punta del Este in September 1986, but already in December 1988 – during the Mid Term Review in Montreal – it became clear that the agricultural dispute with the European Community was hindering real progress. So even if Bush did not propose the FTA with Mexico or the NAFTA, as soon as the proposal was put on the table he saw the benefits of it in the multilateral realm. Indeed, he believed that by creating a North American free trade area, he could scare his partners in the WTO – especially the European Union and Japan – with the perspective that the United States – in case of a failure of the Uruguay Round – would form its own trading bloc (cf. Anderson and Blackhurst, 1993: 3). In itself this idea was not new. Already during the Reagan Administration, William E. Brock, Reagan's first USTR perceived the CUSFTA not as a way to close the North American market but to promote multilateralism in trade by increasing the pressure on the US's trading partners.[68] And it basically worked. Indeed, the risk of an American regionalism outside the GATT after a failed Uruguay Round was an important factor in convincing the EU to show more openness towards changes in its agricultural policies. As Vernon (1996: 625) has put it:

> The emergence of a NAFTA possibility offered the Americans a splendid opportunity to send a signal to the negotiators in Geneva that, if those negotiations [the Uruguay Round negotiations] failed, the United States had an attractive option, namely, to build its own trading block from a North American base.

Other authors (cf. Abbott, 1995: 119; Rolle, 1995: 472; Peterson, 1996: 122; Randall, 1995: 40) come to the same conclusion.[69]

APEC, the Asian-Pacific Economic Cooperation, which acts as a transpacific forum for the promotion of multilateral trade liberalization through what Bergsten (1997) has called 'open regionalism' can be seen – at least from the American perspective – to serve the same purposes (see also Economic and Social Committee, 1995: 2; see also Cuyvers and Van den Bulcke: 6; Buelens, 1997: 45).

One can see here how US regionalism occupies a completely different place in US trade policies, than EU regionalism does in the EU. Whereas the latter has been an end in itself, a way to shape the EU's establishment of special trade relations with other countries, and to achieve market access in specific countries and/or regions, the former has aimed at serving multilateralism in the first place. However, for two reasons US regionalism is evolving to a position in US trade policy similar to the one of its EU counterpart in the EU's trade policies. First, the US is increasingly using RTAs as an end in itself. Second, the EU's approach to RTAs has become much more cautious. The effects of the EU's RTAs on multilateral commitments are much more taken into account than they used to be, and EU's activism on RTAs has been declining as a consequence of this.

In the case of the United States, a number of recent initiatives show that the US is starting to look at RTAs in the same way as the EU has been doing. The proposal to accept Chile as a member of NAFTA is an example of this. The critical effect of this on the multilateral system would be limited, and it would certainly not serve any US interest in the ongoing negotiations in the WTO, as the NAFTA negotiations and the creation of APEC did.

Another, more important, initiative is the FTAA, the Free Trade Area of the Americas proposal. The FTAA aims at nothing less than the creation of a free trade area in the Western Hemisphere. The deadline would be 2010. During the Clinton Administration it has reached a prominent – if not the first – place on the Administration's trade policy agenda. The purposes of this initiative are clearly regional in the first place. No direct multilateral purpose can be discerned.

Why Using Regionalism as a Trade Policy Instrument?

Why has regionalism gained a prominent place on the US trade policy agenda, and why does the US increasingly resort to RTAs to achieve both its regional and its multilateral trade objectives? A number of factors are at work, including declining US hegemony and the proliferation of RTAs around the world.

Erosion of the US hegemony The position of the United States in the multilateral trading system today is quite different from the one during the days in which this system has been built, right after W.W.II. The difference exists in two respects. First, by the fact that the dependency of the US on trade is now more than double what it was during the fifties and sixties.[70] Second, the fact that US preponderance in the multilateral system has declined. With it, US trade hegemony has disappeared. From a unipolar trading system in the first two decades after W.W.II, the system has evolved to a multipolar system. Besides the United States other major trading powers such as the European Union and Japan have emerged.

Faced with these changes, the US has looked for ways to cope with them. The result has been a policy-mix which combines multilateral, bilateral (regional), and unilateral strategies. Whereas the unilateral strategy had emerged during the seventies and had acquired a prominent place during the eighties, largely in response to the drastically increasing trade deficits, bilateralism and regionalism are much more recent phenomena.

During the first two decades after the Second World War, the situation was quite different. The United States created the GATT/ITO and in this creation American domestic politics has played a prominent – if not preponderant – role. According to Hody (1996: 151) the main features of the GATT system have been determined by what was acceptable in the United States. As she has observed, the influence of the US on the shaping of the GATT was not limited to what was not acceptable for the domestic US actors in trade policy. It was largely influenced – if not determined – by the way in which these actors were thinking about trade, both domestic and foreign. In this way, as Hody has observed:

> (..) the establishment of a postwar trade regime based on nondiscriminatory liberalization was contingent on the institutionalization in the United States of the power-sharing alternative to trade policy-making. The results of this process (..) go a long way toward explaining the scope and limitations of the trade regime that emerged in the years after World War II.

Moreover, the fact that GATT was a provisional agreement and not an organization was due to the anticipation by the US negotiators that there was a high probability that the US Congress would refuse to approve the Havanna Charter and the ITO (Hody, 1996: 156). By limiting the scope of GATT, the US negotiators avoided that at least the GATT-agreement – not the ITO-charter – could escape the advice and consent requirement (and its concomitant two-thirds majority requirement) in the US Senate (cf. Milner, 1997: 136-137). Due to its limited scope and its lack of an institutional structure, the GATT could be approved as an executive agreement without congressional involvement (Destler, 1995: 35).[71] Equally, the Protocol on Provisional Application was meant to appease possible objections in the US Congress. As a conclusion therefore, one could say that the postwar multilateral trading system not only reflected American interests in international trade but even more importantly American values about economy and trade (Boyer, 1996: 44). That is not to say that the Americans were the only ones to determine what was possible and what wasn't in GATT – the French and the British, for instance, could only accept the MFN-principle on condition that it would be applied flexibly, given the preferential systems they applied in their respective colonial empires. As some have observed, making concessions to other countries is a necessity for hegemons to maintain the hegemonic system that reflects their values and interests. That is clearly what the US did in the two decades after W.W.II. But it is certain that the terms of the trade debate had been largely determined by Washington. As Milner (1997: 137) has observed:

> (..) the GATT before 1960 (..) required much less of an adjustment of US policies in return for, or anticipation of, the adjustment of other states' policies (..).[72]

With the emergence of the European Community and of Japan in the world trading system, and with the increasing US dependence on trade – which made the US more vulnerable to the externalities of others' trade policies – US hegemony started to decline in the seventies. With this decline, US propensity to use multilateralism as an instrument to open markets and to deal with domestic opposition against trade declined as well. This didn't happen overnight and already in the 1960s the signs of these changes in the international trading system became visible. First, by the success of the EC common market and second by the rise of the Japanese economy at the end of the 1960s.

Already in 1962, during the discussions on the Trade Expansion Act president Kennedy pointed to the increasing importance of the EEC. In his message concerning this act to Congress, Kennedy indicated 'five fundamentally new and sweeping developments [that] have made obsolete our traditional trade policy' (US House of Representatives, 1962: 2). The first of these five was 'the growth of the European Common Market.' As a consequence, JFK not only asked for general negotiating authority in order to reduce the tariffs of the US and its trading partners by 50% in 'reciprocal negotiations', but also 'special authority to be used in negotiating with the EEC, to reduce or eliminate all tariffs on those groups of products where the United States and the EEC together account for 80% or more of world trade in a representative period' (Ibid.: 6-7). JFK saw this special authority as a way to allow the US to intensify multilateral trade liberalization through negotiations with the EEC, that '(..) economy which may soon nearly equal our own.'[73] Such negotiations would liberalize world trade because concerted tariff reductions would be universally applied through MFN. Kennedy saw these negotiations clearly as a tool to open the EEC market, not just for American products, but for products from elsewhere as well, as the following quote from his message indicates (Ibid.: 2): 'The need for new markets for Japan and the developing nations has also been accentuated as never before, both by the prospective impact of the EEC's external tariff and by their own need to acquire outlets for their raw materials and light manufactures.'[74]

Twelve years later, in 1974, when president Nixon was in need of trade negotiating authority, the language would not save Japan as it had done in 1962. On the contrary, Japan was one of the major – if not the main – target of the introduction of what later has been called 'aggressive unilateralism' through Section 301 of the 1974 Trade Act. Not that the importance of Japan in world trade suddenly rose in 1973 or 1974 although it was an extremely rapidly growing economy at that time.[75] What really made the difference was the fact that the US started to have a trade deficit in 1971.

According to Destler (1995: 49) this fact '(..) was treated as offering clear evidence that the United States was losing out in the world marketplace.'

In the run-up towards the start of the Uruguay Round in Punta del Este in September 1986, this weakened American position in the international trading system was emphasized on two important occasions. First in November 1982 when the Reagan administration tried to launch a new round of multilateral trade negotiations but failed, mainly because of European and Japanese resistance against negotiations on agricultural subsidies (Bayard and Elliott, 1994: 15)[76] and because of the developing countries' suspicions about the intentions behind the US' proposal for a new round. As Preeg (1995: 32) has indicated 'the biggest roadblock to the U.S. strategy for a new round in any event would be the developing countries', largely because of their suspicions about newly proposed subjects for such a round, like trade in services, TRIP's, and TRIM's.

In 1986 the Reagan Administration finally succeeded in launching a new MTN whose agenda was, according to some '(..) so paper thin that the prospects of an early and substantive engagement on the major issues were also rated to be slim' (Hart, 1994: 190), and according to others '(..) a watershed for the world trading system' (Preeg, 1995: 9).

As the Uruguay Round – paralyzed by the Euro-American agricultural trade dispute – dragged on for years however, and as the American trade deficit – especially with Japan, and a number of Asian NICs – continued to grow, the search for alternatives to multilateralism intensified, especially in Congress. At the same time however, successive US administrations tried to resist as much as possible Congress' temptation to pursue a policy of aggressive unilateralism. According to Destler, part of this demand was just symbolic politics, largely for electoral consumption. But one thing was clear, the US was negotiating trade concessions in a largely different world from the one of the fifties and sixties, even the seventies. Besides the EU – gradually reinforced by its internal market program and therefore scaring many American businessmen for a largely fictitious 'Fortress Europe' (cf. Abbott, 1995: 119)[77] – and Japan, a large group of developing countries started to play an active role in the MTNs. This was indeed, a new phenomenon. As Preeg (1995: 1) has observed:

> Developing countries (..) faced a growing maze of quota restrictions in industrialized-country markets. The GATT was thus becoming less and less relevant to rapidly growing trade between industrialized and developing countries, and the new round of negotiations would be the decisive test to restore its credibility.

For that reason, 'many developing countries were very active participants in the Uruguay Round both individually and in coalition with industrial countries' (Martin and Winters, 1996: 1). This was already the case during the first US attempts to start a new GATT Round in 1981-82 (Preeg, 1995: 32-33), during the Punta del Este Conference and would remain the case during the seven years that the Uruguay Round took to come to a conclusion (Kerremans, 1996).

Regional trade agreements became an attractive alternative to multilateralism in the changing global trading system. As such regionalism became part of a mixed trade policy strategy that consisted – besides of regionalism (or minilateralism) and bilateralism – of unilateralism and, what Richardson (quoted in Bayard and Elliott, 1994: 18) has called 'contingent multilateralism', which means 'multilateralism where possible, minilateralism where necessary'. In addition, the so-called minilateralism contained a 'grievance minilateralism' based on voluntary export restraints and comparable sectoral agreements such as the Structural Impediments Initiative (SII) with Japan (Ibid.: 19).[78]

In the pursuit and development of US trade regionalism two objectives can be said to be central. The first involves gaining broader and deeper[79] market access through bilateral or regional agreements.[80] This is the most obvious objective of the two. It basically serves as an alternative to multilateralism now that the US faces more difficulties in defending its trade interests in the multilateral realm (cf. Hart, 1994: 46).[81] As Congress has been most sensitive on this – and on the rising trade deficit, bilateralism and regionalism became part of the administration's response to this. In this way, successive US administrations have tried to turn the tide of the rising attractiveness of more mercantilist policies on Capitol Hill.[82]

In addition, however, American regionalism is supposed to serve the purpose of increasing the pressure in favor of market access in the multilateral trading system. This was obvious in the case of NAFTA but certainly also in the case of APEC (cf. Salvatore, 1994: 29). This second objective can be served in either a direct or an indirect way. The direct way is the pressure that US regionalism engenders with the other large trading partners in the WTO. Such pressure results from the fear that US regionalism would draw the US' attention away from the WTO and that this could weaken existing US commitments to multilateralism.

Indirectly, US regionalism can lock in more liberal trade policies of other countries, which could in itself promote the long term commitment of these countries towards an open multilateral trading system. That was one of the objectives of NAFTA (as far as Mexico is concerned), of the APEC

– where cooperation with the Asian-Pacific countries is a tool to avoid that
– as far as trade is concerned – a three-bloc world would emerge in which
the United States would be necessarily tied to the Western Hemisphere
(Lawrence, 1996: 86-87) – and of the current steps towards the FTAA. The
same purpose would be served by free trade agreements with Sub-Sahara
African countries where free trade policies are a precondition for better
access to the US market.[83]

The proliferation of RTAs and competitive trade bloc expansion   The
United States has not been the only one in initiating regional trade
agreements, as the table at the top of this chapter has indicated. The EU has
already a much longer tradition in this field. And more recently, a new zeal
for regional trade agreements has emerged in Latin-America, Southern
Africa, and South-East Asia. As already has been indicated above, this has
changed the attitude of the EU towards RTAs and has resulted *inter alia* in
a stronger EU demand for more WTO-enforced discipline in the matter.

What is interesting about these new forms of regionalism is that they
involve a number of emergent economies. That is especially the case for
South-East Asia and Latin-America. Certainly for the latter, the new zeal
for regionalism has gone hand in hand with new directions in the economic
and foreign trade policies of the countries concerned. Indeed, most of them
have changed their import-substitution policies of the seventies and eighties
into market-led growth policies. That has made these countries much more
attractive for countries or entities like the US and the EU than before.[84]

The creation of Mercosur has in addition engendered the concern in
both Washington and Brussels that the South American customs union
could damage their export interests due to trade diversion. Many of these
fears are reminiscent of the fear for the common market in the 1960s and
Fortress Europe in the 1980s.

This combination for fear of exclusion (through trade diversion) and
the attractiveness of the markets concerned has resulted in an interest from
the part of both the European Union and the United States for access to the
markets of these countries concerned. The WTO can provide a framework
for gaining and improving such access but that is clearly not sufficient. In
recent years both the EU and the US have tried to get that access through
preferential trade agreements or through promises to negotiate such
agreements with them. The more one has showed interest for such
agreements, the more the other has tried to conclude such agreements as
well. Mexico is an example. The EU's interest in Mexico has increased
tremendously since the creation of NAFTA[85] and that is not a coincidence.

On December 8, 1997 it concluded an Economic Partnership and Cooperation Agreement with Mexico that contains the commitment to start negotiations with the Mexicans on improved market access.[86]

In the case of Chile, it seems that the United States and the European Union are engaging themselves in a kind of competition to conclude a free trade agreement with that country. In the case of the US there is the objective of a Chilean accession to NAFTA, an accession that has largely been hindered by the failure of the Clinton Administration to get fast-track authority from the US Congress in the course of 1995-1997.[87] In the meantime, the European Union did exactly the same as what it did with Mexico. In June 1996, it concluded a Framework Cooperation Agreement that contains the objective of negotiations on improved market access.[88]

But maybe the most obvious battleground for competition between the EU and the US has become the Mercosur. Far from claiming that the main and only objective of the US in striving for a trade agreement with the Mercosur – through the FTAA-negotiations – would be the possible benefits accruing to the EU after the conclusion of a Mercosur-EU agreement, it certainly plays a role and the Clinton Administration has made no secret of this. Indeed, it became one of the arguments of the administration to convince Congress to grant it fast track authority in 1997.[89] It is ironic, however, that both the EU and the US will have to face the same kind of hurdles before an agreement with Mercosur (either on a interregional or a hemispheric basis) will be possible: dealing with market access for agricultural produce.[90]

Conclusion

Regional trade agreements have occupied a completely different place in the foreign trade policies in the European Union and in the United States. Whereas the EU has already a long-established tradition of RTAs, the US only recently started to use them as major instruments of foreign trade policy-making. But there is a certain convergence discernible between the two. In the EU, questions are increasingly raised as to the extent to which the large array of EU initiated RTAs can be kept or made compatible with WTO-rules. As this results in a less prominent place for RTAs than in the past, the US is increasingly engaging itself in a proactive RTA-policy. That means that more than in the past, both the EU and the US will use a mixture of multilateralism and regionalism in their approaches to improving market access in third countries. For the EU this means more concerns for multilateralism than in the past. For the US, it is the opposite: a more prominent place for RTAs.

There is another similarity between the two. Both the EU and the US face problems in the domestic context of trade policy-making, which are partly related to RTAs. In the EU, the increased pressure in favor of the WTO-compatibility of its RTAs, leads to more resistance against such RTAs because of agriculture. As WTO-compatibility clearly means that free trade agreements have to encompass liberalization on agriculture as well, the political stakes against such RTAs have become stronger. Recent developments concerning free trade negotiations with Mercosur, Chile, and South Africa corroborate this. RTAs are, therefore, becoming less attractive as a central part in the EU's trade policy-making.

In the US, the conclusion of NAFTA has triggered a strong movement against free trade. These opponents, which have shown to have a strong voice in the US Congress among both Democrats and Republicans, have increased the political risks for US administrations and legislatures alike to conclude new RTAs. Indeed, more than multilateral trade agreements, RTAs seem to be associated with the risks of environmental dumping and job losses. For opposition groups against a particular RTA it suffices, therefore, to talk about NAFTA (an extended NAFTA in the case of the FTAA, or an African NAFTA in the case of the recent African Growth and Opportunity Act) to strike a sensitive cord among large parts of the congressional constituents, both organized and unorganized. That raises the stakes of concluding such RTAs and makes them less attractive as a trade policy-making tool.

As a conclusion, therefore, one can claim that despite the differences in the place that RTAs occupy in the trade policies of the US and the EU, it seems that in both cases the domestic context puts serious limits on the unlimited use of RTAs as tools of trade policy-making. Moreover, the interplay between WTO-rules and the way in which these affect the options of political actors domestically, puts additional limits on the unlimited use of RTAs as tools of trade policy making. With a stronger WTO and maybe with even clearer WTO-rules on RTAs in the future, it seems premature therefore, to express fears for the end of multilateralism and the emergence of two or three insulated trading blocs in the international trading system. Theoretically, this means that the dynamics of trade bloc formation and trade bloc expansion have to be looked for at different levels (multilateral, regional, and domestic) and in the interplay among these. It is only in this way that the significance of RTAs and trade bloc expansion for the multilateral trading system can be fully understood.

Notes

[1] Third countries are countries other than EU member states.

[2] Following Bhagwati (quoted in Srinivan, 1998: 335), we will use the following definition of an RTA: '[a] preferential reduction of trade barriers among a subset of countries that might, but need not, be geographically contiguous. The emphasis, presumably, is on the fact that preferences are restricted to a subset, and not extended to the whole set of countries of the world trading system.'

[3] Both devices 'to counter APEC' (Bergsten, 1997: 552).

[4] As has been indicated by the WTO Committee on Regional Trade Agreements (1996: 1), nearly all members of the WTO are currently Parties to at least one RTA notified to the GATT or the WTO.

[5] Sources: Own calculations based on European Commission (1996a: 11-15); WTO Committee on Regional Trade Agreements (1996: 7-8; 1997: 4-5). Only those years in which RTAs have been reported to the GATT/WTO are included in the graph.

[6] See SEC (95) 322.

[7] See *EU-Bulletin*, 6-1996, point I.20.

[8] See also Bergsten (1997: 548).

[9] Cf. the 1960 GATT Working Party on EFTA (referred to in De Laet and Fletcher, 1996: 2) which concluded that 'substantially all the trade has a qualitative as well as a quantitative aspect.' This means 'that it should not be taken as allowing the exclusion of a major sector of economic activity. For this reason the percentage of trade covered, even if it were established to be 90 per cent, was not considered to be the only factor to be taken into account.'

[10] A similar meaning has been given to the 'substantial sectoral coverage' of Article V GATS. This means that on services RTAs '(..) should not provide for the a priori exclusion of any mode of supply' (De Laet and Fletcher, 1996: 2).

[11] See also its qualification of the Understanding as something that '(..) provided real elements of technical clarification in respect of customs unions and the compensation process under Article XXIV: 6, but little else of substance' (European Commission, 1996a: 5). This opinion is shared by others, including the WTO itself (see WTO, 1995b: 20; Srinivasan, 1998: 332).

[12] According to Srinivasan (1998: 332) exactly the same problem exists for article V GATS as this article '(..) corresponds in many ways to article XXIV on goods trade (..).'

[13] Note that this expert group didn't necessarily expressed the official opinion of the European Commission or DG VI.

[14] Better known as the Buckwell Report.

[15] De Laet and Fletcher (1996: 3) come to a similar conclusion, but in more general terms: 'To the extent that the parties want to protect substantial sensitive sectors, the conclusion of free trade agreements has become a more demanding general policy option following the Uruguay Round.'

[16] This opinion has been widely shared, as Baldwin (Baldwin, 1997: 865) has indicated, among economists. Sager (1997: 240) phrases it as follows: 'Regional Trade agreements have reduced the importance of the multilateral trading system as the sole set of rules governing world trade, but have not produced a negative impact on world trade.' The same goes for RTAs initiated by the US and Canada (Baldwin, 1997: 865). Some economists argue however, that differences have to be made between the effects of RTAs and Customs

Unions on international tariff cooperation during their formation and after they have been formed. In the case of free trade agreements (Bagwell and Staiger, 1997a), the effects would not be negative after their formation. In the case of Customs Unions however, the effects could be negative because of the market power engendered by such union (Bagwell and Staiger, 1997b). The case of the EU's common agricultural policy could be an example of this (cf. Weyerbrock, 1998).

[17] NAFTA basically reduced these barriers between the US and Mexico, and between Canada and Mexico, as the US and Canada already concluded the Canada-United States Free Trade Agreement (CUSFTA) in 1988.

[18] According to Japanese manufacturers, the same holds for Japanese exports (Lloyd, 1993: 699). The problems are said to be due to the rules of origin in the agreement (cf. Nowicki, 1997: 360-362). It mainly concerns rules of origin that apply to automobiles, apparel and textiles (see Gruben and Welch, 1994: 39-40; European Commission, 1997a: 13). Trade diversion may thus be an effect of NAFTA, as it has been the effect of preferential agreements concluded by the EU as well, that is still a far cry from claiming that NAFTA would violate Article XXIV GATT or would threaten multilateral trade liberalization. That is certainly not the case. For Mercosur, the assessment could be different as it has entailed more trade diversion than trade creation and as its discrimination against nonmember states is substantially higher than in both the EU, EFTA, or NAFTA (see Yeats, 1998).

[19] See *2003rd Council Meeting – General Affairs, Luxembourg, 29/30 April 1997*, in: document PRESS/97/129, May 13, 1997 p. 4.

[20] As a matter of fact, the WTO Secretariat has recognized that this is already the case, especially with the EU Association Agreements, although it has equally warned against the effects of these agreements on trade diversion (WTO, 1997a: 24).

[21] In claiming this, one has to take into account, as Bergsten has done, that the EU-initiated RTAs have partially offset the trade diversion effects due to the creation and existence of the EU itself (Bergsten, 1997: 552).

[22] Switky (chapter 2) has referred to the role of such a regional hegemon as a regional variant of the hegemonic stability theory (HST).

[23] One could rather say that it reinforced such a constituency as West Germany equally had an interest in reinforcing trade relations with the Alpine EFTA members.

[24] See *Official Journal of the EC/EU* (hereafter referred to as *OJ*), 1972, L300, p. 2 (FTA with Austria); 1973, L328, p. 2 (FTA with Finland); 1972, L300, p. 293 (FTA with Iceland); 1973, L171, p. 2 (FTA with Norway), 1972, L300, p. 97 (FTA with Sweden); 1972, L300, p. 189 (FTA with Switzerland).

[25] For an overview of the period before 1989, see Maslen (1989: 85). Between 1988 and 1990, the EC concluded Trade and Cooperation Agreements with most of these countries (see De la Serre, 1991: 530-531).

[26] The agreements with the Czech Republic and Slovakia were based on the original agreement with Czechoslovakia.

[27] At this moment, there are no plans for such agreements with these states, after they still have to cope with the aftermath of the civil wars. In 1997, the EU adopted a range of unilateral measures in favor of trade with Macedonia (officially the FYROM). Negotiations with Croatia have been hindered by Croatia's poor record on minority rights and the freedom of the press.

[28] In the same vein, directly after the fall of the Berlin Wall and the collapse of communism in the Central European countries, the Organization for Economic Cooperation and Development (OECD) adopted the PHARE-program (Poland/Hungary Assistance for

Economic Restructuring) that contained, in addition to the elimination of quantitative restrictions on industrial imports, a number of financial support mechanisms (Sarat, 1990; Goybet, 1991). The European Community, especially the European Commission, played a very important role in this. The European Community equally played a large role in the foundation of the European Bank for Reconstruction and Development (EBRD) that provides loans for public and private sector projects (De la Serre, 1991: 531).

[29] Exports are of paramount importance for Central and Eastern Europe. This means primarily that the economic development of these countries will depend largely (as it already did in the past few years) on their access to the markets of the Union. Or, as it is stated in an ECE report (1994: 86): 'Given the large external debt of most East European countries and their growing import requirements once recovery gains momentum, development strategies will have to be based on export-led growth. In this respect improved access to western markets will be important.'

[30] Six years in the agreement with Slovenia (see article 8 of that agreement), four years in the agreements with Latvia and Lithuania (see articles 8 in these agreements), and no period of transition in the agreement with Estonia, on the explicit of Estonia itself (see article 8 of the agreement with Estonia).

[31] See *OJ*, L 347, p. 1 (Hungary); *OJ*, L 348, p. 1 (Poland).

[32] Note that the sensitive products account for more than 55% of the Polish exports to the EU (AE, n° 5456, p. 9), 46% of the Hungarian exports and 26% of the Czech and Slovak exports to the EU (AE, n° 5519: 7). Trade statistics of the effects of the market opening in these sectors clearly indicate that the EU is on the 'losing side' in most of them (not in textiles), but that this is compensated by positive trade balances for most manufactured goods (Schumacher, 1996, table 5).

[33] See Protocol 2 Interim Agreements.

[34] See Protocol 1 Interim Agreements.

[35] See chapter II of the Interim Agreements.

[36] In general, these protocols increased the tariff quotas with 25% in volume (by the year 2000) and established a duty preference of 80% compared with other third countries (see WTO, 1997a: 29).

[37] See article 15 and annex Xa of the Interim Agreements.

[38] Both the EU and the CEEC have made extensive use of these safeguards in the sensitive sectors (cf. the recent conflicts with the Czech Republic on Czech quotas on EU-apples and the EU's retaliation (*Financial Times*, March 2, 1998: 4).

[39] The coup also engendered EU interest in concluding Europe Agreements with Bulgaria and Rumania (see Beach, 1998: 47). Negotiations with these countries – especially with Bulgaria – would be long and difficult because of agriculture.

[40] Council for Mutual Economic Assistance, better known as the Comecon.

[41] Between 1989 and 1995, Germany was the only EU member state that imported more than it exported to the CEECs. As Schumacher (1996: 1) has concluded: 'These trends for Germany as a whole conceal a significant expansion of west German trade with Eastern Europe and a dramatic initial fall in east German trade with the region.'

[42] The expected growth of trade between Germany and the CEECs would range between 30 and 50%.

[43] Due to lower labor costs.

[44] Cf. the Volkswagen plant in the Czech Republic.

[45] As Dinan (1994: 33) has phrased it 'Only by guaranteeing clauses in the EEC Treaty that favored France's overseas possessions and promising to include agriculture in the proposed common market did the [French] government carry the day [in the Assemblée nationale].'

[46] Articles 131-136 EEC Treaty.

[47] The Dutch insistence on the elargement of the conventions was supported by the demand of the British who were negotiating an accession treaty with the EC. Because of De Gaulle's veto these negotiations were not concluded with a British accession to the EC. But the British demand on the conventions continued to play a role in the conclusion of the Yaoundé Convention.

[48] The so-called Associated African States and Madagascar (AASM).

[49] All these new provisions became part of what became called the Lomé Conventions. The developing countries (currently 70) that have signed these conventions, are known as the ACP Countries (Africa,, Caribbean, and Pacific countries).

[50] The instrument through which the EU finances the projects that are provided by the Lomé Conventions, such as Stabex, Sysmin and the Structural Adjustment Facility. For a brief overview of these conventions, see Babarinde (1995: 471-472).

[51] In these agreements a cumulation of origin is provided for imports from the EU, Tunisia, Morocco, and Algeria (Hoekman and Djankov, 1996: 400).

[52] As March Pujol (1997: 9) has phrased it: '(..) Spain has managed to formulate a truly Euro-Latin American policy - that is, a policy of the European Community toward the Latin American countries.' Roy (1997: 28; 51-53) has characterized Spain as a 'bridge between the European Union and Latin America.' Moreover, others have claimed that this Spanish policy towards Latin America has been '(..) one of the factors leading Spain to gain an important role within Community Councils' (Martinez, Crespo, Jerez, 1997: 109).

[53] As most Latin American countries enjoy a GSP status, these Cooperation Agreements are still a far cry from the kind of preferences granted by the EU to the ACP countries or to the Mediterranean countries (Galinsoga Jorda, 1992: 171).

[54] In this sense, the definition of this concept is analogous to the meaning of externalization in economic theory.

[55] For most of them, more than 50% of their exports went to the EC, and the EC was the most important source of their inward-FDI.

[56] *European Parliament Debates*, 1989, 2-373, 17-1-89, pp. 79-80.

[57] In those days the term 'European Economic Space' was also used.

[58] Politically, joining the EC was out of the question for most of these states. Neutrality (Austria, Sweden, Finland, and Switzerland) and domestic political opposition to EC-membership (Sweden, Norway, and Switzerland) were the most important reasons for this. In the case of Iceland, EC-membership would have meant the opening of its fishing grounds to EC-vessels, which was (and still is) – given the predominance of fisheries in its economy – politically unfeasible. Ironically, for most of the countries concerned, EEA-membership became an important – if not the most important – factor to eventually become EC-members, as the EEA required them to adopt EC-legislation on a large number of issues, without them being involved in the decision-making on these issues (the EEA-members were only involved in the decision-*shaping*, not the decision-*making*) (Kerremans, 1992). Baldwin (1997: 872) has called this 'regulation without representation.'

[59] It was originally hoped that the EEA-Agreement would enter into force at the same day as the completion of the Internal Market, thereby underlining the relationship between the two.

[60] This can be seen in the same figures as those mentioned above. A deepening of an existing RTA means in legal terms that an old RTA with the countries concerned is replaced

by a new one (in the EU jargon, a 'new generation'). These new ones have to be reported as new RTAs to the WTO even if they build on old ones.

[61] Already during the end of the 19th centrury, the United States was interested in, and indeed concluded trade agreements with Canada.

[62] The objective of negotiating free trade areas is mentioned in the fifth objective of the bill that has been adopted by the House, see H.R. 1432, Section 2(5), in: *Report* 105-423, Parts I and II.

[63] See *Bridges Weekly Trade News Digest*, Vol. 2, n° 11, March 30, 1998.

[64] According to Blank (1993: 22) CUSFTA was less about improving market access – which was already high before CUSFTA – but about stabilizing '(..) an emerging environment in which vast and rapidly increasing interdependencies made each side vulnerable to actions by the other.'

[65] Orne (1993: 23) has typified the respective roles of Mexico and the US in the creation of NAFTA as follows: 'If Salinas and Bush are the parents of the North American free trade agreement, Ronald Reagan is the godfather.' That he mentioned Reagan was due to the fact that he defended the idea of a North American common market in his 1980 presidential campaign. During the Reagan years the idea has not been implemented, largely due to two reasons: first the fact that Mexico had to settle its 1982 debt crisis first, and second the reservations of the then Mexican president Lopéz Portillo (Ibid.: 24). Equally in the US many foreign policy specialists believed that such a common market 'would contradict the U.S. commitment to multilateral trade negotiations under GATT' (Ibid.: 25). But in 1990, largely due to Mexican president Salinas, the idea of NAFTA started to become reality. As Orne (1996: 39) has put it: '(..) it was Reagan who told Mexican leaders that if they wanted to join a continental free trade zone, it was their move. That was the invitation – repeated by Bush in 1988 – that Salinas, to Washington's great surprise, accepted.'

[66] Canada's demand was – despite domestic opposition to a new free trade agreement after CUSFTA – due to Canadian fear that an American agreement with Mexico would hurt its exports to its largest export market: The US (Walker, 1993: 14). In this vein, following Orne (1993: 27), one could say that CUSFTA '(..) laid NAFTA's structural foundation.'

[67] In this vein, Orne (1996: 292) has observed that NAFTA is '(..) at bottom (..) the codification and regulation of an integration process that is already well advanced and that would have continued (though more slowly and unpredictably) even without a free trade agreement.'

[68] ....and on Congress. By striking a 'hard' deal with Canada that would clearly reflect US trade interests, the second Reagan Administration hoped to get a new mandate for the Uruguay Round negotiations from Congress. As Hart (1994: 243; see also 319) has put it: 'It wanted to prove Congress that it could drive a hard bargain, thereby gaining a renewed mandate to take to the Uruguay Round of talks.' But the MTN's also had a negative affect as the US couldn't accept any agricultural concessions in CUSFTA as long as the GATT negotiations on this subject were not finished. Such concessions would have been a precedent that could enhance the position of the EC in the GATT (Hart, 1994: 262). France, by the way, used the same approach in the negotiations with the Central and Eastern European countries.

[69] Abbott, for instance, claims that one of the major factors behind the US-attitude towards NAFTA consisted of '(..) the developments involving the European Union.' It was not however, the fear for a Fortress Europe that was decisive, but the fact that the EU would assemble so much bargaining power that it could create a 'sufficient risk of imbalance in future trade negotiations with the United States' (1995: 119).

[70] As Wade (1996: 64) phrases it: 'In the US, the biggest US firms typically faced two to five competitors in 1960, almost all of them other US based firms playing by the same rules. Today, the firm may have ten or more serious competitors, half of them foreign, playing by different rules.'.

[71] Note that Congress, during the several extensions of the Reciprocal Trade Agreements authority, never forgot to emphasize that it had never approved GATT and that the concerned extensions could never be explained as being tantamount to a congressional approval of the agreement.

[72] Hart (1994: 38) has phrased it even more straightforwardly: 'Throughout this period, the role of the United States in the management of the international economy and international institutions cannot be overestimated. The negotiation of new international rules frequently involved the internationalization of US domestic legislation or ideology.'

[73] At that time, JFK was only referring to an EC of six member states.

[74] For an overview of the US-EEC negotiations in the Kennedy Round, see Coffey (1993).

[75] According to Destler (1995: 51) this could not but lead to serious problems with the US as leading trade hegemony, as 'any large country rising so rapidly was bound to cause problems for the world trading system.'

[76] The consolation for the Americans was the creation of the Committee on Trade in Agriculture (CTA) at that meeting. As Josling et. al. (1996: 112) have observed, 'the CTA foreshadowed the Uruguay Round negotiations on agriculture because it discussed the various options for how improvement in GATT rules for agriculture could be negotiated.'

[77] Abbott (1995: 119) has emphasized that it was not Fortress Europe in itself that played an importantfactor in the creation of NAFTA but the fact that the EU would assemble so much bargaining power that it could create a 'sufficient risk of imbalance in future trade negotiations with the United States.'

[78] According to Preeg (1995: 222) such bilateral agreements with Japan became 'the initial centerpiece of the Clinton Administration trade strategy vis-à-vis Japan in 1993.'

[79] Deeper refers to the promotion of market access not only through the removal of tariff barriers to trade or the traditional NTBs (such as quotas), but also through regulatory cooperation, coordination, if not regulatory harmonization.

[80] Cf. the FTAA that would secure US market access to the rapidly expanding markets of the Mercosur-countries and would secure these countries' market access to the US (cf. Lang, 1997).

[81] According to Hart (1994: 46-47) it was the Reagan Administration that started to see regionalism and bilateralism in this way, largely as a result of the disappointment following the hesitant attitude of Japan, the EC, and a range of developing countries to engage in a new round of MTNs (what would later become the Uruguay Round).

[82] Cf. Green (1993: xix) as far as Bush and the Enterprise for the Americas Initiative (EAI) is concerned.

[83] Cf. Section 4(a) of H.R. 1432.

[84] Cf. the testimony of deputy USTR Jeffrey Lang to the House Ways and Menas Committee (Lang, 1995) in which said the following: 'Latin America alone, if current trends continue, will exceed both Japan and Western Europe combined as an export market for U.S. goods by the year 2010. Already, Latin America is our fastest growing export market, even though the tariffs within the region average four times higher than the average U.S. tariff' (see also the testimony of Ambassador Brown to the House Subcommittee on International Economic Policy and Trade, April 29, 1998). Equally, the following from a report of the Belgian Senate on the agreement between the EU and Mercosur speaks for itself: 'Mercosur

représente une population de 200 millions d'habitants (soit 45 % de la population sud-américaine totale), et il occupe, avec un P.I.B. de plus de 600 milliards de dollars U.S., la quatrième place dans le classement des puissances économiques, après l'A.L.E.N.A., l'U.E. et le Japon. Le Mercosur dispose en outre d'un potentiel de croissance important, d'une grande richesse en matières premières et il constitue un marché en expansion, tant pour les biens d'équipement que de consommation.'

[85] It is ironical to see how president Salinas opted for the NAFTA-solution after the Western European countries showed no interest for his demands for aid and investments (Orne, 1996: 32).

[86] The agreement doesn't contain the reference to a free trade agreement, but refers instead to an agreement 'in accordance with the WTO-rules, in particular article XXIV GATT' (article 5), and 'article V GATS' (article 6).

[87] In 1995 Chile broke off the negotiations with the US on NAFTA accession because negotiating with the US administration on such accession was considered to be useless until Clinton would have got fast track authority from the Congress. See for instance, *Congressional Records*, Extension of Remarks, November 6, 1997: E2210.

[88] The provisions are similar to those in the agreement with Mexico (see article 2, Agreement with Chile; see also *European Parliament Report*, A4-23/96).

[89] Cf. the testimony of USTR Charlene Barchefsky to the House Subcommittee on Trade, March 18, 1997.

[90] Cf. *Bridges Weekly Trade News Digest*, Vol. 2, n° 5, February 16, 1998 (concerning FTAA), and *Financial Times*, July 16 and July 17, 1998 (concerning a Mercosur-EU Trade Pact).

References

Abbott, F.M. (1995), *Law and Policy of Regional Integration: The NAFTA and Western Hemispheric Integration in the World Trade Organization System*, Martinus Nijhoff, Dordrecht.

Anderson, K., Blackhurst, R. (1993), 'Introduction and Summary', in K. Anderson, R. Blackhurst (eds), *Regional Integration and the Global Trading System*, Harvester Wheatsheaf, New York, pp. 1-18.

Babarinde, O.A. (1995), 'The Lomé Convention: An Aging Dinosaur in the European Union's Foreign Policy Enterprise?', in C. Rhodes, S. Mazey (eds), *The State of the European Union, Vol. 3: Building a European Polity?*, Lynne Rienner, Boulder, pp. 469-496.

Bagwell, K. and Staiger, R.W. (1997a), 'Multilateral Tariff Cooperation During the Formation of Free Trade Areas', in *International Economic Review*, vol. 38, 1997, no. 2, pp. 291-319.

Bagwell, K. and Staiger, R.W. (1997b), 'Multilateral Tariff Cooperation During the Formation of Customs Unions', in *Journal of International Economics*, vol. 42, 1997, no. 1-2, pp. 97-123.

Baldwin, R.E. (1997), 'The Causes of Regionalism', in *The World Economy*, vol. 20, 1997, no. 7, pp. 865-888.

Bayard, T.O., Elliott, K.A. (1994), Reciprocity and Retaliation in U.S. Trade Policy, Institute for International Economics, Washington DC.

Beach, D. (1998), 'The Negotiation of the Europe Agreements with Poland, Hungary, and Czechoslovakia', Aarhus, *TKI Working Paper on European Integration and Regime Formation*, no. 31/98.

Belgian Senate (1998), 'Projet de loi portant assentiment à l'Accord interrégional de coopération entre le CE et le Mercosur – Westontwerp houdende instemming met de Interregionale Kaderovereenkomst tussen de EG en de Mercosur', in *Stukken Senaat*, 1-721/2, Session 1997-1998, February 11, 1998.

Bergsten, C.F. (1997), 'Open Regionalism', in *The World Economy*, vol. 20, 1997, no. 5, pp. 545-565.

Black, S.W. (1995), 'Europe's Economy Looks East: Implications for Germany and the EU', in *Economic Studies Program Conference Report*, n 1, American Institute for Contemporary German Studies, The Johns Hopkins University, November 1995.

Blank, S. (1993), 'The Emerging Architecture of North America', in A.R. Riggs, T. Velk (eds), *Beyond NAFTA: An Economic, Political, and Sociological Perspective*, The Fraser Institute, Vancouver, pp. 22-35.

Boyer, R. (1996), 'The Convergence Hypothesis Revisited: Globalization but Still the Century of Nations?', in S. Berger and R. Dore (eds), *National Diversity and Global Capitalism*, Ithaca, Cornell University Press, pp. 29-59.

Buelens, F. (1997), 'After the Presidential Elections: Will the US 'Open Door' Trade Strategy Continue?', in *Intereconomics*, vol. 32, 1997, no. 1, pp. 41-50.

Coffey, P. (1993), *The EC and the United States*, Pinter, London.

Cuyvers, L. and Kerremans, B. (1997), *Internationale economische organisaties*, Garant, Leuven.

Cuyvers, L. and Van Den Bulcke, D. (1996), 'Regionalisering van de wereldeconomie: een goede zaak?', in *Noord-Zuid Cahier*, special issue on Regional Integration and the World Economy, vol. 21, 1996, no. 3, pp. 5-21.

De Laet, J.P. and Fletcher, I. (1996), *The Multilateral Rules on Free Trade Agreements and Customs Unions: Some Implications for the Accession of CIS States to the WTO*, paper published by the European Commission, DG I, Brussels.

De La Serre, F. (1991), 'La Communauté européenne et l'Europe centrale et orientale', in *Revue du Marché commun*, 1991, pp. 529-534.

Destler, I.M. (1989), 'United States Trade Policymaking in the Uruguay Round', in: Nau, H.R., *Domestic trade Politics and the Uruguay Round*, Columbia University Press, New York, pp. 191-207.

Destler, I.M. (1995), *American Trade Politics*, Institute of International Economics, Third Edition, Washington DC.

Dinan, D. (1994), *Ever Closer Union? An Introduction to the European Community*, Macmillan, European Union Series, London.

Donges, J.B. and Wieners, J., 'Foreign Investment in the Transformation Process of Eastern Europe', in *The International Trade Journal*, vol. VIII, 1994, no. 2, pp. 163-191.

Drevet, J.F., 'La Géographie incertaine du continent', in *Le Monde Diplomatique*, Mars 1996, p. 4.

Economic and Social Committee (1995), *Information report on Relations between the European Union and the United States* (Rapporteur: Mrs. Davison), Brussels, CES-Report 978/95.

Enders, A. and Wonnacott, R.J. (1996), 'The Liberalisation of East-West European Trade: Hubs, Spokes, and Further Complications', in *The World Economy*, vol. 19, 1996, no. 3, pp. 253-272.

European Commission (1995), *The European and Latin America. The Present Situation and Prospects for Closer Partnership, 1996-2000*, Brussels, European Commission, DG IB, CAB III/164/95-EN.

European Commission (1996a), *WTO Aspects of EU Preferential Trade Agreements with Third Countries*, Brussels, COM (96) 2168 final.

European Commission (1997a), *Report on United States Barriers*, Brussels, European Commission, DG I, July 1997.

European Commission (1998a), *The New Transatlantic Marketplace. Communication by Sir Leon Brittan, Mr Bangemann, and Mr Monti*, Brussels, European Commission, DG I, March 1998.

Expert Group (1997), *Towards a Common Agricultural and Rural Policy for Europe, Report of the Export Group convened by the European Commission*, Directorate-General VI/A1, European Commission, Brussels.

Ganster, P. (1995), 'United States – Mexico Transborder Interdependence', in S.J. Randall, H.W. Konrad (eds), *NAFTA in Transition*, Calgary University Press, Calgary, pp. 141-177.

Gerber, J., Kerr, W.A. (1995), 'Trade as an Agency of Social Policy: NAFTA's Schizophrenic Role in Agriculture', in: S.J. Randall, H.W. Konrad (eds), *NAFTA in Transition*, Calgary University Press, Calgary, pp. 93-111.

Goybet, C. (1991), 'Aide à l'est: les douze en première ligne', in *Revue du Marché commun*, 1991, pp. 425-428.

Green, R.E. (1993), 'Introduction', in: R.E. Green (ed), *The Enterprise for the Americas Initiative. Issues and Prospects for a Free Trade Agreement in the Western Hemisphere*, Praeger, Westport, pp. xv-xxv.

Grilli, E.R. (1994), *The European Community and the Developing Countries*, Cambridge University Press, Cambridge.

Grossman G.M. and Helpman, E. (1995), 'The Politics of Free-Trade Agreements', in *The American Economic Review*, vol. 85, 1995, no. 4, pp. 667-690.

Gruben, W.C. and Welch, J.H. (1994), 'Is NAFTA Economic Integration?', in *Federal Reserve Bank of Dallas Economic Review*, Second Quarter 1994, pp. 35-61.

Hanson, B.T. (1998), 'What Happened to Fortress Europe? External Trade Policy Liberalization in the European Union', in International Organization, vol. 52, 1998, no. 1, pp. 55-85.

Hart, M. (1994), *Decision at Midnight: Inside the Canada-US Free-Trade Negotiations*, UBC Press, Vancouver.

Hody, C.A. (1996), *The Politics of Trade: American Political development and Foreign Economic Policy*, University Press of New England, Hanover.

Hoekman, B. and Djankov, S. (1996), 'The European Union's Mediterranean Free Trade Initiative', in *The World Economy*, vol. 19, 1996, no. 4, pp. 387-406.

Galinsoga Jorda, A. (1992), 'The Central American Policy of the EC: Balance and Perspectives (A Spanish View)', in: J. Roy (ed), *The Reconstruction of Central America: The Role of the European Community*, Iberian Studies Institute, Miami, pp. 165-186.

Ginsberg, R.H. (1989), *Foreign Policy Actions of the European Community: The Politics of Scale*, Lynne Rienner, Boulder.

Josling, T.E., Tangermann, S., Warley, T.K. (1996), *Agriculture in the GATT*, Martin's Press, New York.

Kennedy, D., Webb, D. (1993), 'The Limits of European Integration: Eastern Europe and the European Communities', in *Common Market Law Review*, vol. 30, 1993, no. 6, pp. 1097-1117.

Kerremans, B. (1996), *Besluitvorming en integratie in de externe economische betrekkingen van de Europese Unie*, Koninklijke Academie voor Wetenschappen, Letteren en Schone Kunsten, Brussels.

Kittelmann, P. (1997), 'Report on the Proposal for a Council Decision on Laying Down the Procedure for Adopting the Community's Position in the Customs Union Joint Committee', in *European Parliament Reports*, A4-0276/97, September 24, 1997.

Lang, J. (1997), 'Testimony by Ambassador Jeffrey Lang, Deputy USTR, to the House Ways and Means Committee', Hearing on the North American Free Trade Agreement, September 11, 1997.

Laurent, P.H. (1992), 'To the Backburner: The European Community - Central American Relationship', in J. ROY (ed), *The Reconstruction of Central America: The Role of the European Community*, Iberian Studies Institute, Miami, pp. 155-164.

Lawrence, R.Z. (1996), *Regionalism, Multilateralism, and Deeper Integration*, Integration National Economies Series, The Brookings Institution, Washington DC.

Lloyd, P.J. (1993), 'A Tariff Substitute for Rules of Origin in Free Trade Areas', in *The World Economy*, vol. 16, 1993, no. 6, pp. 699-712.

Mango, A.J. (1997), 'Testing Time in Turkey', in *The Washington Quarterly*, vol. 20, 1997, no. 1, pp. 3-20.

March Pujol, J.A. (1997), 'The Making of the Ibero-American Space', in: J. Roy, A. Galinsoga Jorda (eds), *The Ibero-American Space: Dimensions and Perceptions of the Special Relationship between Spain and Latin America*, Iberian Studies Institute, Miami, pp. 7-20.

Maresceau, M. (1989), 'A General Survey of the Current Legal Framework of Trade Relations between the European Community and Eastern Europe', in: M. Maresceau, *The Political Framework of Trade Relations between the European Community and Eastern Europe*, Martinus Nijhoff Publishers, Dordrecht, pp. 3-20.

Marquez Perez, P.G. (1995a), 'The Social Neo-Liberal Policies of Carlos Salinas de Gortari', in: S.J. Randall, H.W. Konrad (eds), *NAFTA in Transition*, Calgary University Press, Calgary, pp. 47-55.

Marquez Perez, P.G. (1995a), 'The Mexican Automobile Industry', in S.J. Randall, H.W. Konrad (eds), *NAFTA in Transition*, Calgary University Press, Calgary, pp. 215-236.

Martinez, A., Crespo, I., Jerez, A. (1997), 'Between Europe and Ibero-America: The Political Discourse of the Spanish Government', in J. Roy, A. Galinsoga Jorda (eds), *The Ibero-American Space: Dimensions and Perceptions of the Special Relationship between Spain and Latin America*, Iberian Studies Institute, Miami, pp. 107-118.

Maslen, J. (1989), 'European Community - CMEA: institutional relations', in M. Maresceau, *The Political Framework of Trade Relations between the European Community and Eastern Europe*, Martinus Nijhoff Publishers, 1989, Dordrecht, pp. 85-92.

Massey, D.S. (1998), 'The March of Folly. U.S. Immigration Policy After NAFTA', in *The American Prospect*, 1998, no. 37, pp. 22-33.

Mayer, H. (1997), 'Early at the Beach and Claiming Territory? The Evolution of German Ideas on a New European Order', in *International Affairs*, London, vol. 73, 1997, no. 4, pp. 721-737.

Milner, H.V. (1997), *Interests, Institutions, and Information. Domestic Politics and International Relations*, Princeton University Press, Princeton NJ.

Nau, H.R. (1995), *Trade and Security. U.S. Policies at Cross-Purposes*, The AEI Press, Washington DC.

Nowicki, L.W. (1997), 'Rules of Origin and Local Content Requirements: Protectionism after the Uruguay Round', in *The International Trade Journal*, vol. XI, 1997, no. 3, pp. 349-387.

Orne, W.A. (1993), *Continental Shift. Free Trade and the New North America*, The Washington Post Company, Washington DC.

Orne, W.A. (1996), *Understanding NAFTA. Mexico, Free Trade, and the New North America*, University of Texas Press, Austin.

Peers, S. (1995), 'An Ever Closer Waiting Room?: The Case for Eastern European Accession to the European Economic Area', in *Common Market Law Review*, vol. 32, 1995, no. 1, pp. 187-213.

Pomfret, R. (1997), *The Economics of Regional Trading Agreements*, Clarendon Press, Oxford.

Rolle, J. (1995), 'EU Enlargement and the World Trade System', in *European Economic Review*, vol. 39, no. 3-4, pp. 467-473.

Roy, J. (1997), 'Spain's Relations with Latin America', in J. Roy, A. Galinsoga Jorda (eds), *The Ibero-American Space: Dimensions and Perceptions of the Special Relationship between Spain and Latin America*, Iberian Studies Institute, Miami, pp. 21-56.

Rubio, L., Rodriguez, C., Blum, R. (1989), 'Mexico's Trade Policy and the Uruguay Round', in: Nau, H.R., *Domestic trade Politics and the Uruguay Round*, Columbia University Press, New York, pp. 167-190.

Sager, M.A. (1997), 'Regional Trade Agreements: Their Role and the Economic Impact on Trade Flows', in *The World Economy*, vol. 20, 1997, no. 2, pp. 239-252.

Sarat, D. (1990), 'L'assistance de la Communauté à la Pologne et à la Hongrie', in *Revue du Marché commun*, 1990, pp. 14-17.

Schumacher, D. (1996), 'More Employment in the EU Through Foreign Trade with the Transition Countries', in *Economic Bulletin*, German Institute for Economic Research, vol. 33, 1996, no. 3, pp. 3-10.

Sekwat, A. and Lynch, T.D., 'The World's Trading System in the Post Cold War Era: Implications for Public Administration', in *International Journal of Public Administration*, vol. 18, 1995, no. 11, pp. 1753-1773.

Senti, R. (1994), 'Die Integration als Gefahr für das GATT', in *Aussenwirtschaft*, vol. 49, 1994, no. 1, pp. 131-150.

Srinivasan, T.N. (1998), 'Regionalism and the WTO: Is Nondiscrimination Passé?', in: A.O. Krueger (ed), *The WTO as an International Organization*, The University of Chicago Press, Chicago, pp. 329-349.

United Nations Economic Commission for Europe (ECE) (1994), *Economic Survey of Europe 1992-1993*, United Nations, Geneva, 1994.

United States House of Representatives (1962), *Hearings before the Committee on Ways and Means on H.R. 9900*, March and April 1962, GPO, Washington DC, Parts 1-5.

Vernon, R. (1996), 'Passing Through Regionalism: The Transition to Global Markets', in *The World Economy*, vol. 19, 1996, no. 6, pp. 621-633.

Verrier, M. (1995), 'La Turquie Piétine aux portes de l'Europe', in *Le Monde Diplomatique*, Mars 1995.

Verrier, M. (1996), 'Espoirs d'Ankara et fantasmes européens', in *Le Monde Diplomatique*, Juin 1996, p.18.

Wachtel, H. (1998), 'Labor's Stake in the WTO', in *The American Prospect*, 1998, no. 37, pp. 34-38.

Wade, R. (1996), 'Globalization and its Limits: Reports of the death of the National Economy are Greatly Exaggerated', in: Suzanne BERGER and Ronald DORE (eds), National Diversity and Global Capitalism, Cornell University Press, Ithaca, pp. 60-88.

Walker, M.A. (1993), 'Free Trade and the Future of North America', in A.R. Riggs, T. Velk (eds), *Beyond NAFTA: An Economic, Political, and Sociological Perspective*, The Fraser Institute, Vancouver, pp. 13-21.

Weidenfeld, W. (1996), *A New Ostpolitik – Strategies for a United Europe (short version)*, Bertelsmann Foundation Publishers, Gütersloh.

Weyerbrock, S. (1998), 'Reform of the European Union's Common Agricultural Policy: How to Reach GATT-Compatibility?', in *European Economic Review*, vol. 42, 1998, no. 2, pp. 375-411.

Whitehead, L. (1992), 'The Identity of the New Europe and the San José Process', in: J. Roy (ed), *The Reconstruction of Central America: The Role of the European Community*, Iberian Studies Institute, Miami, pp. 139-153.

World Trade Organization (1995b), *Regionalism and the World Trading System*, Geneva, WTO.

World Trade Organization (1997a), *Trade Policy Review- European Union*. Report by the Secretariat, Geneva, WTO, WT/TPR/S/30.

WTO Committee on Regional Trade Agreements (1996), *Report (1996) of the Committee on Regional Trade Agreements to the General Council*, Geneva, WTO, WT/REG/2.

WTO Committee on Regional Trade Agreements (1997), *Report (1997) of the Committee on Regional Trade Agreements to the General Council*, Geneva, WTO, WT/REG/3.

Yeats, A.J. (1998), 'Does Mercosur's Trade Performance Raise Concerns about the Effects of Regional Trade Agreements?', in: *The World Bank Economic Review*, Vol. 12, 1998, no. 1, pp. 1-28.

6 Competition and Cooperation between Blocs: The Case of North America and Europe

BART KERREMANS

Introduction

If there is one issue on which there exists consensus between the two sides of the North-Atlantic, it is that the European Union and the United States are linked to each other by extensive trade and investment relations and by common security interests. Indeed, each and any of the numerous statements on transatlantic relations issued since the fall of the Berlin Wall has emphasized this. And there are many reasons to agree with this.

First, there is NATO that binds the security policies of the U.S. and Canada together with those of an increasing number of European countries.

Second, there is the impressive record on transatlantic trade. According to the Office of the United States Trade Representative (USTR, 1998a), the EU and US trade about $300 billion in goods annually (in 1996, ECU 277 billion), accounting for about 20% of world trade in goods. About 20% of this trade was trade in high technological manufactures, an indication that a large part of the Transatlantic trade is intra-industry trade. European products compete with similar U.S. products on the Transatlantic market (Commission, 1998a). Furthermore, agricultural trade alone accounted for $15 billion in 1997.[1]

The picture for trade in services is similar although this sector is still in full development, given the difference between its share in the GNP of both the U.S. and the EU, and its lower share in the exports of these customs territories. But in terms of bilateral trade, services accounted for ECU 124 billion which was about 35% of world trade in services.[2] If all trade is taken together the EU, the U.S. and their bilateral trade account for about 60% of world trade whereas US trade accounts for approximately 20% of EU imports and exports (goods and services combined, see following tables).

Table 6.1   EU Trade, U.S. Trade, and Transatlantic Trade

	1994		1995	
	Value	%	Value	%
Tot. EU Exports	523640.4	100.0	572839.9	100.0
Of Which to the U.S.[3]	103669.9	19.7	103298.9	18.0
Tot. EU Imports	518499.2	100.0	545129.5	100.0
Of Which from the U.S.[4]	99956.8	19.2	103643.3	19.0
Tot. Balance	+5141.1		+27710.4	
Trade Balance with the U.S.	+3713.0		-344.35	
	1996		**1997**	
	Value	%	Value	%
Tot. EU Exports	625084.1	100.0	717884.6	100.0
Of Which to the U.S.[5]	114417.1	18.3	140705.5	19.6
Tot. EU Imports	581464.6	100.0	667357.1	100.0
Of Which from the U.S.[6]	112781.4	19.4	136480.5	20.4
Tot. Balance	+43619.5		+50527.5	
Trade Balance with the U.S.	+1635.6		+4225.0	

Sources: House of Commons (1998); USTR (1998b)

The investment relationship has been equally impressive.   While the European Union acts as the biggest foreign investor in the United States – being responsible for 59% of the FDI stock in the U.S. – the United States is equally the biggest foreign investor in the EU with a share of 51% of the FDI stocks in the European Union (Ibidem). As a result, about 3 million Europeans work for American companies in the EU while about the same number of Americans work for European companies in the U.S. (House Ways and Means, 1998).[7]

Clearly, a transatlantic marketplace needs not to be invented. It already exists. And it is created and recreated every day in the numerous transactions between the two sides of the Atlantic. Still, it seems that there is a need for political structures to sustain this marketplace, to smoothen its transactions, to further enhance mutual trade and investment, and to remove remaining barriers of all kinds. In addition, the transatlantic marketplace doesn't operate in a vacuum. It works in an environment of regulated trade and investment. And part of this regulation is not transatlantic but multilateral in nature. Transatlantic trade regulations and practices cannot have anything but a large effect on the operation of this multilateral system because EU-US trade accounts for 20% of world trade in goods and 35% of world trade in services. In addition, the EU and the U.S. are the two largest trading blocks in the multilateral trading system. Seen from that perspective, transatlantic trade policies are not only transatlantic in nature but multilateral as well, or, as Jeffrey Lange, Deputy USTR, has phrased it in his testimony to the Ways and Means in July 1997 (House Ways and Means, 1997: 21; see also Green Cowles, 1997: 1):

> (..) it's safe to say that most U.S. efforts to further open markets and increase the rule of law in international trade, particularly on a multilateral basis, cannot advance without the positive participation of the European Union.[8]

Since the end of the Cold War, one can observe a new enthusiasm, a new zeal for the strengthening of the transatlantic relationship. A number of reasons can be put forward to explain for this.

First, there is the end of the Cold War itself. Quite soon after the fall of the Berlin Wall, politicians on both sides of the Atlantic started to wonder what the effect of this would be on the transatlantic relations. James Baker, George Bush's Secretary of State was one of the first to realize this. In his December 1989 visit to Berlin on the verge of the German reunification process, Baker stressed the continuing importance of the security ties across the Atlantic. Similarly in Europe, voices were raised about the nature and extent of the American commitment to Europe's security now that the Cold War was over and the Warsaw Pact soon dissolved. In those days, ideas started to emerge that trade linkages would provide a stable basis for the continuation of the mutual security commitments. As trade and investment would bring the two sides of the Atlantic closer together, the security ties between them would become closer as well. The New

Transatlantic Declaration, as adopted in December 1990, directly stemmed from this.

Second, there was the GATT's Uruguay Round. If the Uruguay Round made one thing quite clear, it was that without agreement between the U.S. and the EU on major issues of trade policy, no multilateral trade cooperation in the GATT/WTO, or elsewhere would be possible. The EU and the U.S. clearly held each other hostage in the multilateral trading system just like the multilateral system itself was a hostage of transatlantic cooperation and agreement.[9] In addition, as the Uruguay Round dragged on, it made regional bloc formation more attractive for the United States (Jütte-Rauhut, 1995; Economic and Social Committee, 1995: 2; Buelens, 1997: 5). The EU thus had an additional argument to keep the Americans on the multilateral track (Abbott, 1995: 119; Rolle, 1995: 45). This was a remarkable evolution since the EU itself has traditionally been the champion of regional trade agreements and regional trade policies. But the emergence of U.S. interest in regional trade agreements – first through CUSFTA and NAFTA, then through APEC, and now through the FTAA – changed the picture. As the Commission Forward Studies Unit remarked (1995: 15):

> Regional projects are now important variables on both sides of the Atlantic, and their development, at varying speeds, will be one of the primary contextual factors shaping Transatlantic relations.

Furthermore with the Asian financial crisis of 1997 both the EU and the U.S. have to function as a 'market of last resort.' Especially on the American side complaints have been issued about the lack of economic growth in the European Union and the necessity for the EU and the U.S. to share the role of market of last resort as a way to avoid the emergence of protectionism in the U.S. (cf. *Financial Times*, February 25, 1999, p. 1).

These developments led to the following two conclusions. First, the role of trade, and therefore of trade policy, in sustaining and cementing a security partnership was even more important after the Cold War than during.[10] As the aforementioned Jeffrey Lang testified in July 1997:[11]

> As U.S. cooperation with Europe on security matters formed the bedrock on which the post-Second World War peace was built, the U.S.-European trade relationship has been the anchoring point for the international trading system since the General Agreement on Tariffs and Trade came into force in 1947.[12]

A second conclusion was that the intensity of transactions and interactions in the transatlantic marketplace could not be taken for granted. In order to reap the full benefits of these transactions, they had to be underpinned by political commitments and by a large array of rules – both bilateral and multilateral. Otherwise stated, besides the transatlantic marketplace of trade transactions and investment – the one that already exists for a long time – there was a need for a transatlantic Marketplace – with a capital 'm' – built on trade agreements and rules. The search for such a marketplace started quite quickly after the fall of the Berlin Wall and is – to a certain extent – still going on.

The aim of this chapter is to highlight the problems and the challenges that had to be met in order to make this endeavor a success. In doing so, it will become clear why cooperation is still difficult between two major trading blocks with such a large and deep trading relationship. Indeed, the paradox of the transatlantic partnership is exactly that its depth is inextricably linked to the occurrence of conflicts, and that its weight in the multilateral system has almost inevitably intensified these conflicts. This has put a serious burden on transatlantic cooperation, and has required serious political investments in it.

The Road to the 1995 New Transatlantic Agenda (NTA)

Our search for transatlantic cooperation starts with the emergence of the New Transatlantic Agenda in the course of 1995. The process that led to it generated a qualitative leap in the transatlantic relationship because it went beyond pure declaratory politics (which was largely the case with the 1990 Transatlantic Declaration). It not only created constant communication at high political levels between the U.S. and the EU (which proved to be helpful when problems arose during negotiations on trade agreements such as the ITA, veterinary equivalence, and customs cooperation), but it was also evolutionary in nature. The New Transatlantic Agenda (NTA) was not meant to be the end of the search for improved relations. It was a stepping stone, meant to create new political momentum in favor of deeper trade, security, and political relations, and to provide the start of a new process in which new frameworks for these relations would be looked for and created.

The NTA was – at least from the perspective of trade – also a 'qualitative' leap in that it started from a new paradigm (Stern, 1996; Jackson, 1996). Instead of letting the governments do all the work and determine what would be put into the relationship, business – and later, in

1998, also civil society – were directly involved. Moreover, it was government that basically brought businesses from the two sides of the Atlantic together in order to clarify how from a business point of view, Transatlantic trade relations could be promoted. The initiative to this came from the U.S. Dept of Commerce, namely from its Secretary, the late Ron Brown. For the U.S. this approach was not completely new given its propensity for self-regulation rather than regulation by decree.

For the European Union, this was less evident. Indeed, the EU has undergone a major shift in its attitude to the business approach, i.e. an approach in which businesses play an important role as identifiers of problems and agenda setters. When the U.S. Commerce Department issued a proposal on a business-inspired approach towards Transatlantic trade relations[13] the reactions in the European Union, including the Commission, were highly skeptical.[14] The original proposal was called the 'Expanded New Vision for Trade with Europe' and later changed into the 'Transatlantic Business Dialogue'. But European politicians didn't see the added value of such an initiative given the existence of several international forums – like the G7, the annual EU-US summits, the OECD, and the Quad. For the European Commission, a dialogue inspired by business could only be accepted on condition that after an initial test period, a withdrawal from it would be possible.

There were also questions in business circles. Some. company leaders wanted to have more guarantees about the extent to which the dialogue would get a real input in the intergovernmental transatlantic relations. Others had to be convinced that the required investment in such a dialogue would pay off with trade liberalization and the removal of regulatory barriers.

The Commerce Department ultimately succeeded in enticing both businesses and the European Commission. The first was seduced by the emphasis on the complementarity of this initiative and its expected effect on trade liberalization with the ongoing liberalization process in the WTO (which just had started to operate). The emphasis, therefore, was largely put on regulatory issues such as standards, product testing and certification, and on public procurement, intellectual property rights, and national treatment in foreign investment.

The Commission was convinced by the promise to make the new approach a 'trial' and by the concomitant consequence that participation in it didn't commit neither the Commission nor the EU member states on any subject of trade liberalization. In addition, the prospect for cooperation on a 'level playing field' in third markets – the Central and Eastern European

Countries' integration in the WTO, and the Asian emerging economies – was put forward as an 'appetizer'. Indeed the skepticism was extremely high on the European side.

Gradually, however, the idea of more than just a dialogue started to emerge, especially on the European side. One of the main reasons for this was the end of the Cold War and the concerns in some member states, not to the least Germany, that this could lead to a weakening of the security ties between Europe and the United States. As a consequence, the idea of a transatlantic free trade area started to emerge (Peterson, 1996: 58). Political leaders such as John Major and Klaus Kinkel first referred to the new transatlantic relations in this way. The Commission, however, remained cautious. It realized that the compatibility of such an approach with the brand new WTO rules would require that such an area would have to cover 'substantially all the trade' between the EU and the US (Kerremans, 1998). This would certainly mean that a TAFTA would cover agricultural trade as well. Given the difficulties in the Uruguay Round, such an approach was just not realistic. Sir Leon Brittan proposed, therefore, an approach that emphasized business facilitation, mutual recognition of standards and certification and an intensified Transatlantic business dialogue.

This approach was largely shared by the Americans as they believed that the negotiation of a major trade liberalization agreement so soon after the termination of the Uruguay Round and the difficulties in the U.S. ratification process would be risky. More and more, the U.S. Commerce Department and the European Commission shared the conviction that the first step in the amelioration of trade relations had to be provided by the business dialogue and by business facilitation. As Leon Brittan put it in December 1995: 'The best way to identify and discuss all (..) [the] problems is to let the businessmen speak' (*Agence Europe*, n° 6599: 5). From May 1995 on, therefore, they embarked on a strategy of which the Transatlantic Business Dialogue would become the centerpiece and in which different initiatives for the removal of obstacles to Transatlantic business development would be gathered in one single framework. The idea was that separate initiatives on business facilitation would never attract sufficient investment from higher political levels. This could be the case, however, if many initiatives were to be grouped into one large project. In that case, there was a possibility that it would attract the active interest from the U.S. president, and European government leaders. This became indeed the main objective of the new initiative: attracting political attention and interest. That would be its added value to the large array of already existing agreements and negotiations. At the same time, it would avoid that the search for an improvement in Transatlantic trade relations would have to concentrate on the creation of a Transatlantic Free Trade Area, a formula which was clearly out of the question for both the Commission and the Clinton Administration (Kerremans, 1998).

Two politicians, U.S. Commerce Secretary Ron Brown, and European External Trade Relations Commissioner Sir Leon Brittan, took the lead. At the end of April 1995, they sent a letter to more than a hundred large European and American companies and business associations asking them to participate in a Transatlantic Business Dialogue. As the letter indicated:[15]

> The goal is to provide a means for U.S. and EU companies and organizations to develop an agenda of key issues that could be addressed by the European Commission and the U.S. Administration so as to improve and deepen the transatlantic business relationship.

And it continued:

> We believe that a direct business perspective could make a constructive contribution to defining our vision of the future shape and direction of that relationship.

Businesses seemed to be interested in the initiative as the U.S. Commerce Department received many (more than 300) positive reactions and as the European-American Business Council took the lead in further institutionalizing the emerging business dialogue (cf. European Commission, 1996b). Most of the companies had clear demands on regulatory issues and the question of mutual recognition of testing and certification. At the same time, the highest political levels started to react as well. At a meeting[16] between President Clinton, Commission president Jacques Santer and French President Jacques Chirac (who held the presidency of the European Council), a new High Level Working Group was created to develop a new Transatlantic agenda. This agenda was clearly meant to include more than just trade. It had to encompass security and other political aspects of the Transatlantic relationship as well. The group had to prepare this agenda against the US-EU Summit of December 1995 in Madrid.

In addition, both the Commission and the U.S. Administration started to conduct studies in order to find out the level of political support for the idea and the issues and objectives for the new initiative. In its study, the Commission clearly focussed on regulatory issues (including testing and certification, and early warning of regulatory changes) and emphasized that close cooperation on regulation and competition could make contingency protection (such as antidumping) obsolete in what the Commission called 'the Transatlantic Economic Space.' In addition, the recurrent question of a TAFTA was resolved by proposing a 'joint US-EU feasibility study' that would include the precise gains and losses of such a free trade area. Furthermore, a distinction was made between bilateral and multilateral issues. As far as the former was concerned, the Commission proposed 'an overall approach' in which different ongoing negotiations would be brought together and in which a clear timeframe would be defined. As far as the latter was concerned, the idea was that the EU and the US together had to take a leadership role in the WTO in order to complete the 'unfinished business of the Uruguay Round', especially in the area of telecommunications and maritime services, and to expand the WTO-agenda in areas such as competition policy[17] and investments (cf. TABD, 1996b: 22).

At the September 29, 1995 meeting of the EU-Council of Ministers (General Affairs) however, many member states expressed their reservations about a drive towards a TAFTA or even concrete concessions on tariff reductions at this stage. But the Council principally approved the search for deeper transatlantic relations. During the debate, it became clear, however, that some member states' objections went deeper. The 'substantially all the trade' requirement of article XXIV GATT would require the inclusion of agriculture and textiles in a TAFTA-agreement, and that was clearly unacceptable to member states like France, Belgium, Greece, and Portugal, and to a lesser extent to Spain,[18] Austria, and Italy. These member states didn't even want to include a reference to TAFTA in the joint feasibility study that the U.S. administration and the Commission would set up jointly. Including such a reference would be tantamount to passively committing to TAFTA, according to these countries.[19]

Also on the U.S. side some work was done in preparation of the Madrid Summit. But here, relatively more emphasis was put on the multilateral aspects of the Transatlantic agenda. For many U.S. officials, the Madrid Summit had to 'lock in' EU support for trade liberalization in the WTO and more concretely for commitments in this vein in the upcoming WTO ministerial in Singapore. In this respect, the Americans were trying to garner European support for zero tariffs by 2000 on information technology (what would become the ITA 1 agreement). In addition, the US sought to reinforce cooperation in the framework of the OECD notably on investment rules (the MAI-negotiations[20]).

But on the American side – just like on the EU side – a certain divergence of opinion emerged among the different trade-related bureaucracies. The United States Trade Representative (USTR) tried to emphasize a cautious approach in which a TAFTA would be avoided and in which a political impetus was sought for the 'overall approach.' Issues like regulatory cooperation and the acceleration of tariff reductions were considered to be much more important than the politically risky track of TAFTA. Such an approach would have two benefits. First, it wouldn't trigger Congressional opposition which would certainly be the case with TAFTA. The difficulties with the Uruguay Round Agreement and with NAFTA provided ample evidence of this. Second, tariff reductions would not directly and automatically require new trade negotiating authority for the president.[21] This was clearly an advantage given the difficulties that the administration faced in getting new 'fast track' authority from Congress (cf. Kerremans, 1999).

The State Department was more in favor of a TAFTA, however. That was not a coincidence as State perceived a TAFTA in a larger security perspective. A TAFTA would tie both sides of the Atlantic and would avoid disruptive trade conflicts. This would strengthen the preparedness of the Europeans to continue the North Atlantic security cooperation now that the Cold War was over and new security problems had emerged (i.e. the Yugoslav War and the U.S. diplomatic involvement in it).[22]

Because of the objections against an FTA-approach on both sides, a subcabinet meeting on September 28, 1995 retained a 'building block approach.' Instead of working with a free trade area, a transatlantic marketplace would be created by gradually concluding trade liberalization agreements, not by concluding one agreement that would cover all the subjects concerned. But the conclusion of these agreements would become part of a predetermined timeframe. In addition, such agreements could only be concluded where they would be complementary to currently existing WTO-agreements or would be explicitly allowed for by these agreements. In this sense, tariff reductions would become part of EU-US efforts inside the WTO,[23] not of separate bilateral deals. As a consequence, the 'building block approach' would largely result into agreements on regulatory issues. Ongoing negotiations on such issues – like the question of testing and certification – would be integrated into the new initiative so as to give them a new political impetus.

In the remainder of 1995 two important things happened in the transatlantic relations. First, the Transatlantic Business Dialogue was institutionalized, largely due to efforts by U.S. Commerce Secretary Ron

Brown and EU Commissioners Sir Leon Brittan and Martin Bangemann. This institutionalization meant *inter alia* that the TABD would continue to play a role – would even be formally involved – in defining and developing the Transatlantic trade agenda.[24]

Second, the EU-US Summit of December 3 in Madrid resulted in the adoption of the New Transatlantic Agenda (NTA) and of an attached Action Plan. The agenda covered a whole range of issues – ranging from actions against cross-border criminality, over trade, security, and cultural and educational exchanges. The Action Plan also provided for a dialogue, not only for businesses, but also for labor unions and environmental groups.

Progress was being made on other fronts as well. There was, of course, the multilateral agenda which included 'the unfinished business of the Uruguay Round'[25] and the initiation of new issues in the WTO, especially in the light of the upcoming Singapore ministerial. Even the bilateral relations had to be perceived and assessed in this perspective. Bilateral deals between the two sides of the Atlantic were not supposed to be an end in itself but only a way to initiate, promote, and stimulate the negotiation of multilateral agreements on the same subjects either in the WTO or in other multilateral frameworks such as the OECD.

In the light of the conclusions of the Madrid Summit, the decision was taken to set up a joint EU-US study – not on a TAFTA as was originally suggested but rejected by some EU member states – but on 'reducing or eliminating' remaining EU-US barriers to trade and on trade facilitation. The reference to 'reducing or eliminating' was included on the demand of France which didn't want to commit itself to 'eliminating' only.

The conclusion of the New Transatlantic Agenda has not been easy. Both the governments and the business representatives (in the European and the American groups of the TABD) had there own sensitivities and priorities and these were not always exactly the same on both sides of the Atlantic. The Americans wanted European commitment on the acceleration of tariff reductions,[26] particularly in sectors such as agriculture (e.g. oilseeds), information technology,[27] and telecommunication services. The European side stressed the importance of non tariff barriers and trade liberalization in maritime services, and financial services, and the importance of a multilateral steel agreement. But at the end of the day, the momentum created by the idea of a new relationship proved to be decisive.

From NTA to NTM, and from NTM to TEP

Problems with the NTA

The New Transatlantic Agenda was not particularly successful in terms of its effect on transatlantic relations was concerned.[28] To a certain extent, the effect of the NTA on multilateral relations was more significant than the effects on US-EU bilateral relations.

The Bilateral Agenda There are a number of reasons why the bilateral track proved to be much more difficult than the multilateral one. First, there was the role of the U.S. Congress. During the period in which the New Transatlantic Agenda was adopted, Congress was working on two bills that would poison Transatlantic relations. The first one was the Helms-Burton Act (on Cuba)[29] and the second the D'Amato Act[30] (on Libya and Iran). Both acts were extraterritorial in nature in that they were designed to punish non-U.S. companies for actions outside the United States (respectively in Cuba, and Iran and Libya). As some European companies were hard hit by this measure, and as the EU considered the extraterritorial effects of the two laws to be violations of international trade law, the acts resulted in a major trade conflict between the European Union and the United States (cf. House of Commons, 1998: 33).

Second, the kind of bilateral issues with which the Transatlantic Agenda tried to deal, proved to be more complicated and controversial than was originally expected. Issues such as testing and certification opened the door to discussions on the equivalence of EU and US standards, and the tests on these standards. A typical example here was the conclusion by the EU that American slaughter procedures for chickens didn't reach the EU veterinary standards.[31] In the case of testing and certification on pharmaceuticals, there was the resistance from the Food and Drug Administration to allow EU products certified by EU pharmaceutical inspection services on the U.S. market. At the same time, the U.S. Congress increased the pressure on the administration by allowing U.S. wines to use European regional designations as generic wine categories.[32] An amendment proposed by Senator D'Amato (R-NY) gave federal legal blessing to a U.S. practice that already existed for a long time but that has never been accepted by the EU.

In the same vein, EU ecolabelling was considered to be a potential hidden trade barrier instead of a genuine environmental measure.[33] In Congress, irritation about the EU's Common Agricultural Policy started to grow, and with it the pressure on the U.S. administration[34] not to accept anything from the Europeans unless something was done about the negative trade effects of the CAP and the European stances on sanitary and phytosanitary regulations (see House of Representatives, 1998a).

Most of the problems on the bilateral agenda had to do with regulatory issues in the environmental area (where besides ecolabelling, fur and leghold traps were the issues), bioengineering in foodstuffs (the so-called GMOs), electronic commerce (encryption, data protection), and veterinary and phytosanitary regulations (ranging from the use of hormones in beef to hygiene in slaughter houses). Part of these problems were a consequence of the ambitions of the agenda itself. Dealing with regulatory issues is more than just liberalizing trade. It is – in addition to the removal of trade barriers – an effort that aims at establishing or maintaining a certain level of safety, health, environmental, and eventually labor standards. Since the definition of what is needed here can be quite different on the two sides of the Atlantic (e.g. the beef hormone question), this is an area where conflicts can easily and strongly erupt (Vogel, 1997: 23-24 and 58-59). As Lawrence (1996: 7) has put it, '[O]nce tariffs are removed, complex problems remain because of differing regulatory policies among nations.'

Other problems were the consequence of longstanding disputes (such as the 11-year old hormone question) and the fact that the political impetus provided by the NTA was clearly not sufficient to resolve them. But in the background the discussion on the Helms-Burton and the D'Amato Act loomed. It impeded any serious political input – especially from the European side – into the Transatlantic Agenda and prevented any serious progress on bilateral issues. A major conflict in the WTO – which would have risked to jeopardize the WTO dispute settlement system itself – could just be avoided.[35]

The Multilateral Agenda The picture of the multilateral agenda was quite different despite the fact that problems had emerged here as well. However, on many issues, cooperation between the EU and the US proved to be decisive in getting things done in the WTO. The Information Technology Agreement, the Agreement on Basic Telecommunications, and the Financial Services Agreement were all concluded after major efforts by both the EU and the US to convince others – especially the newly industrialized countries – to grant concessions on the subjects concerned.

The Search for a New Initiative: the NTM

As the bilateral part of the NTA experienced difficulties, and as the multilateral part proved to be successful, the European Commission started to look into ways to renew the political commitment of the NTA. In its point of view, this had to be done in two ways. First by removing the Helms-Burton and D'Amato cases as major obstacles in the bilateral relations. The second involved presenting a new plan for market integration that could trigger new enthusiasm for Transatlantic trade relations, and that could engender a new political momentum. The conclusions of the joint study had to act as a guide in this.

By looking for a new initiative, however, the Commission was looking further than just bilateral trade relations. First, the security perspective was taken into consideration. The old idea with which it all had started in 1989-1990 (the Transatlantic Declaration) and which played a role in the launching of the NTA in 1995, became prominent again when the 'new initiative' was being prepared. The ideas was that good trade relations would advance the quality of the security integration on the two sides of the Atlantic. And the period between 1991 and 1998 had provided ample and sufficient evidence that this kind of integration was still important after the end of the Cold War. Wasn't it NATO that was playing a central role in the peacekeeping and peace enforcing efforts in Bosnia-Herzegovina? Wasn't everybody looking at the US again when in February 1998 new violence erupted in Kosovo, this time with an even larger spillover risk than Bosnia? Clearly, forging stronger security links between the two sides of the Atlantic was not outmoded yet.

In addition, many in the European Union– especially Commissioner Leon Brittan–were looking at the WTO as well. In December 1999 new negotiations on agriculture had to be started and that would be as difficult a case for the EU as for transatlantic relations. During the second half of 1997 and the first of 1998, there was ample reason to believe this. World market prices for some major crops were dropping, and in the United States the pressure for opening foreign agricultural markets became overwhelming at a time when the Clinton administration faced tremendous difficulties in getting new trade negotiating authority from Congress. Leon Brittan was, therefore, thinking in terms of a new all-encompassing round of multilateral trade negotiations. For the first time since the creation of the GATT – and a fortiori of the WTO – the Europeans would initiate such a round, the Millenium Round. But in order to do so, both the United States and most EU member states had to be convinced. And he had to react quickly as the list of potential trade conflicts became longer and longer. There was not only the issue of agriculture but also of electronic commerce (data privacy protection), beef hormones (where a WTO-panel ruled), food safety,[36] the use of specified risk materials (SRMs) in animal products, and bananas.[37] The momentum created by launching a new major initiative in Transatlantic trade relations, could be helpful therefore. This initiative would become the New Transatlantic Marketplace. As Leon Brittan has described its significance:[38]

> The New Transatlantic Marketplace is a specifically tailored package of measures to address the real barriers that exist in the EU/US trading relationship. It represents a huge leap forward for Europe's relationship with the US, bringing not only strong economic benefits for both business and consumers, but also a new political momentum to relations across the Atlantic.

In March 1998, after months of careful preparations, the European Commission officially submitted its proposal on a New Transatlantic Marketplace (NTM). The NTM proposal may have served the Commission's agenda on the WTO quite well, it was to a large extent a logical outcome of the NTA. Indeed, the NTA had produced its joint feasibility study in November 1997 and had formulated a number of recommendations to the EU-US Summit of December 1997.[39] As a consequence, Sir Leon Brittan had formulated four areas on which Transatlantic cooperation in the field of trade had to be concentrated: technical barriers to trade (with an emphasis on the extension of the MRA[40]), trade in services, the elimination of industrial tariffs, and issues that should be dealt with on a multilateral scale such as government procurement (where new negotiations are scheduled in the WTO[41]), investment (cf. the then ongoing MAI-negotiations), and intellectual property. Despite this broad agenda, the initiative was meant to fall short of a free trade approach. Such an approach was clearly unacceptable to both the U.S. Congress and to several EU member states.

The Commission's NTM proposal – as endorsed on March 11, 1998 – was both ambitious[42] and controversial. Immediate reactions followed, first from the U.S. Congress, than from the EU member states.

The reactions from the U.S. Congress were no surprise. During the informal meetings between the EU and the US – and specifically between USTR Charlene Barchefsky and EU External Trade Commissioner Leon Brittan, it had become clear that the American approach towards the NTM was more careful and restrictive than the Commission's. Barchefsky had underlined this in one of her numerous letters on the subject to Congress. In her February 11 letter she had enumerated the five following principles that had to guide the new NTM:[43]

> First, any initiative must be in the interest of the United States. Second, it must be trade creating, not trade diverting. Third, it must enhance the global trading system and build a model for the future. Fourth, it must not prejudice the resumption in 1999 of global talks on the WTO built-in agenda, most notably in agriculture. And finally, it must in no way detract from our ability to enforce aggressively our existing agreements with the EU. If we can develop a proposal that adheres to all of these principles, we will then have a solid basis for moving forward.

The second principle was clearly a warning against an FTA approach or anything close to it. The third principle – widely shared by the European Commission[44] – pointed at the complementarity between the NTM and the WTO and at the role of the Transatlantic relationship in promoting multilateralism. The fourth principle was a way to calm concerns in Congress that the EU could use the NTM to 'drown' the question of agricultural liberalization – a matter that was on the 1999 WTO agenda anyway – into negotiations on a larger agreement. The fifth principle pointed at pending conflicts such as the beef hormones and the banana regime. An NTM could in no way be used to provide a bargaining chip in negotiations on these matters.

But despite the guarantees on these principles, many in Congress were unhappy about the EU Commission's proposal. In press statements, the chairmen of the Senate Finance Committee and of the Senate Finance Subcommittee on Trade, stressed that the NTM served European interests to the detriment of issues that were of particular importance to the United States. There were reasons for that. First, there was the explicit exclusion of agricultural tariff reductions, export subsidies and internal support systems.[45] According to the Commission, since negotiations on these issues would start in the WTO anyway, parallel negotiations as part of the NTM would not be very 'helpful.' For many members of Congress, this was far from evident.[46]

In addition, the NTM implicitly excluded other sensitive issues. Fish and fish products would have to be dealt with as agricultural products, thus to be excluded from the NTM. Audiovisual services would be, according to the Commission, excluded since these had received an exemption in the final stages of the Uruguay Round and this exemption 'must be fully preserved and therefore excluded from the NTM negotiations.'

In the same vein, the proposal included many subjects that were extremely difficult for the United States to negotiate about. Examples are the maritime services (excluded from the Uruguay Round services agreement thanks to U.S. opposition), foreign ownership levels in satellite-based telecommunications services companies, state-level restrictions on the provision of professional services, the question of 'first-to-file' or 'first-to-invent' in the case of patents,[47] and the upcoming question of the use by U.S. wine producers of EU appellations of origin.

It was maybe not surprising that the Commission paid attention to its own agenda in the first place. It was after all, a Commission proposal and it had to be acceptable for the EU member states in the first place. But it remains remarkable that – given the numerous informal meetings that preceded its adoption by the EU executive – it failed to take into account Congressional concerns to such an extent, especially since the failure of President Clinton to get new trade negotiating authority in November 1997 indicated quite clearly the new assertiveness of Congress on trade issues. A contentious issue thrown into the mix was that of agriculture (Kerremans, 1998).

But even if there may have been a focus on the EU member states themselves, the proposal was far from uncontroversial to these. The first opportunity to discuss the proposal formally was at a Council meeting on April 3, 1998 and at subsequent meetings of the Committee of Permanent Representatives (COREPER) and a special working group on transatlantic relations. At these meetings, several member states raised questions about the compatibility of the proposal with the EU's WTO obligations. This was especially the case concerning the absence of agriculture. Would this jeopardize the legality of an NTM in the perspective of the 'substantially all the trade' requirement of article XXIV GATT, even if the NTM was not meant to be the basis of a free trade agreement?

Equally, questions were raised about the effects of a transatlantic dispute settlement system – as spelled out in the proposal – on the obligations of the EU under the Dispute Settlement Understanding (DSU) of the WTO.

In the same vein, doubts were expressed about the proposed free trade area in services with the ongoing services agenda of the WTO.

But not all member states expounded these concerns with the purpose of targeting the NTM as such. Most of them welcomed the proposal on condition that it would be clear what kind of problems and obligations it could entail for the EU and its member states as WTO members. In this sense, the position of France (and perhaps the Netherlands) was slightly different. For France, the NTM as proposed by the Commission was unacceptable, partly because of its potential problems with the WTO, and partly because of the extent of the proposal itself. The big political importance that France attached to the question could be seen by the personal intervention of both president Jacques Chirac and prime minister Lionel Jospin. Both complained that the Commission had failed to consult the member states sufficiently on the NTM proposal – an allegation that was vigorously rejected by Leon Brittan – and about the possible inclusion – either explicitly or implicitly – of agriculture and (audiovisual) services in the NTM negotiations. At the April 27 Council of Ministers meeting the consequence of these complaints and objections became clear. France, supported by other member states, rejected the NTM-proposal. The Council – on the demand of those that supported the NTM – asked the Commission to conduct talks with the Americans aiming at '(..) promoting multilateral liberalization, as well as enhanced bilateral cooperation by progressively reducing or eliminating barriers that hinder the flow of goods, services and capital.' In other words, while the NTM was rejected, many of its pieces were approved. In addition – and some say that this was the real objective of Leon Brittan – the Council formally endorsed Brittan's proposal on the organization of a new round of multilateral trade negotiations in the WTO, the so-called Millenium Round. Both the Round and transatlantic trade relations would be part of the Commission's mandate for the May 18 EU-US Summit in London. But all these decisions were conditional upon the acceptance by the United States to repeal the Helms-Burton and D'Amato Acts or to waive parts of them.

Inside the Commission, the search for an alternative for the defunct NTM almost immediately started. Already after the first contacts with the US it became clear that a new initiative had to be more modest and would probably cover regulatory issues only or almost only. Issues such as the elimination of industrial tariffs by 2010, a free trade area in services, investment, and procurement soon dropped out.

At the May 18 Transatlantic Summit, the idea of a Transatlantic Economic Partnership (TEP) was launched with a Declaration on the Transatlantic Partnership.[48] At that time it was still more an idea than a plan but it clearly distinguished itself from the NTM. It did not contain a proposal for a free trade area for services but only a reference to negotiations 'with the aim of substantially improving opportunities for market opening' in this sector and an emphasis on the importance of the planned WTO negotiations in this field (point 9.b. TEP Declaration). It excluded any talks on agricultural tariffs and subsidies but offered clear perspectives on agricultural regulatory issues.[49] As far as industrial tariffs were concerned, the TEP didn't refer to their elimination against 2010 but to 'a broad WTO work program for the reduction of industrial tariffs.'[50]

As for technical barriers to trade, the TEP was pretty close to what was proposed in the NTM. Moreover, in the TEP, such barriers would become the centerpiece of transatlantic negotiations. These would aim at 'the elimination or substantial lowering of the remaining barriers' (point 9.a. TEP Declaration) and would concentrate on the extension of the already existing mutual recognition agreement between the US and the EU, especially as far as testing and approval procedures are concerned. In addition, cooperation between the standard-setting and regulatory bodies would be promoted and intensified.

Attached to the TEP-Declaration was a Declaration on Political Cooperation which contained the commitment to enhance the political cooperation established by the NTA of 1995, especially with the aim of promoting international stability and security. This Declaration was not unimportant since it maintained the linkage that had been made quite explicitly in the NTM proposal. This linkage envisioned good trade relations as part of an overall strategy to intensify the political and security partnership between the two sides of the Atlantic (European Commission, 1998b: point 2.b.).

The Transatlantic Economic Partnership was still largely an idea, a vague commitment, when it was endorsed at the May 18 summit. In the following months, this idea had to be translated into an Action Plan that would guide its concrete realization. But this was no easy task. Almost immediately after the adoption of the Declaration, criticism started to mount in Congress. Both the chairman of the Senate Finance Committee, Sen. William Roth, and the chairman of the Senate Finance Subcommittee on Trade, Chuck Grassley, issued press statements in which they rejected the approach of the TEP.

Roth's statement left no doubts about his feelings on the TEP. As he stated it:[51]

> While I am a strong supporter of further trade liberalization with our European trading partners, we have to understand that we cannot expect the support of the American people for further initiatives on trade if we cannot demonstrate how they serve their fundamental interests. (..) I have made clear, as have a number of members of the Finance Committee, which I chair, that any

bilateral initiative on trade with the European Union worthy of investment must address the difficult issues that divide us, particularly those of European agricultural tariffs and subsidies. The proposed arrangement would simply defer progress on those issues, while taking up an agenda shaped by European, not U.S. interests.

These remarks had to be taken seriously, even if their strong language had to serve political (and constituency) purposes as well. But given the important role agricultural interests played (and play) in gathering the necessary majorities to give the president new trade negotiating authority (which failed in 1997 and 1998), and given the fact that indeed agriculture is the 'shining star' in the quickly rising U.S. trade deficit, both the U.S. administration and the EU Commission had an interest in not neglecting the meaning of these messages in particular and congressional criticism on the TEP in general.

There were equally problems inside the European Union. First, there was the ever recurring problem of the Helms-Burton and D'Amato Acts. The problem rose as a consequence of confusion among the EU member states about the precise commitment that Washington had made (*Financial Times*, May 20, 1998). This confusion emerged after U.S. officials made clear that the commitment of the administration to seek a permanent waiver on Title III of the Helms-Burton Act (legal suits against companies that have invested in expropriated assets in Cuba) only meant that it had to see what the sense of Congress on this issue was and whether such an amendment would be feasible. It didn't mean, however, that the administration had to seek agreement with Congress on this issue.

The EU member states reacted promptly. During the preparations of the May 29 Council meeting, several member states – among which France, Belgium, Spain, and Portugal – made clear that they would neither support nor approve a mandate for TEP negotiations in case the two laws hadn't been changed in line with the Understanding of May 18 (*Financial Times*, June 2, 1998). The unilateral declaration issued by European Council president Tony Blair and Commission president Jacques Santer, stressed more or less the same. This basically means that the Commission will not be enabled to negotiate on the TEP (which means on the implementation of the TEP Action Plan) with the United States unless Congress has amended the two laws. In this way, the EU again expressed its irritation about the extraterritorial effects of the two laws but postponed the effects of this irritation to the implementation stages of the TEP. Hence, Sir Leon Brittan could pursue his work on the TEP Action Plan.

But there was not much time left. First, an Action Plan had to be drafted and approved. Then, negotiations on this plan had to be started with a clear deadline at the end of 1999. Hence the emerging idea to work on an Action Plan with stages. Thereby, a first group of issues to be dealt with in the course of 1999 would be identified. A second group of issues would be dealt with in negotiations that could take place after December 1999.

The limited time span had another effect as well. Ever more, all efforts started to be concentrated on the issue of regulatory cooperation. Two strategies emerged: the strategy of harmonization of regulations, taking into account that this would be a time-consuming and laborious way of working, and the strategy of mutual recognition. The latter would be used whenever the former would prove to be unfeasible or too time-consuming. The matter was now to identify the issues and sectors on which this endeavor would be undertaken. The U.S. side directly demanded negotiations on the harmonization of the approval process for bio-engineered agricultural products. This request was not surprising given the difficulties that the U.S. faced with its genetically modified corn on the EU market. At the same time, the United States Trade Representative (USTR) published a request for suggestions from industries on the subjects that should be negotiated as part of the TEP.[52] From these reactions, it became clear that besides regulatory cooperation (including on agriculture), demands had been expressed for TEP-talks on intellectual property rights (cf. pharmaceuticals, new digital media and such rights), talks on specific services sectors (intermodal transportation, air auxiliary services, distribution, warehousing, customs, postal, telecommunications, logistics, brokerage, insurance and freight forwarding), and on government procurement (e.g. the EC's Utility Directive and its application in the telecom sector). [53] The U.S. Chamber of Commerce further asked for tariff reductions (up to elimination) in the fifteen sectors that were dealt with in the tariff negotiations of APEC.[54]

The preparation of the Action Plan took place through a range of formal meetings – themselves prepared by informal meetings at lower official levels – that convened in the course of July, August, and September 1998. Some of these were meetings between Barchefsky and Brittan (July 7, September 25, October 19), others were meetings of the Senior Level Group, and the NTA Task force (see following table).

Table 6.2   Structure for the Development of the TEP Action Plan

Format	Meetings	Level
U.S. – EU Summit	Semi-Annual	Presidential
Bilateral meetings between Barchefsky and Brittan	Regular	Cabinet-level/ Ministerial level
Senior Level Group	Regular (six to eight times a year)	Subcabinet level/ Ambassadorial level
NTA Task Force	Regular: Through either video conferences or in person	Workinggroup-level Officials

In these meetings a number of problems showed up and had to be resolved. Discussions concentrated first on commitments concerning trade in services where the U.S. administration had proposed a standstill agreement and an agreement on the improvement of existing GATS-rules. For the EU this was problematic as it feared that this would violate the provisions of article V GATS (regional trade agreements), which would entail an obligation to extend the granted concessions to all the WTO members. This would confront the EU and the US with a free rider problem.[55] The solution to this – as defended by the American side – would be that a services agreement would have to be large in scope so that it wouldn't violate the 'substantially all the sectors' requirement of article V GATS. But that created problems for the EU since some member states – among which France – wanted to exclude a services agreement that would liberalize services trade 'across the board', clearly with an eye on the possible inclusion of audiovisual services.[56]

The outcome of the process was twofold. First, the EU and the US agreed to start negotiations with the aim of preparing a joint approach to the WTO negotiations of 2000. One of the subjects in these would be the development of additional disciplines 'to strengthen market access' and to work on the guarantee 'that services can be supplied in a pro-competitive environment' by *inter alia* the drafting of pro-competitive regulatory principles, as was done in the 1998 WTO agreement on basic telecommunications services.

Second, the question of regulatory cooperation emerged. One question dealt with the approach to be used. It became clear from the start that there should be a focus on the harmonization of standards. In all cases where that would be difficult, mutual recognition would be sought.[57] However, since the Commission was looking for a Council mandate by September 1998, there was no time left to determine the sectors for which such agreements would be sought. As a consequence, the conclusion of the Action Plan mainly pointed to the identification of the sectors that had to be included in such negotiations. It didn't determine which sectors would be included.[58] After this identification – which would last until January 1999 – substantial negotiations aiming at the principles of cooperation in this field would start. During that stage the U.S. and the EU would compare their regulatory regimes. After that, negotiations on testing and certification would start, and – according to the planning – be terminated by the end of 1999. After that date, talks on newly identified sectors could begin.

In the integrated approach that emerged, all sectors that are included in the MRA-talks would become part of a single general agreement. In this agreement, general principles and rules for all the sectors concerned would be defined, including a dispute settlement system. In additional annexes to this agreement, concessions for the specific sectors – either based on a positive or on a negative list – would be exchanged.[59] This approach would maintain consistency and transparency, and would reconcile consistency with an open-ended dynamic process through which new sectors could be added without forcing the parties to start the whole process all over again. In the case of regulatory cooperation, this is not unimportant. With fast technological developments – e.g. electronic commerce – new rules are needed all the time and old ones quickly become redundant. This implies that cooperation between the two sides of the Atlantic has to be permanent and continuous in order to be effective. And this concern was clearly reflected in the approach that came out of the Summer 1998 deliberations between the European Commission and the U.S. Administration.

A second problem with regulatory cooperation was its place in the Transatlantic Economic Partnership, compared with other issues. Whereas the EU emphasized the central importance of this kind of cooperation within the TEP, the U.S. preferred to focus more on the liberalization of services. One of the reasons for this was the U.S. concern that MRA negotiations would be difficult because self-regulating agencies (such as the FDA, the FAA, and the FCC) and state-level authorities had to be involved, the latter especially on the subjects in which the EU was interested: professional standards for engineers and architects. But the conclusion (reached Mid-October 1998) was that indeed MRAs would occupy a central place in the services negotiations.[60] The outcome of the other discussions was relatively vague. No mention was made about a standstill agreement or of focussed negotiations on the removal of existing barriers (except of course the above mentioned MRA negotiations). Instead, transatlantic cooperation would focus on the discussion of any policy proposals 'that could have an adverse effect on conditions for service providers.' In the course of 1999, talks on services negotiations would continue, first with a focus on engineering.

Besides services and regulatory cooperation, a third problem that emerged in the preparation of the TEP concerned the approach towards government procurement. There, the Clinton Administration preferred the multilateral approach, through the GPA.[61] A reason for that was the U.S. expectation that such an approach would largely concentrate on procedural issues (such as bidding procedures and electronic tendering) and would leave sensitive issues such as 'buy America', military procurement and exemptions for small and medium-sized enterprises (SMEs) relatively untouched (cf. TABD, 1996b: 30). In addition, an important request by the EU to extend the rules to the state-level and to local authorities, was clearly unfeasible within the GPA-framework.[62] After laborious negotiations during October and November 1998, a compromise was reached in which the two sides agreed 'to explore possibilities for the balanced expansion of market access opportunities for U.S. and EU companies in U.S. and EU procurement markets.' No mention was made of 'buy America' on the explicit demand of the U.S. side.

The fourth problem concerned the patent system mentioned above, namely the question of 'first-to-invent' (applied by the U.S.) or 'first-to-file.'[63] While the EU continued to insist on the inclusion of this matter in the TEP, the U.S. rejected this.[64] Even EU questions 'to explore the consequence of the two systems' were not acceptable.

The fifth problem consisted of cooperation inside the WTO on an 'accross the board' reduction and harmonization of industrial tariffs. While the EU defended this approach, the U.S. expressed concerns about the free rider problem due to MFN.

The sixth problem consisted of the place of investment rules inside the WTO, an approach defended by the EU. The U.S. showed more reservations in this field, partly because of rising domestic opposition against such rules in the WTO, but mainly because the U.S. doesn't expect that any serious agreement on this issue would be feasible in the WTO.[65] The U.S. wanted to reinvigorate the MAI-negotiations instead of declaring them dead, like the EU wanted to do. For the EU, a key issue was the fact that the French government played an important role in the collapse of the MAI-negotiations claiming that the EU doesn't have the exclusive competencies in this field.[66] The MAI is, therefore, a 'dead end' for the EU and the only way out of it is an investment deal in the WTO. This would allow the negotiations to restart 'from scratch', would avoid negotiations exclusively concentrated on a confrontation between the EU and the U.S., and would provide the developing countries the opportunity to participate in them. But the U.S. government didn't support this approach and insisted on a resumption of the MAI-talks in Paris.

This divergence of opinion between the two sides of the Atlantic was clearly not only a matter of difference of opinion between governments but between companies. This became clear at the TABD meeting of November 1998 in Charlotte, NC.

The seventh problem was the issue of regulatory cooperation in the field of agriculture, more specifically veterinary equivalency and biotechnology. The outcome here was a deal to establish an 'early warning system' to avoid acrimonious disputes in the food safety, plant and animal health areas. Specific steps would be undertaken to promote administrative cooperation in this field. In addition, an 'overarching group' would be created. Its function would consist of the monitoring of discussions on technical issues in the field of biotechnology with the purpose of taking 'into account their potential trade effects with the objective of reducing unnecessary barriers to trade.'

In the meantime, it seemed that USTR Barchefsky succeeded in convincing the House of Representatives that the TEP would in no way weaken the United States in agricultural tariff and subsidy negotiations with the EU. On July 28 she testified in that sense before the House Subcommittee on Trade. The day after this testimony, House Ways and Means Chairman Bill Archer (R-TX) changed a proposed resolution for a non binding sense of Congress – H. Con. Res. 213 – from a clear criticism on the EU's market access policies for agriculture into a resolution that referred to barriers in agricultural trade in general and their negative effect on U.S. farm exports in particular.[67] In addition, however, the resolution also urged the USTR not to start the TEP-negotiations with the EU if she would determine that these would 'undermine the ability of the U.S. to achieve a successful result in the upcoming WTO talks on agriculture' (point 7, H. Con. Res. 213RFS).

The agreements on the different issues opened the door for the formal adoption of the TEP Action Plan at the U.S.-EU Summit of December 18,

1998. It was maybe a pity that this happened in the shadow of the impeachment proceedings in the U.S. House, as the summit took place one day before the vote on this issue, and the day after bombings on Iraq had started. For that reason, the issue of trade was almost absent from the summit and the discussions concentrated largely on security questions. But the Action Plan was formally adopted and this provided the basis for its implementation from 1999 on.

As has been indicated above, the action plan not only provides for a range of commitments on negotiations on particular issues but also a time frame, at least for some of its topics. It equally provides for such negotiations with the purpose of concluding bilateral agreements and in addition with the purpose of influencing, even reinforcing, the process of multilateral liberalization in the WTO.

Conclusions

The Wider Implications of the Transatlantic Relationship

The discussions on the transatlantic relations and particularly on the Transatlantic Economic Partnership have showed that conflict and cooperation are an integral part of the Transatlantic relations and that this has a consequence on the operation of the WTO as well.

Cooperation is a rational option when the two largest trading blocks in a multilateral trading system in which none can dominate on its own and where – partly as a consequence of the accession of developing countries – the EU and the U.S. find themselves increasingly on the same side of major issues.[68] The U.S. and the EU clearly realize this as they endeavor to deepen their cooperation on issues that are dealt with in the WTO and its concomitant negotiating process or that are expected to be dealt with in the WTO in the future (e.g. investments).

Equally, the cooperation in the Transatlantic Marketplace has never been remote from wider questions of political relationships and security. This has been emphasized by many European and American politicians and was quite obvious in the Commission's March 1998 proposal for a Transatlantic Marketplace. As the Commission emphasized (Commission, 1998b):

> The proposal [the Transatlantic Marketplace] is more than a trade policy initiative. It is also an important initiative for the EU's broader policy towards

the United States, and should be considered in that light. Since the end of the Cold War we have taken a number of steps to restructure and refocus the EU's links with the US, which remains our most important and complex external relationship, and to reinforce US support for European stability. (..) [The Transatlantic Marketplace] is designed to use an economic instrument to give a much broader impetus to the overall political relationship; to produce important economic benefits; and to provide a new mechanism and stronger incentives to prevent and resolve disputes between us.

Questions such as the crisis in Kosovo have re-emphasized the importance of this relationship. Typical in this respect was the answer given by the Department of State's spokeman, James Rubin, to a question related to the U.S.' interest in Kosovo. Rubin's answer clearly pointed at the way in which this interest was clear and present but at the same time dependent on the commitment of the Europeans in this particular question. The significance of his answer was wider than just Kosovo. It basically pointed at the transatlantic security relationship that has emerged after the end of the Cold War and its implicit division of labor between the U.S. and the West-European countries as far as European security is concerned. Rubin – talking about the U.S. interest in Kosovo –put it in the following way:[69]

We believe that we do have an interest; but not so big that we'll do all the work or we'll take the overwhelming risk. What we've done here is arrange for the Europeans to bear the brunt of the military responsibilities as well as the brunt of the financial responsibilities if there is an agreement.

The Coexistence of Cooperation and Conflict

The Kind of Conflicts Despite the interests in a deepened relationship both for economic, political, and security reasons conflicts continue to arise between the two sides of the Atlantic. Some of these conflicts have been bitter, i.e. the Helms-Burton, agricultural subsidies, and the banana case. Many have even posed a danger for the operation and credibility of the WTO (the bananas are a case in mind, just like Helms-Burton is). And it was this danger that played a role in appeasing the conflict, that stimulated creativity in finding a way out, and that intensified attempts to avoid similar conflicts on other issues.[70]

By looking at the recent trade conflicts between the United States and the European Union, a distinction between different categories of trade conflicts can be made. Some of them are idiosyncratic in nature, others are related to more structural features of the transatlantic trade relationship. If these two features are considered as the two extremes of a continuum, the following three categories can be discerned: idiosyncratic conflicts, conflicts rooted in a strong and structural domestic base, and conflicts due to the features of Transatlantic trade.

In the first category, one can find conflicts that are due to a whole range of domestic policies but that are transient. It concerns particular policy decisions that come and go with particular majorities or administrations and that go as easily as they have come. The Helms-Burton case is rooted in a particular U.S. policy and in particular ideas about the extent to which the U.S. can oblige its trade partners to abide by the rules created by its own domestic sensitivity on this issue. Nothing tells us, however, that the laws concerned will stay there when another administration would be in office or another congressional majority.

In the first category, one can find conflicts that are due to a whole range of domestic policies but that are transient. It concerns particular policy decisions that come and go with particular majorities or administrations and that go as easily as they have come. The Helms-Burton case is rooted in a particular U.S. policy and in particular ideas about the extent to which the U.S. can oblige its trade partners to abide by the rules created by its own domestic sensitivity on this issue. Nothing tells us, however, that the laws concerned will stay there when another administration would be in office or another congressional majority.

First, the policies concerned are less transient because they engender a high level of political mobilization. For that reason, the political price of changing course is – even for a new administration or for a new majority – more politically risky.

Second, the base for mobilization in the domestic realm is structural. It doesn't consist of a coincidental coalition or interest. Rather it concerns social groups or actors that are seriously and structurally affected by the policies and that are quite well organized therefore. For them it consists of a matter of (economic) life and death, as it consists for their political representatives.

In the third category, the conflicts are directly related to the kind of trade relations between the U.S. and the EU. They are not necessarily related to particular domestic policies or groups but to the extent of trade and economic integration between the two sides of the Atlantic. They basically reflect the depth of this integration and wouldn't exist in case there wasn't such deep integration. They are – to a certain extent – a reflection of the existence of a Transatlantic marketplace in which trade and investment have come to play such an important role. They also reflect the fact – so prominent in the transatlantic trade relationship, as in the transpacific relationship (i.e. between Japan and the U.S.) – that deeper cooperation enhances the probability of conflicts while simultaneously providing for instruments to contain and to prevent conflict escalation, and to resolve them. As Deputy USTR Lang has put it (House Ways and Means, 1997: 27):

> No international economic relationship as vast and intricate as that binding the United States and Europe could operate without problems. The very dynamism which propels this machinery inevitably results in a certain amount of friction, especially as the pace of innovation and adaptation in the business world continues to accelerate.

For all the three categories however, a multiplier effect is at work. Because of the size of the U.S. and the EU as trading blocks and of their mutual trade relations, Transatlantic trade conflicts have serious consequences for the WTO, at least if they cover issues that fall within the scope of the WTO rules, are dealt with in WTO negotiations or are supposed to be dealt with in WTO negotiations soon.

Structural Roots of Transatlantic Conflicts It can be expected that the future of Transatlantic relations will be haunted by the second and third categories of conflict. This doesn't mean that the first group won't play a role, but it means that for this group the occurrence, resolution, and disappearance of conflicts is relatively unpredictable as they depend on idiosyncratic factors.

In the case of the second and the third categories, the situation is different. They are more deeply rooted in respectively factors of domestic mobilization (for the second category), and factors endemic to the depth of Transatlantic market integration.

For the second category, the domestic-structural one, the continuous existence of the conflicts concerned will depend on the extent to which particular national policies will be changed. First and foremost, this is the case for agriculture. As long as the EU's Common Agricultural Policy remains as it is today, major transatlantic conflicts on this issue will erupt, either in the WTO, or in other international forums. The same is true for the risks that regional trade agreements concluded by either the United States or the EU bring with them for the transatlantic relationship. The banana dispute is a reflection of this as it basically refers to the problems between multilateral rules and the philosophy of preferential trade relations.

For the third category, the endemic one, the continuous existence of conflicts can be expected. But that is not a dramatic conclusion. This basically reflect the health and magnitude of the relationship. Most – if not all – of these conflicts are related to regulatory issues. These are typically issues that show up when all other barriers to trade – cross-the-border-barriers – have been removed. The remaining 'behind-the-border' barriers inevitably lead to conflicts since they are more deeply rooted in the political and social systems in which they have been created. In addition, many of these so-called barriers act as barriers not because they were intended to do so but because their effect on trade has latent consequences. Their intended consequences are mostly related to issues such as health, security, social welfare, the environment, and consumer protection. These are areas that typically considered domestic and have been shaped by domestic concerns without any explicit attention for their consequences on trade.

The problem with these measures is twofold. First, making the distinction between intended and unintended effects on trade is not easy. Measures that seem to be intended for non-economic purposes such as consumer, health or environmental protection can be intended to provide a barrier to trade as well. Measures that seem to be intended to impede trade can, however, be rooted in domestic concerns unrelated to trade. That is a general problem for all non-tariff barriers to trade, especially the technical ones (the so-called TBTs), and especially for the kind of regulatory barriers that have been so prominent in recent transatlantic trade conflicts. And the problem is compounded by the scientific foundation (or alleged scientific foundation) of these barriers as the hormones dispute has shown.[71] Indeed, if one looks at these conflicts, the presence of such issues has been prominent. The following table provides an indication of the Transatlantic trade conflicts that emerged during the period between the adoption of the New Transatlantic Agenda (December 1995) and the adoption of the TEP Action Plan (December 1998). In this table, a distinction has been made between problems of the first (idiosyncratic), the second (domestic-structural), and the third category (endemic).

Table 6.3   Types of Trade Conflicts in Transatlantic Relations

Type	Conflict
I	Helms-Burton Act
	D'Amato Act
	U.S. Trademark bill
II	Consequences of the 1995 EU Enlargement (Agriculture)
	ITA: Sectoral coverage[72]
	Tariff classification of Local Area Network equipment (LAN)
	EU subsidies on barley
	China's WTO accession as a developing country
	ITA: Staging of tariff cuts
	MAI: Exeptions for regional economic integration organizations
	Allocation of tariff-quotas for rice
	EU subsidies for canned fruit
	EU certification of wine exports
	EU banana regime
	Boeing – Mc Donnell Douglas merger
	Wine: Use of generic geographical designations
	Fish and fish products: exclusion from the NTM
	EU imports of products that could carry BSE
	Audiovisual commitments by Latvia (as part of its WTO-accession)
III	MRA: Standard certification or just testing
	Consequences of the 1995 EU Enlargement (Agriculture)
	ITA: Sectoral coverage
	MRA: Role of FDA in testing and certification of medical equipment and pharmaceuticals
	EU data privacy directive
	MRA: Transitional period for medical devices
	MRA: Confidence-building period for pharmaceuticals[73]
	European approval processes for biotechnological products
	Veterinary equivalency agreement: Poultry and poultry products
	EU ecolabelling rules
	Growth hormones in beef
	Animal protection: leghold trap case
	Foreign ownership levels in satellite-based telecommunications

services companies
'first to file' versus 'first to invent' in patent systems
Negotiations on competition disciplines in the Millennium Round
EU's Utility Directive: Telecommunications equipment
U.S. foreign sales tax provisions
EU mandatory standard for third generation of digital wireless
services and equipment (3G)
Strategy on investment: WTO or OECD
Wine-making practices
UN Convention on Biological Diversity, Biosafety Protocol

The endemic problems have been prominent and have therefore, caught the attention of the designers of the different proposals for a deepening of the Transatlantic partnership and of the Transatlantic Business Dialogue (1997; 1998). This is not surprising as many of the regulations that have been put into question are rooted in quite different political, social, and economic traditions. Sometimes, the traditions concerned are continental in scope (federal in the case of the U.S., the EU-level in the case of the EU). Sometimes they are national (in the EU) or subnational (in the U.S.) in nature. Sometimes they deal with the role of particular societal values and principles, sometimes with the role of particular institutions that enjoy public trust.[74]

The United States and the European Union have similar political-economic approaches in general, and both clearly support a market-based economy. These similarities are only real at a high level of aggregation. As soon as one digs deeper into lower levels of political-economic aggregation – such as the relations economy-society, the relation state-economy, and the relation state-society – differences between the U.S. and the EU, and among EU member states start to show up. As long as the removal of trade barriers is limited to cross-the-border barriers, the relevance of these differences is relatively limited as both the U.S. and the EU share the conviction that the removal of tariff barriers free trade is beneficial for their own economic prosperity as it is for global welfare. As soon as the barriers refer to 'behind-the-border' issues, the differences in domestic political-economic approaches becomes relevant. Elsewhere (Kerremans, 1998: 74), I have called this the 'fallacy of commonality', a phenomenon of relevance for transatlantic relations that has been recognized by many practitioners and scholars (cf. Vogel, 1997). According to one of these (Ives, 1997: 27), this is especially the case in issues related to the mutual recognition agreements. As Ives has stated:

(..) the differences when diving into something like MRAs tend to emerge much more readily than the similarities. (..) the differences seem to stand out more than our wish to cooperate and find common ground.

This conclusion leads to another. The depth of transatlantic trade relations and the kind of demands that it engenders are evidence of the fact that the transatlantic marketplace is not just a concept for international trade; it is also situated somewhere between traditional international trade and trade within an integrated market. It is not an internal market, as there still are a number of non-tariff barriers to trade. It is not even supposed to be an internal market as there is no preparedness to tie decision-making on tariff and non-tariff barriers together to the extent that it is necessary to sustain such a market.

Transatlantic relations thus, go deeper than the traditional concept of international trade. It is featured by extensive mutual investment and by a large extent of business and trade integration beyond the level of removed cross-border barriers. This puts a burden on transatlantic relations as far as institutions and policy-making are concerned. As far as the latter is concerned, it leads to a larger vulnerability and therefore sensitivity to the domestic policies of 'the other.' In a market integrated to such an extent, domestic policy-decisions of many kind are not exclusively 'domestic' in nature as they directly affect the other side of the Atlantic. Many issues that traditionally belong to the domestic realm have acquired therefore a transatlantic relevance and engender transatlantic conflict potential, just like policy decisions engender conflicts and political mobilization domestically. They are indeed barriers and they have an increasing political significance both Transatlantically and domestically.[75] It seems that political leaders realize this increasingly as they have been expanding the dialogue between societal actors of the two sides beyond business. In the course of the development of the TEP Action Plan, both the European Commission and the Office of the United States Trade Representative have made clear that they wished to create a Transatlantic Consumer Dialogue, a Transatlantic Environmental Dialogue, and a Transatlantic Labor Dialogue. As Assistant USTR for Europe Cathy Novelli phrased it at the TABD meeting of November 1998 in Charlotte (NC): 'It is necessary to have a trade policy that includes all civil society views.'[76]

As far as the institutional consequences of this evolution are concerned, taking into account the transatlantic consequences of domestic policies requires a permanent dialogue in the real sense of the word. It needs to be permanent and that requires – to a certain extent – its institutionalization. This is probably the most obvious in the area of standardization where rapid technological developments require new standards, new rules and the adaptation of old ones. International trade agreements – as agreements at one fixed moment in time – just don't suffice for that. What is required here is the creation of institutions that enable quick and joint responses to these developments. The 'Overarching Group for Biotechnology' that will be created as part of the TEP Action Plan will be the first in a necessarily expanding list of bodies that can bring together regulators from the two sides of the Atlantic. But the task won't be easy as many issues – because they are regulatory in nature – touch upon non-trade social sensitivities and rule-setting traditions.

In the case of the latter, a point of conflict between the United States and the European Union is the extent to which governments need to be involved in the process of standard-setting. In the U.S. there is a clear and old tradition of private sector standardization, in most EU member states it is a government driven process. Quite recently, this difference has proved to be relevant in the case of the biotechnology dispute between the U.S. and the EU, and even more on the question of privacy protection in electronic data transactions.[77] And the problem is quite complicated because it goes much deeper than dealing with jurisdictions. It is a matter of public trust and confidence. In the U.S. the public in general accepts – even thinks that it is normal – that the private sector sets its own standards as long as they respect certain levels of consumer, health and safety protection and provide for a credible enforcement. In the European Union, this is not the case. There, people associate credibility much more with government involvement in setting the standards and enforcing them. Bridging this difference will not be easy, especially if transatlantic (or international) harmonization becomes the objective.

The Case for Cooperation Conflicts are unavoidable when countries seek cooperation. This is certainly the case for the transatlantic trade relations, and there is no reason for panic on this front. The only question concerns the intensity of the conflicts than can be reconciled with the maintenance of cooperative structures. There are two reasons why this question has to be answered carefully in the case of transatlantic relations and both have a multiplication effect.

First, there is the weight of the two 'territories' – this term is used because the EU cannot be considered a state – in the World Trade Organization and the market power that this entails. Their conflicts – as far as they are related to WTO issues – set more than others precedents and determine more than others the extent to which the WTO members will be able to reach a consensus on issues. As transatlantic conflicts have large multilateral ramifications, their conflict potential becomes larger as there is much more at stake.

Second, there is the prevalence of behind the border issues in transatlantic relations which more clearly links domestic politics, and therefore domestic mobilization and questions of trade policy legitimacy, to the transatlantic relations. Such mobilization can easily lead to the emergence of conflicts. Conversely, conflicts can also trigger such mobilization more easily, which basically complicates cooperation further as it makes it more difficult for decision-makers to turn from a conflictual dynamic to a cooperative one.

The conclusion is, therefore, that conflicts in transatlantic trade relations are not by definition negative – they can even be healthy. In addition, they have to be contained in order to avoid that they would hinder or even jeopardize cooperation. In the recent banana regime case, this border line has clearly been crossed and has created the risk that this particular conflict would spill over to other transatlantic trade issues because of the climate of bitterness that it created. Conflict containment is, therefore, recommended for transatlantic policy-makers, rather than conflict management. In order to do so greater involvement of social actors – not just businesses – is advisable. Second, it is equally important to provide for early warning systems – as has been provided by the Transatlantic Economic Partnership Action Plan – and for conflict prevention systems. In doing this, Transatlantic trade relations will be able to find a healthy combination of civilized conflicts and constructive cooperation.

Notes

[1] In that year the EU had a deficit of $2 billion on its bilateral agricultural trade balance with the U.S.
[2] The overall U.S. trade balance for services was positive in 1997 ($87.8bn).
[3] The five largest EU exporters (goods) to the United States were in 1997 (in order of importance): Germany, United Kingdom, France, Italy, and Belgium/Luxembourg.
[4] The five largest EU importers (goods) from the United States were in 1997 (in order of importance): United Kingdom, Germany, France, Netherlands, and Belgium/Luxembourg.
[5] The five largest EU exporters (goods) to the United States were in 1997 (in order of importance): Germany, United Kingdom, France, Italy, and Belgium/Luxembourg.
[6] The five largest EU importers (goods) from the United States were in 1997 (in order of importance): United Kingdom, Germany, France, Netherlands, and Belgium/Luxembourg.

[7] Equally, about one-third of American exports that go to the European Union supply U.S. companies located there.

[8] And indeed, one could give the Information Technology Agreement and the WTO Agreement on Basic Telecommunications as convincing evidence of this.

[9] This was, of course, in the first place the case for the question of trade in agricultural products (cf. Josling, 1998: 18).

[10] Indicative of this may be the fact that the House Ways and Means Committee devoted in July 1997 a hearing that focussed exclusively on the trade relations with the EU and the US, something which – according to Rep. R. Matsui (D-CA) hadn't happen in 18 years (House Ways and Means, 1997: 15).

[11] Written statement by Ambassador J. Lang (House Ways and Means, 1997: 23). USTR Charlene Barchefsky testified in the same sense (USTR, 1998c: 2). The European Commission clearly shared this opinion as is indicated by its statement that '(…the Cold War has changed the nature of the Transatlantic relationship. There is no longer a single, common adversary and the need to guarantee military security has ceased to be the overriding feature of the relationship. (..) There can be no return to the time when political and economic issues were subordinate to the central question of security. Today it is necessary to demonstrate anew why this unique relationship is more valid than ever, for reasons which have more to do with the future than a past common heritage' (European Commission, 1995a: 2).

[12] During the same hearing, Timothy Hauser, Acting Under Secretary, International Trade Administration, put it this way: 'The U.S.-European partnership has never been one only of military and security concerns, but has also developed common ground in trade and economic interests. With the end of the Cold War, the commercial aspect of our relationship has taken on greater importance, and trade and economic growth are the focus at the top levels of our bilateral meetings and institutions' (House Ways and Means, 1997: 34).

[13] The idea has been flouted first by the late Ron Brown, the then Commerce Secretary, in a December 1994 speech before the American Chamber of Commerce in Belgium.

[14] Hugo Paemen – since 1996 European Commission ambassador to the US – later (in January 1996) recognized that the Commission first felt some 'apprehension' on the TABD as it was initially too much 'Department of Commerce driven.'

[15] Quoted in *Inside U.S. Trade*, Vol. 13, n° 8, May 5, 1995.

[16] On June 14, 1995 in Washington DC.

[17] The EU and the US already had a Competition Agreement since 1991. In 1995 this agreement has been renewed (see *OJ* L95 of April 27, 1995, as corrected by *OJ* L134 of June 26, 1995).

[18] Its position as Council President prevented Spain from expressing its opposition too explicitly.

[19] Their objections were issued at the Council meeting of October 2, 1995. In the same vein, the countries concerned rejected any reference to a speeding up of tariff concessions made during the Uruguay Round. Other member states supported a feasibility study that would include the FTA-approach. In this position were the United Kingdom, Germany, Ireland, Finland, Sweden, and Denmark. The position of France was somewhat peculiar. Whereas the French foreign minister Hervé De Charette rejected a feasibility study on the FTA-approach and the tariff acceleration, he emphasized that a renewal of the Transatlantic relations had to be concentrated on political issues such as 'the United States' disengagement in matters of aid to development (..) as well as the question of the funding of the UN and that of currency stability.' Especially the last has been emphasized by French

diplomats during the shaping of the NTA. See *Agence Europe*, n° 6575, October 2-3, 1995, p. 8.

[20] The MAI-negotiations had started in May 1995.

[21] As the president still had some residual tariff reduction authority from the previous fast track law (it concerns the July 1993 extension of the trade authority based on the 1988 Trade and Competitiveness Act).

[22] As the U.S. Deputy Chief of Mission to the EU, Tony Wayne, said in November 1995: 'Though trade and economics have often been the focus of the U.S.-EU relationship, non-trade issues are the growth areas of the relationship' (quoted in *Inside U.S. Trade*, Vol. 13, n° 45, November 10, 1995).

[23] This doesn't apply of course to those tariff issues that had been left out of the Uruguay Round negotiations, among which the products covered by the ITA 1 agreement and products such as white spirit, fertilizers, nonferrous metals, oilseeds and oilseed products, photographic film, wood, electronics, flashlights, soda ash, and certain cameras (see *Inside U.S. Trade*, Vol. 13, n° 44, November 3, 1995 & TABD Group II Report).

[24] As a matter of fact, the role of the TABD went beyond this. In November 1996, during the negotiations on the Mutual Recognition Agreement, the TABD meeting in Chicago played a decisive role in pushing through an agreement (TABD, 1996). As was testified by Timothy Hauser (House Ways and Means, 1997: 40 & 45) the involvement, especially the insistence, of the TABD people during their meeting in Chicago played a decisive role in keeping the MRA talks on track and in unblocking them. The Commission (1996b) defined the role of that TABD meeting as '(..) contributing to (..) progress on by providing the occasion for an important conceptual breakthrough on the negotiations for a Mutual Recognition Agreement (..).' De Vink called it a typical example of how 'entrepreneurial diplomacy' can contribute to the Transatlantic relationship (House Ways and Means, 1997: 63). But one could rather call it an example of successful triangular diplomacy in which the two government sides (the U.S.' FDA, and the Commission's DG I and DG III) and business representatives (from the TABD) negotiated deals on controversial issues (especially pharmaceutical good manufacturing practices). The contribution of the TABD can best be summarized from De Vink's testimony (Ibidem: 66): 'By helping government negotiators understand more precisely the practical ramifications of the policy decisions before them, we helped facilitate an agreement.'

[25] Such as maritime services, telecommunications, financial services, and government procurement.

[26] The American demand for accelerated tariff reductions or even elimination was not a coincidence. It is partly related to the structure of U.S. tariffs (generally low tariffs, with peak tariffs in sensitive sectors such as food products, textiles, footwear, leather goods, jewellery, ceramics, glass, trucks, and railway cars, see European Commission, 1997: 10; 1998d: 12; World Trade Organization, 1999b) and partly related to the absence of any new trade negotiating authority for the U.S. president. This limited the leeway of the administration in the field of tariff reductions to the residual authority from the previous fast track laws (the July 1993 extension of the 1988 OTCA). The combination of the two basically meant that the U.S. was proposing accelerated reductions in sectors that would benefit them, much less the EU which complains about the peak tariffs, especially on textiles (cf. the Commission reply to the TABD proposals in TABD, 1996b: 26).

[27] Contrary to the request from the TABD, no deadline, neither for the agreement nor for the tariff elimination was provided for. The TABD had asked for the December 1996 for the first, and 2000 for the second.

[28] Cf. the comments by Bruce Stokes (Council on Foreign Relations) in the *Financial Times* (May 14, 1998).

[29] Public Law 104-114. The law originated in two bills: H.R. 927 (104th Congress) submitted by Rep. Dan Burton (R-IN), and S. 381 (104th Congress) submitted by Sen. Jesse Helms (R-NC).

[30] Better known as ILSA. The Act was introduced as S. 1228 (104th Congress) by Sen. Alfonso D'Amato (R-NY) and became public law 104-172.

[31] *Agence Europe*, n° 6957, April 18, 1997.

[32] See however, article 23 ('Additional Protection for Geographical Indications for Wines and Spirits') of the TRIPs Agreement. Whereas the EU claims that some U.S. geographical wine appellations violate this article, the U.S. claims that article 23 has to be read in conjunction with article 24 TRIPs. This article provides for exceptions to article 23 provisions (TABD, 1996c: 67).

[33] *Agence Europe*, n° 6578, October 6, 1995. As the U.S. Administration indicated in its comments on TABD proposals: 'The U.S. Government remains concerned that the ecolabel development committee was not transparent to industry and afforded insufficient means to influence the development of criteria (..)' (TABD, 1996c: 28).

[34] The relevance of this question gradually grew as in the fall of 1997 it became obvious that president Clinton would only be able to get trade negotiating authority from Congress if such authority would be supported by representatives from the agricultural states (see House Committee on Agriculture, 1997; Senate Committee on Agriculture, Nutrition, and Forestry, 1997).

[35] On April 18, 1997 the EU and the U.S. reached an Understanding in which the U.S. Administration promised to suspend Title III of the Helms-Burton Act (suing of European companies that have invested in expropriated assets in Cuba) in return for a European promise 'to step up efforts to promote democracy in Cuba' (*Agence Europe*, n° 6958, April 19, 1997: 6).

[36] As part of the negotiations on a veterinary equivalency agreement.

[37] Where a WTO-panel, and later the WTO Appellate Body ruled against the EU (World Trade Organization Appellate Body, 1997a).

[38] Statement by Sir Leon Brittan, following the official launching of the NTM-proposal, March 11, 1998.

[39] On the U.S. side the study was conducted by the International Trade Commission.

[40] Such an extension would include telecommunications, chemical products, and motor vehicles.

[41] Emphasis would be put here on an EU commitment to national treatment (which would give third suppliers the benefit of internal market rules), and the extension of public procurement rules to defense-related procurements. In the background of this discussion looms – of course – the question of the Massachusetts Burma Law, currently under legal attack by the federal American government and by the European Commission.

[42] In his March 18 speech at Harvard University, Leon Brittan described the NTM proposal as follows: 'This is a major initiative, and deliberately so. It is designed to tackle the most serious impediments to transatlantic trade, by far the biggest economic relationship in the world, and to bring major economic benefits to business and consumers in the EU and the U.S.'

[43] Quoted in *Inside U.S. Trade*, Vol. 16, n° 7, February 20, 1998.

[44] Cf. Brittan's March 20 speech at the National Press Club in Washington DC in which he emphasized the role of the NTM in promoting multilateral trade liberalization. As he put it:

'[W]hat we are doing is not at the expense of other countries or the multilateral economic system. It is rather a way to reinforce the joint leadership of Europe and the United States and to provide a building block in the next step forward in the evolution of the multilateral system.' This was clearly meant to appease any concern – *inter alia* by third countries – that the Transatlantic partnership could jeopardize or hinder multilateral trade liberalization or commitments in that sense.

[45] As far as agriculture was concerned, the proposal suggested to include talks on phytosanitary standards, veterinary equivalency, and animal welfare (which includes the sensitive issue of production of fur on the basis of animals captured by leghold traps).

[46] However, within the Clinton Administration support was shown for the exclusion of agricultural tariffs and subsidies from the NTM – since these would be dealt with in the WTO anyway – and the focus on regulatory issues concerning this sector (cf. sanitary and phytosanitary measures, GMOs). This clearly didn't satisfy the members of Congress. During the April 21 hearing in the Senate Finance Subcommittee on Trade, the rationale behind this was clearly expressed by Sen. Brownback (R-KS) in his reference to a letter sent to him by former USTR Clayton Yeutter. The letter, as quoted by Brownback, said the following: 'Where they've [the Europeans] successfully isolated agriculture from other trade issues, we've not been able to do much because we've not had much agricultural trading stock of interest to the EU.' So even if subsidies and tariffs would be dealt with in WTO negotiations, the US could use bilateral talks – and especially the European anxiousness to conduct these on a wide array of regulatory issues – as a bargaining chip to get agricultural concessions beyond regulatory issues from the EU.

[47] The United States being the only country that uses the 'first-to-invent' principle.

[48] This was only possible after the two parties negotiated a deal on the Helms-Burton and D'Amato Acts (*Agence Europe*, n° 7224, May 18-19, 1998: 6-6bis).

[49] This happened in the context of an escalating conflict on the GMOs after a rumour was spread that the French government had decided not to approve the import of two strains of genetically modified corn. As the U.S. doesn't separate its unmodified corn from its GMOs, this would have blocked all U.S. corn imports in the EU. This would have (and indeed initially did) outraged U.S. agricultural interests. The Commission was anxious therefore, to offer the Americans the prospect of Transatlantic talks on the subject. At the end of July it became clear however, that the French government had approved the two strains of corn. The problem of these particular strains was thus resolved, but not the transparency of the approval procedure. Hence the fact that this procedure continued to occupy a prominent place on the agenda of the Transatlantic trade talks.

[50] As far as the WTO is concerned, the TEP Declaration also referred to Transatlantic cooperation on the WTO accessions. This is notably important for the questions of the Chinese and Russian applications for WTO accession.

[51] Senate Committee on Finance, Press Release #105-325, May 18, 1998.

[52] Published on June 9, 1998.

[53] The Commission excluded the binding of government procurement negotiations in the WTO to bilateral U.S.-EU negotiations on the issue (cf. TABD, 1996b: 29).

[54] *Inside U.S. Trade*, Vol. 16, n° 27, July 10, 1998. The negotiations had to be concluded in November 1998 without a clear outcome because of Japanese resistance against tariff concessions in particular sectors. What has been conceded however, will be submitted for tariff negotiations in the WTO (see World Trade Organization, 1999a).

[55] Concerns in this sense were not only expressed by the European Commission but also by France.

[56] Cf. the French fear for a 'negative list formula' in the services negotiations that have to start in 2000 in the WTO. This formula has been agreed upon by the Quad members in the course of 1998.

[57] This approach is not new for the Transatlantic trade relations. In May 1998 the US and the EU signed their first MRA agreement on testing. It covers a wide range of sectors such as pharmaceuticals, medical devices (with some exceptions), recreational craft, telecommunications equipment, and products that must be inspected electromagnetic compatibility and electrical safety. The agreement basically provides for one testing procedure that will be recognized (certified) when products are imported in the market of the other party to the agreement. In December 1998, right before the December 18 Summit, the U.S. proposed to extend the coverage of the MRA to six new areas in three sectors: road and marine safety equipment, and calibration devices. See *Inside U.S. Trade*, Vol. 16, n° 49, December 11, 1998. The EU didn't want to agree with this extension immediately.

[58] Although it was clear that each of the parties had particular sectors in mind. The U.S. the audiovisual services, the EU the mutual recognition of professional standards. As far as the EU was concerned, the MRA approach to services would have as an additional benefit that it would not fall under the MFN obligations and that it would, therefore, avoid the free rider problem. The fact that the EU didn't want to include audiovisual services was quite obvious, certainly after the EU had insisted (and convinced) that Latvia could not include commitments on this sector in its WTO accession negotiations with the U.S. and other WTO members. This in the perspective of a future EU membership of this country.

[59] This is clearly the format of the 1998 Mutual Recognition Agreement where the agreement consists of two parts: a framework, and sectoral annexes.

[60] *Inside U.S. Trade*, Vol. 16, n° 42, October 23, 1998.

[61] Government Procurement Agreement, an agreement that was part of the Uruguay Round but that was only plurilateral in nature. The extension of the coverage of the GPA was planned for 1999, as part of the 1994 agreement in the Uruguay Round.

[62] A typical example of the problems faced here by the US is the Massachusetts Burma Act, which has been challlenged by both the U.S. Administration (for being unconstitutional) and by the EU (for violating the U.S. commitments in the WTO) (see European Commission, 1998d: 29).

[63] The EU defends the 'first-to-file' system because it avoids claims that the first inventer was somebody else than the one that first filed the invention.

[64] As the U.S. Administration already indicated in 1996: '(..) there is currently no consensus in the United States, including in the U.S. Business community, to go forward with patent harmonization negotiations largely because they would require the United States to change to a first-to-file system for issuing patents and to make other changes that are not supported by U.S. industry' (TABD, 1996c: 64).

[65] This opposition manifested itself quite strongly against the MAI negotiations in the OECD.

[66] The MAI-negotiations were declared 'dead' after a six months suspension of the talks in April 1998. The 'declaration' itself was issued by the French prime minister, Lionel Jospin on October 14, 1998 in the Assemblée nationale, the French lower house of parliament (cf. Assemblée nationale, 1998: 22).

[67] In the original proposal (H. Con.Res. 213 IH) the focus was explicitly on the EU.

[68] As USTR Barchefsky has put it recently (USTR, 1999a): '(..) it is the U.S. relationship with Europe that provides the cornerstone for a liberal trading regime.'

[69] Interview of State Department Spokesman James Rubin on Fox Morning News, February 22, 1999. Distributed by the State Dept. Listserver.

[70] Cf. a remark made by a U.S. official on the beef hormone dispute between the U.S. and the EU that 'both sides want to foster a dialogue on this issue in order to avoid a contentious fight in the WTO such as on the ongoing dispute over bananas' (*Inside U.S. Trade*, Vol. 17, n° 7, February 19, 1999).

[71] Questions that aroused here concerned the question of the risk assessment (what kind of evidence is legitimate to underpin regulations that act as barriers to trade), the question of the risk itself (what is a risk and how serious has the risk to be in order to be legitimate as a basis for a *de facto* trade barrier), the question of proportionality (is banning a product better than regulating its substance, a question that is related to the problem of import control), and the kind of proof that is necessary to show that a regulatory regime is a 'disguised restriction on international trade' (World Trade Organization Appellate Body, 1998).

[72] Among which *inter alia* the inclusion of fiber optic cables.

[73] Including the conditions for the reinspection of European drugs by the FDA (the EU asked for an automatic recognition of European drug inspections, while the FDA wanted to keep the right for reinspection, see TABD, 1996c).

[74] In the case of the U.S. , for example, there is the resistance of some regulatory agencies against any loss of autonomy due to international agreements. Opposition of the Food and Drug Administration, the Environmental Protection Agency, and the Occupational Safety and Health Administration to parts of the 1997 MRA are cases in mind. But on the European side, similar problems exist. An example of this is the role of the European Telecommunications Standards Institute (ETSI) that recently sparked a new Transatlantic conflict with its proposal to set one European standard for wireless services (3G) in Europe and which has chosen a standard that is mainly used by European telecom companies (W-CDMA) and that is incompatible with a standard that is used by most American telecom companies (cdma2000).

[75] As Hauser has indicated (House Ways and Means, 1997: 42) the costs engendered by such regulatory barriers are not just born by large companies but also – even disproportionately – by small and medium companies (which is by the way recognized in the preamble of the 1997 MRA between the US and the EU, see International Trade Administration, 1997: 2). As a matter of fact, for many of these companies regulatory cooperation – i.e. through mutual recognition – is a matter of access or no access. On the question of testing for instance, many SMEs just cannot afford to do the testing and are unable to bear the cost of outsourcing such tests to international labs. With mutual recognition, the cost of testing decreases (since oversees testing disappears) and becomes affordable. It is normal that these companies have achieved a strong voice in the TABD through the Transatlantic Small Business Initiative (TASBI).

[76] *Inside U.S. Trade*, Vol. 16, n° 50, December 18, 1998.

[77] Directive 95/46/EC.

References

Assemblee Nationale (1998), Rapport d'information (rapport préliminaire) déposé par la délégation pour l'Union européenne sur les relations économiques entre l'Union européenne et les Etats-Unis, Assembléee nationale, Paris, rapport n° 1150.

European Commission (1995a), Communication from the Commission to the Council: Europe and the US: the Way Forward, Office for Official Publications, Luxembourg, COM (95) 411 final.

European Commission (1995b), Eleventh Report on United States Barriers to Trade and Investment, Services of the European Commission, Brussels, May 1995.

European Commission (1996a), Twelfth Report on US Barriers to Trade and Investment, Brussels, Services of the European Commission, Brussels, May 1996, also available on Internet.

European Commission (1996b), Report on the Conference of the Transatlantic Business Dialogue (TABD), Chicago, 8-9 November 1996, DG I & DG III, Brussels, internal unpublished document.

European Commission (1997), 1997 Report on the United States Barriers to Trade and Investment, Services of the European Commission, Brussels, July 1997.

European Commission (1998a), Draft Action Plan for Transatlantic Economic Partnership, European Commission, DG I, Brussels, Press Release.

European Commission (1998b), The New Transatlantic Marketplace. Communication of Sir Leon Brittan, Mr Bangemann and Mr Monti, DG I, Brussels, Press Release.

European Commission (1998c), Prospects for Agricultural Markets, 1998-2005, European Commission, DG VI Homepage, October 1998.

European Commission (1998d), Report on United States Barriers to Trade and Investment – 1998, European Commission, DGI, Brussels.

Green Cowles, M. (1997), 'The Limits of Liberalization: Regulatory Cooperation and the New Transatlantic Agenda: A Conference Report', in The Limits of Liberalization: Regulatory Cooperation and the New Transatlantic Agenda, American Institute for Contemporary German Studies, The Johns Hopkins University, Washington DC, pp. 1-25.

House Committee on Agriculture (1997), Fast Track Negotiating Authority. Hearing of the Subcommittee General Farm Commodities – September 23, 1997, House of Representatives, Washington DC, House Committee on Agriculture Homepage.

House of Commons (1998), Cuba and the Helms-Burton Act, London, House of Commons Research Paper, #98/114, 14 December 1998.

House of Representatives (1998a), Sense of Congress Regarding Elimination of Restrictions on Imports of United States Agricultural Products, Report to Accompany H. Con. Res. 213, GPO, Washington DC, House Report 105-672.

House Ways and Means Committee (1997), New Transatlantic Agenda Hearing before the Subcommittee on Trade, GPO, Washington DC, Report #105-20, July 23, 1997.

House Ways and Means Committee (1998), Hearing on Trade Relations with Europe and on the Transatlantic Economic Partnership – July 28, 1998, Washington DC, House Ways and Means Committee Homepage, 105th Congress.

International Trade Administration (1997), Agreement on Mutual Recognition between the United States of America and the European Community, Washington DC, Dept. Of Commerce, ITA Homepage.

Ives, R. (1997), 'The ABC of MRAs', in The Limits of Liberalization. Regulatory Cooperation and the New Transatlantic Agenda, American Institute for Contemporary German Studies, The Johns Hopkins University, Washington DC, pp. 27-33.

Jackson, S. (1996), 'The Transatlantic Business Dialogue: An Entrepreneurial Force Behind the New Transatlantic Agenda', in ECSA Review, vol. 9, no. 3.

Josling, T. (1997), Implications of Regional Trade Arrangements for Agricultural Trade, FAO Economic and Social Development Paper no. 133, Rome.

Josling, T. (1998), Agricultural Trade Policy: Completing the Reform, Institute for International Economics, Washington DC.

Kerremans, B. (1998), 'Transatlantic Trade Policy Relations: Bilateral and Multilateral Implications of the Emerging Marketplace for Goods', in Implementation of the New Transatlantic Agenda and Future Prospects, Final Report, Trans-European Studies Association, Brussels, pp. 59-88.

Lawrence, R.Z. (1996), Regionalism, Multilateralism, and Deeper Integration, The Brookings Institution, Washington D.C., "Integrating National Economies" Series.

Office of the United States Trade Representative (1998a), Statement by USTR Barchefsky concerning the U.S.-EU Summit Trade Discussions, USTR, Washington DC, Press Release 98-112.

Office of the United States Trade Representative (1998b), Trade Policy Agenda 1998 & the 1997 Annual Report of the President of the United States on the Trade Agreements Program, USTR, Washington DC.

Office of the United States Trade Representative (1998c), Testimony of Ambassador Charlene Barchefsky before the House Ways and Means Subcommittee on Trade, July 28, 1998, USTR, Washington DC, Homepage.

Office of the United States Trade Representative (1999a), USTR Barchefsky Statement in Bonn, USTR, Washington DC, February 1, 1999.

Peterson, J. (1996), Europe and America: The Prospects for Partnership, Routledge, London.

Senate Committee on Agriculture, Nutrition, and Forestry (1997), Hearing of Senate Committee on Agriculture, Nutrition and Forestry – June 18, 1997, U.S. Senate, Washington DC, Senate Committee on Agriculture Homepage.

Stern, P. (1996), The Transatlantic Business Dialogue: A New Paradigm for Standards and Regulatory Reform Sector-by-Sector, Unpublished Paper, available on the TABD-Homepage.

Transatlantic Business Dialogue (1996a), Chicago Declaration, November 9, 1996, TABD Fax Release, Brussels-Washington DC.

Transatlantic Business Dialogue (1996b), Comments by Services of the European Commission on the TABD Progress Report of 23 May 1996, TABD Unpublished Document, Brussels.

Transatlantic Business Dialogue (1996c), U.S. Government Comments on the Transatlantic Business Dialogue Progress Report of 23 May 1996, TABD Unpublished Document, Washington DC.

Transatlantic Business Dialogue (1998), Charlotte Statement of Conclusions, November 5-7, 1998, TABD Homepage.

Vargo, F. (1997), 'Prepared Statement by Franklin J. Vargo before the Subcommittee on International Economic Policy and Trade of the House Committee on International Relations', in USIS Washington File, September 10, 1997, pp. 1-9.

Vogel, D. (1997), Barriers or Benefits? Regulation in Transatlantic Trade, The Brookings Institution, Washington DC.

World Trade Organization (1999a), Preparations for the 1999 Ministerial Conference: APEC's Accelerated Tariff Liberalization (ATL) Initiative – Communication from New Zealand, WTO General Council, Geneva, Report WT/GC/W/138, January 26, 1999.

World Trade Organization (1999a), Preparations for the 1999 Ministerial Conference: Negotiations in Industrial Products – Communication from Australia, WTO General Council, Geneva, Report WT/GC/W/132, January 21, 1999.

World Trade Organization Appellate Body (1997a), European Communities – Regime for the Importation, Sale, and Distribution of Bananas, WTO, Geneva, Report WT/DS27/AB/R, September 9, 1997.

World Trade Organization Appellate Body (1998), EC Measures Concerning Meat and Meat Products (Hormones), WTO, Geneva, Report WT/DS26/AB/R & WT/DS48/AB/R.

7 The Politics of Domestic Ratification Across Democratic Institutions
SHERRY L. BENNETT AND ERICK DUCHESNE

Introduction

As the general theme of this book suggests, free trade areas have a profound impact on both inter-regional trade and multilateral trade institutions. In this chapter we turn our attention to the 1989 free trade agreement between Canada and the United States (FTA). This agreement is important because it came in response to a perceived lack of progress in multilateral trading institutions and is widely touted as the impetus for future encompassing trade blocs in the Americas. Because free trade agreements shape trade patterns between states, it is important to examine not only the political factors responsible for the initiation of free trade agreements, but also the institutions that structure the ratification process. To explain how democratic states successfully ratify international trade agreements we integrate and extend theoretical insights from scholars that have pondered variations in the policy making process across parliamentary and presidential Democracies (Milner, 1997; Tsebelis, 1995; Weaver and Rockman, 1993; Lijphart, 1992; Steinmo, 1989). Specifically, in this chapter, we focus on the combination of constitutional and electoral structures that shape decision-making authority in Canada and the United States. Both have been used to explain why democratic states choose different public policies. We also find that both are important institutional determinants for explaining whether and when democratic states are able to secure cooperation on international trade liberalization. We illustrate how variations in political institutions across democratic states shape ratification outcomes. Moreover, we argue that scholars must appreciate the pre-existing milieu of a state's trade institutions as a significant factor in

213

predicting cooperative outcomes. In short, institutions are part of an interactive relationship with the policies that emerge from them. By taking this approach, we are able to demonstrate how ratification was more likely in Canada than in the United States, even though Canada had strong embedded institutional roots in favor of protection in contrast to the United States, which had institutional arrangements favoring trade liberalization.

This chapter is divided into four sections. In the first segment we provide a theoretical overview of how the distribution of political authority, electoral structures, and institutional foundations exert influence on trade policy outcomes. In the following two sections we apply our theoretical framework to the discussion and comparison of Canadian and American trade institutions. Finally, we demonstrate how different institutions can lead to similar outcomes, by assessing the road taken by the two North American partners during the pre-negotiation of the FTA. We conclude with general thoughts on the empirical and theoretical significance of the FTA in regards to the expansion of trade arrangements in the Americas.

Theoretical Overview

Political institutions structure collective decisions in a polity, they also serve to structure the advantages and impediments accruing to different groups in the legislative process. For example, the rules of representation govern who participates in the decision making process, and from these constellation of rules, societal interest logically deduce what actions are required to gain influence in the political process. In this sense, institutions structure how political pressure may be exerted over policy outcomes among different interests in society (Milner, 1997; Tsebelis and Money, 1997; Tsebelis, 1995; Steinmo, Thelen and Longstreth, 1992; Steinmo, 1989; Hall, 1986). Thus, it is crucial to center our attention on the interaction of societal and institutional factors in trying to explain why states pursue and ratify free trade agreements (Mansfield and Milner, 1999). We begin our discussion of the theoretical framework by first focusing on the distribution of political authority over trade policy. As we demonstrate, the fragmentation of legislative decision-making is a common, key institutional element that shapes policy outcomes across democratic states. Whether authority is centralized or diffuse, renders valuable insights into the institutional actors vested with constitutional power over policy and the decision-making environment that structures legislative behavior (Milner, 1997; Tsebelis, 1995; Steinmo, 1989).

Afterwards, we examine how electoral structures across democracies interact with the distribution of legislative power.

The Distribution of Political Authority

As Steinmo (1989) convincingly argues, 'the specific loci of decision-making authority for any particular policy arena can vary across polities,' and this point is critical to understanding how states adopt different public policies. Furthermore, it is also critical to the understanding of whether states are able to achieve international cooperation.[1] In democratic states, the bargaining processes that precede a final vote on a policy involve a variety of institutional and partisan actors. According to Tsebelis (1995), these actors represent *veto players* with the power to prevent policy change in democratic political systems.[2] As the number of veto players rise, the more difficult it is to secure agreement. Subsequently, the less likely change from status quo policy will occur.[3]

In the legislative arena, Milner (1997) identifies five powers that structure the fragmentation of political authority in the decision-making process. Vested powers associated with agenda setting (initiation), amendments, ratification (veto), referendums and side payments are factors that determine the relative power of the executive over the legislature (and vice versa) on policy matters. If these power are concentrated in one actor, a state is able to simulate decision making as a unitary rational actor. When these powers are fragmented among political actors a state is governed by polyarchy. Milner (1997) argues that polyarchic states are much more susceptible to distributive particularistic politics. Unitary actors are not. Thus, as unitary actors have few veto players and are less susceptible to distributive politics, logically we might conclude that policy outcomes are easier to secure in states characterized as unitary actors than in polyarchic states with multiple veto players and distributive politics. In particular, we might infer that international cooperation on trade agreements would be more difficult to secure in a polyarchic state than in a state characterized as an unitary actor.

However, policy bias toward particular special interests can be observed across many states with different political processes and institutions. As Lohmann (1998) convincingly argues, inefficient forms of public policy are common not only in the United States but also in countries where monetary contributions to political candidates play an insignificant role, in some cases because campaigns are publicly financed. In this sense, distributive pork-barrel politics is not logically restricted to polyarchic states like the U.S. It may also occur in legislatures controlled by strong parties that enforce majoritarian partyline voting rather than universalistic logrolls or deference to stacked committees. Thus, individuals and special interests may adopt different behavior to exert political pressure on politicians to secure desirable policy outcomes. Thus, the dichotomous distinction between unitary and polyarchic states may underestimate the extent to which distributive politics manifests in states with concentrated political authority. The logic underlying these assertions emanate from factors associated with the electoral structures of democratic states and their attendant influence in shaping legislative behavior.

Electoral Structures

Politicians across all Democracies are fundamentally motivated by the common desire to seek reelection (Taagepera and Shugart, 1989; Cain et al., 1987; Mayhew, 1974; Rae, 1971). As Carey and Shugart (1995) acknowledge, this desire coexists with a tension between the collective electoral interests of a given political party and the individual electoral interests of the politicians who run for office under particular party labels.[4] To be precise, there exists a potential collective action problem for politicians in establishing and maintaining party reputations (Cox and McCubbins, 1993). As Carey and Shugart contend, '[m]aintaining a party's reputation requires that politicians refrain from taking positions or actions that conflict with the party's platform. If the quality of her party's reputation is all that matters to each politician's electoral prospects, then there is no problem – there is no incentive to weaken party reputation by staking out independent positions. But if electoral prospects depend on winning votes cast for the individual politician instead of, or in addition to, votes cast for the party, then politicians evaluate the trade-off between the value of personal and party reputations'(Ibidem: 419). In the latter case, the absence of a programmatic party system can create incentives for legislators to become independent political entrepreneurs (Steinmo, 1989).

According to this logic, the electoral structures of a state shape the extent to which individual politicians benefit electorally by developing personal reputations distinct from those of their party (Mainwaring, 1991; Jacobson, 1990; Uslaner, 1985; and Fenno, 1978). Specifically, the variety of election rules and formulas for allocating seats in office that exist under different electoral systems determine whether politicians value their personal reputation over party labels.[5] Whether politicians have a stake in developing individual versus party reputations should logically determine how constituents and special interests are able to exert political pressure on legislative behavior.

If the configuration of electoral structures in a state shape legislative incentives in favor of cultivating their own personal reputations, then candidates are likely to respond to the interests of their service constituency not the party organization.[6] In this instance, a representatives' electoral fortunes are tied to their local constituencies in a manner that makes them vulnerable to locally defined demands and special interest groups pressures. However, if the configuration of electoral structures in a state shape legislative incentives in favor of cultivating the reputation of their political party, then we anticipate that they are less likely to respond to particular constituency factors. Instead, legislative behavior will be motivated by the party line.[7] Highly specialized interests groups will have little influence on individual representatives per se. To exert any influence special interests will have to form broader coalitions and acquire access to party platforms. Regardless, special interests are able to acquire influence whether parties are weak or strong. The critical point is that distributive political dynamics manifests under both type of states. As we demonstrate, the distribution of political authority on international trade issues and electoral structures that shape legislative behavior explain support for ratification. However, to understand legislative preferences for liberalization, we also need to consider the pre-existing milieu of trade institutions that constrain policy makers.

Institutional Foundations of Trade Policy

Embedded Preferences and Trade Institutions in Canada

Protectionism is at the core of Canadian early economic development and it remained a central feature of its trade policy until the early 1980s The 1879 National Policy, which instituted the structure of protective tariffs, continues to resonate in the trade policy of Canada. As such, protectionist interests have been able to secure trade restrictions that benefit Canadian producers (Lusztig, 1996). Section 91(2) of the 1867 British North American Act stipulates that the regulation of trade and commerce is the sole responsibility of the parliament in Canada. In reality, it means that the Executive has the sole responsibility of negotiating international accords, even without the assent of the provinces or the Canadian Parliament.[8] In surplus, there is no need for domestic ratification of an international agreement, unless the accord overrides domestic legislation.[9]   At its historical roots, the Canadian trading system favors protectionism. Indeed, the passage of the 1879 National Policy created a national system of restrictive tariffs and was primarily responsible for determining the institutional origins of Canada's protectionist history. The impetus for this policy was to support industrialization in Central Canada although this was unpopular in the agriculture dominated Western Canada.[10]

If history is any indication, pursuing free trade is a risky business in Canadian politics. Since McDonald's[11] National Policy, the shadow of protectionism is omnipresent in Canadian history and those who veered from this traditional *modus operandi* have paid a consequential political price. The origins of this risk go back to the unfortunate experience of Wilfrid Laurier, Liberal Prime Minister of Canada in 1911. Laurier went before the electorate campaigning in favor of a reciprocity agreement with the United States, which would have dismantled the system of protective tariffs created under the National Policy. This proved extremely unpopular with Central Canada's electors, and financial and manufacturing interests. It resulted in a resounding defeat for the Liberals at the hands of the Conservatives, who had campaigned to dissolve the agreement (Lusztig, 1996). In 1935 and 1938 Canada signed bilateral trade accords with the United States, but these agreements were modest in scope and did little to dismantle the existing tariff structure, which remains intact today (Lusztig, 1996). The fear of American cultural and economic invasion culminated during the 1970s with the Third Option.[12] This was a short-lived effort by a Liberal led government to restructure the Canadian economy and diversify Canada's foreign economic relations from its southern neighbor. The first pillar of the strategy was the Foreign Investment Review Agency (FIRA), a governmental institution involved in the regulation and screening of foreign investments. Established in the minority Liberal government between 1972 and 1974, FIRA imposed minimal conditions on foreign takeovers of Canadian industries, but it had no jurisdiction over the expansion of foreign interests already in Canada. Despite a strong reluctance by the Canadian cabinet to disallow a foreign claim of Canadian ownership, FIRA became a major irritant to the United States. Another central element of the strategy was the establishment of the National Energy Program (NEP) in 1980. In the wake of the second oil crisis, the NEP increased the 'oil tax,' redistributed the oil revenues in favor of Ottawa, kept the national oil price below the world level, encouraged off-shore development, and promoted the Canadianization of the industry. Not only were these objectives inimical to Western Canadian provinces, which relied heavily on oil revenues, but it also proved to be very unpopular with the American Congress. This reluctance to liberalize continued in the early1980s despite Canada's rise in export interests. Not until 1983 did another administration publicly declare its support for trade liberalization.[13] The Liberal government of Pierre Trudeau initiated sectoral trade negotiations with the United States.[14] This was a clear turnaround in Trudeau's trade policies. His *volte-face* was spurred by an acute bilateral conflict that erupted in 1981 over Canadian national economic policies, especially NEP and FIRA. American officials sent a clear signal to their Canadian counterparts. They focussed on the Canadian trade dependence on the United States and the possible aftermath of American retaliatory measures for Ottawa. At a time when the worse economic crisis since the 1930s was hitting Canada, the American threat was taken seriously (Tomlin, 1989: 263; Clarkson, 1985: 153; 1982: 34-6, 151).

In 1984, the Progressive Conservatives came into power and despite his earlier opposition to free trade, Brian Mulroney's top international priority became the negotiation of a free trade agreement with the United States. The change in big business's opposition to bilateral liberalization affected his decision to abandon protectionism. To be more precise, Mulroney's shift to promote a free trade strategy stems from an electoral calculus. He was constructing a new winning coalition based on support from Québec and Western Canada (Lusztig, 1996; Doern and Tomlin, 1991). In essence, support for liberalization became an important political strategy for the Progressive Conservative Party in its effort to secure electoral majorities and retain control of government.[15]

Embedded Preferences and Trade Institutions in the U.S.

The United States is endowed with domestic trade institutions that strive to promote free and fair trade with other states in the global economy. Historically, this was not always the case. Commercial policy was susceptible to log-rolling coalitions among special interests that sought prohibitive restrictions on trade. Congress, vested with constitutional authority to set tariffs on individual goods, would seek to appease economic interests whose electoral support sustained their tenure in office (Conybeare, 1991; Haggard, 1988). In fact, for many years, it was possible to predict support for trade liberalization by monitoring the outcomes of elections. Typically, when Democrats controlled Congress and the presidency, restrictions on commercial activities would decline, while if Republicans dominated Congress and the presidency, tariffs would generally increase (Keech and Pak, 1995; O'Halloran, 1994; Stewart and Weingast, 1992).[16] As a general trend however, tariffs, regardless of which party was in power, have declined since 1930. In fact, the tone of the United States policy changed most dramatically in the midst of the depression and the ensuing political realignment that followed. And it is at this point in time that the ideological preferences embedded in Congress and the Executive since the end of the civil war began to change.

Broadly speaking, new trends designed to liberalize US trade were ushered in with the New Deal realignment, beginning with the 1934 Reciprocal Trade Agreements Act (RTAA). This trade act delegated authority to the executive to negotiate genuine reciprocal free trade agreements by proclamation alone (Bennett and Smith, 1999b; Bailey, Goldstein and Weingast, 1997; Gilligan, 1997; O'Halloran, 1994). To be precise, the RTAA allowed the president to reduce U.S. tariffs by up to 50 percent. Democrats, frustrated with the Republican party's repeated attempts to prevent unilateral tariff reductions, chose to delegate this authority to the president. This institutional innovation established the basic structure for trade liberalization for the next quarter century (Bennett and Smith, 1999b; Irwin and Krozsner, 1999; Schneitz, 1998; Bailey, Goldstein and Weingast, 1997; Gilligan, 1997; O'Halloran, 1994). In particular, the RTAA fostered two important developments that explain the nature of US trade policy preferences in the Executive and Congress. First, the RTAA and its various extensions would solidify a growing contrast between an Executive office with an overwhelming predisposition to support trade liberalization and a Congress with a general orientation to legislate restrictions on trade. Second, it would create the necessary conditions for economic interests to organize and lobby in support of trade liberalization. In particular, in the years following the passage of the 1934 RTAA, export interests would overcome collective action costs associated with organizing politically, to exert pressure on legislators to support liberalization.

Vested with the authority granted in the 1934 RTAA, the president made great strides in promoting liberalization. Between 1934-47, the president negotiated over twenty-five reciprocal treaties with other countries. Congress however, did not completely abdicate its authority over trade policy matters. In fact, Congressional extensions of executive authority became political as delegation and renewal of reciprocal negotiation authority varied over time. As O'Halloran (1994) convincingly argues, this behavior on the part of Congress was reinforced over time and created back and forth delegation of power from Congress to the Executive that solidified a protectionist institutional bias in Congress that contrasted greatly with the trade liberalization bias inherent in the executive office. Members of Congress maintained their right to relinquish the president's authority to negotiate free trade agreements with other states. And often they would exercise their authority by failing to renew, or imposing restrictions on, extensions of the 1934 RTAA. However, as the RTAA reduced access to legislative mechanisms that supported redistributive bargains and log-rolling coalitions, a political environment was fostered that favored lower tariffs (Irwin and Krosner, 1999; Shepsle and Weingast, 1994).[17] The executive, vested with agenda setting power and interested in serving the economic interests of the nation as a whole, was able to advocate liberalization. Unlike Congress, the president was less susceptible to parochial interests demanding protection (Irwin and Krosner, 1999; Haggard, 1988; Weingast, Shepsle and Johnson, 1981).

Throughout the post WWII era aggregate US exports continued to rise along with export-oriented interest groups who secured increasing levels of influence in the trade policy making process (Gilligan, 1997). Historically, protectionist interests have had an asymmetric policy bias in their favor (Krueger, 1990). Specifically, import-competing interests producers have been able to overcome collective action costs associated with political organization because the benefits have been highly concentrated (Bennett and Smith, 1999a; Gilligan, 1997; O'Halloran, 1994; Olson, 1968). Broadly speaking the costs associated with organizing export interests were too high and benefits too diffuse. However, the institutionalization of reciprocity in RTAA began to concentrate benefits to export interests (Gilligan, 1997). As Irwin and Krozsner (1999) further argue, '[b]y directly tying lower foreign tariffs to lower domestic tariffs (and upsetting the ability of import-competing producers to form logrolls), the RTAA may have fostered the development of exporters as an organized group opposing high tariffs and supporting international trade agreements' (Ibidem: 6). Moreover, the reduced tariffs negotiated under the auspices of the RTAA served to increase the size of the export sector, consequently creating enhanced support for its renewal (Hillman and Moser, 1996).

Taken together, both of these factors signal a change in the commitment of the United States to promote and sustain trade liberalization. However, intermediate demands for protection from domestic producers would surface.[18] These pressures would significantly influence legislative support for liberalization as special interests were able to exert political pressure on representatives to favor trade.

Explaining Variation in the Ratification of CUSFTA

Distribution of Legislative Power in Canada

Canada has a political party system that has strong party discipline. This high level of party discipline in the Canadian House of Commons and, by the same token, a low level of party dissent, signify that important votes, such as the ratification of the FTA, are taken along party lines.[19] Hence, Members of Parliament (MP's) tend to vote according to party preferences instead of constituency preferences (Cox, 1987). As such, in this type of political system, the public votes for the parties rather than individual candidates. Long time students of Canadian political institutions present the issue bluntly when they indicate that in Canada, candidates at general elections have no other alternatives but to 'organize around leaders rather than political principles and ideologies' (Clarke et al., 1991: 8). This is due to the fact that Canada has a closed-list electoral formula with one round (Carey and Shugart, 1995: 426-27). This means that political parties present fixed ballots and voters are allowed a single opportunity to choose among them. According to Carey and Shugart (1995), personal reputation is the least important under this formula. Under these circumstances, an individual candidate is less concerned with representing his district's interests than with pursuing the interests of its party. Consequently, because strong ideological positions by the candidates on the issue of trade do not govern political parties in Canada, the power to negotiate trade agreements is concentrated in the hands of a few high-ranking Canadian officials.[20]

The issue of party ideology in Canada has been and still is hotly debated by scholars. A first group of researchers (Winn and McMenemy, 1976) argues that no basic ideological differences exist between the Liberal and Conservative parties. A second interpretation is that while no fundamental ideological cleavages between parties exist, Liberals and Conservatives have maintained consistent historic policy differences (Mallory, 1971; Dawson, 1963). The third perspective asserts that fundamental ideological differences do exist in Canada and that such ideologies as conservatism, liberalism, and democratic socialism are embedded in contrasting policies pursued by the Liberal, Conservative, and New Democratic parties respectively (Christian and Campbell, 1990; Horowitz, 1978; 1966; Hartz, 1964). On the issue of international trade, we find the second interpretation the most convincing.[21] Liberals and Conservatives have supported trade liberalization and trade protection at different points in history. Historians have generally observed that the

Liberals were historically more continentalist or U.S. oriented and favored lower tariffs. Prior to the 1988 FTA, all previous attempts to increase trade ties with the United States occurred under a Liberal government. In contrast, the Conservatives[22] favored a strong connection with Great Britain and stood for higher tariffs. For instance, the National Policy of 1879, a prohibitive system of tariffs, which protected manufacturing interests of central Canada, was the brainchild of the Conservative Prime Minister John A. McDonald. Such policy differences over trade remained consistent for decades, but recently, traditional perspectives about trade have changed. Pierre Trudeau's Third Option policy reflected the time-honored Conservative views on trade, while Brian Mulroney's vision of a continental free trade area was in unison with traditional Liberal position. This indicates that newly elected prime ministers and their close advisors are not constrained by previous partisan policies over trade. Simply put, trade is a political issue, manipulated by opportunistic political parties in an effort to maximize support for a winning coalition during elections. This institutional feature of Canada's party system manifests a different representation process than that observed in the United States. The structure of the party system in Canada manifests short-term electoral incentives, which promote institutional change in its trade institutions.

Thus, short-term electoral incentives in Canada induce political parties to adopt positions, particularly on trade policy, that they believe will maximize support from the greatest number of electoral districts. Thus, political parties will seize the opportunity to depart from Canada's traditional protectionist trade policy institutions if it is electorally advantageous for the party organization.[23] Consequently, we speculate that Brian Mulroney, in his desire to entrench a permanent political realignment, calculated that a majority of electoral districts would favor free trade with the United States. An historical tight-knit alliance between the Progressive Conservative Party and industrialists adds weight to this argument. While 'big business' traditionally opposed free trade, an increasing fear of American Congress' protectionism provides a logical explanation for its change of heart (Lustzig, 1996). Major business lobbying groups such as the Business Council on National Issues (BCNI), the Canadian Manufacturers' Association (CMA), the Canadian Chamber of Commerce, and the Canadian Federation of Independent Business (CFIB) were exceptionally vocal in their support of the FTA.[24] Doern and Tomlin go as far as mentioning that 'if business interests, led by the BCNI and CMA, had not changed their historic position on the basic issue of trade, the FTA would not exist' (1991: 108). The Canadian business community remains the best-organized and well-funded lobbying group in the country. Its direct access to powerful Cabinet officials makes it a force to reckon with.[25]

Distribution of Legislative Power in the United States

In contrast to Canada, weak party discipline is a characteristic of the American political system. The public tends to vote for individual candidates, not political parties. Since the United States is characterized by weak party discipline, members of Congress compete in candidate-center elections. Thus, members of Congress will adopt electoral strategies to maximize their own support from their constituencies. Typically this results in members servicing the needs of their particular district interests. As a consequence, members of Congress are less concerned with national trade policies and are not predisposed to support trade liberalization if there is no compelling local electoral incentives to do so.[26] As legislators in the United States benefit electorally by developing their own personal reputations, they are motivated to service the needs of their constituent's interests. Hence, distributive political battles oftentimes ensue over trade policy in Congress as legislators seek to fulfill the various demands of their respective district interests. Two major pieces of legislative have had a major influence in structuring the distribution of legislative power on trade policy between the Executive and Congress over time. They are the 1934 RTAA and the 1974 Trade Reform Act.

Beginning with the 1934 RTAA, Congress sought to overcome the negative implications of distributive politics in trade policy by allocating authority to the president to negotiate liberalization agreements with other states. Recognizing that the Executive has a broad-based constituency and has a natural predisposition weigh the national benefits of trade protectionism vs. liberalization. Congress solved its collective dilemma by delegating authority to the president (O'Halloran, 1994). However, congressional delegation was not absolute. Although members of Congress delegated authority to the president to overcome its own collective action problems, it did not abdicate control to the executive. Partial delegation rendered in the extensions of the RTAA permitted members of Congress to maintain some procedural control over the negotiations and formation of trade policy making. As a logical consequence, special interests have been able to maintain some influence in shaping legislative preferences and in the trade policy process in general. Thus, delegation of trade policy making to the executive characterizes modern trade policy making in the United

States, and is partly responsible for the preservation of liberal trade policy in the United States.

The 1974 Trade Reform Act had another significant influence on the distribution of power between Congress and the Executive on trade matters. This legislation overhauled the institutional structure that governed how trade policy was made in the mid 1970s. Specifically, it represents the first time Congress authorized the president to enter into trade negotiations with other nations in an effort to reduce *non-tariff* barriers. In addition, it established special procedures for implementing international trade agreements. These procedures were known as Fast Track, which represent a set of procedural rules that govern voting on treaties, and became the standard rules governing the ratification vote of free trade agreements in the United States. Under Fast Track procedures, only a majority in both houses of Congress is required for an agreement to be enacted and no amendments are permitted at the time of a vote. The vote is a simple up or down. Hence, the amount of product-specific protectionism that plagues most trade legislation is limited. As O'Halloran (1994) convincingly demonstrates, fast track has ex ante and ex post stages, which enable Congress to have considerable veto power over executive actions. Broadly speaking, it entails a sequence of events that pose constraints on negotiating unabated liberalization. These opportunities exist in both *ex ante* and *ex post* stages. Ex ante procedural opportunities constrain the executive's discretionary authority to liberalize throughout international negotiations, while ex post enable Congress to amend or veto an agreement before a final vote is to occur.[27]

More specifically, Fast Track serves three primary functions that structure the distribution of legislative power over free trade agreements. First Congress has veto power over executive actions. There exist three checks on president's negotiating authority. The House Ways and Means and Senate Finance can pass disapproval resolutions within sixty days after the president has expressed intentions to negotiate a free trade agreement and the president will be denied fast track authority. Moreover, both houses can pass resolutions within any sixty-day period stating that the president has failed to keep Congress sufficiently informed about the negotiations and fast track authority can be repealed. And Congress has an up-or-down vote over the final agreement.

Second, fast track procedures provide Congress with information. This is accomplished by participating directly in the international negotiations. In effect Congress is able to monitor the executive branch fulfilling the role of policeman with patrol oversight (O'Halloran, 1994: 142). In addition,

Congress creates executive agents such as the USTR, who act as fire inspectors, which oversee agencies responsible for trade policy and that report directly to Congress. Lastly, constituents enfranchised into the decision-making process through private sector advisory committees and public hearings. Thus, if the president takes actions that are objectionable to particular special interests, they can let their views and opinions are expressed.

Third, fast track procedures enable Congress to clarify their preferred policy. Through direct and indirect oversight legislators know what is going on and can let the president and executive agencies know what sort of policies are electorally feasible for them to support. And during this process, it becomes clear what groups benefit and what groups are injured. This is important because it feeds into the electoral structure. In the United States members of Congress run candidate centered elections and are influence by particularistic interests in their districts.

Taken together, the 1934 RTAA and the 1974 Trade Reform Act have served to preserve the pursuit of trade liberalization by the president of the United States, while at the same time affording Congress the ability to constrain such activities when they are electorally disadvantageous.

The Canadian Road to the Free Trade Agreement

As Brian Tomlin pointed out, 'the decision to negotiate free trade represented a rather dramatic policy shift on the part of the government of Canada, one that could not be anticipated at the outset of the decade' (1989: 255). Canada's Liberal-led government was still pursuing its 'Third Option' policy destined to divert its trade relationships from the United States to other areas of the globe.[28] On the other side of the border, Congress was responding to interest groups growing resentment towards foreign 'unfair' trade practices. The buzzword inside the beltway was 'aggressive unilateralism,' not trade liberalization. Under those circumstances, the spectacle at Québec City's Shamrock Summit in March 1985, where two 'dancing Irishmen' extolled the virtues of North American trade liberalization, certainly seemed uncharacteristic. What had happened in the meantime? Why did Mulroney and Reagan give the green light necessary for the hastening of the negotiations at the historic summit? How and why were two democratic states associated with a large amount of protectionist public sentiments able to ratify the 1988 Canadian-United States Free Trade Agreement (CUSFTA)?

As explained above, a high level of party discipline in the Canadian House of Commons and, by the same token, a low level of party dissent, signify that important votes, such as the ratification of the FTA, are taken along party lines. Indeed, when the FTA finally came to a third reading vote, during a late night special session on December 23, 1988,[29] its outcome was never in doubt. All members of the Progressive Conservative Party who were present in the House at the time voted in favor of the agreement, while the elected officials of the opposition retorted with resounding 'Nays.'[30] Yet, one should not jump to conclusion. Despite strong party discipline in the Canadian political system, a long and winding road, one strewn with numerous stumbling blocks, led from the Liberal Party's decision to open sectoral trade agreements with the United States in 1983 to a full-fledged free trade accord more than five years later.

To elect its representatives in the Lower House, Canada has a single-member plurality electoral system (Majoritarian system). Up until the 1993 elections three contending parties (Liberal, Progressive Conservative and New Democratic) were competing to attract the vote of the electorate in first-past-the-post, single-member, simple-majority elections. The emergence of two new parties in the late 1980s, the Bloc Québécois (BQ) and the Reform Party (RP), served to demonstrate the underlying regional division of the Canadian vote that had already taken hold on the Canadian electoral system, especially during the 1980s. As its name indicates, the BQ concentrates uniquely on garnering votes in Québec, while, despite its claim to a national presence, the RP finds adherents almost solely in Western Canada.

It was to partly the popularity of his party in these two regions that Brian Mulroney owed his party's electoral success in 1984.[31] Traditionally in Canada, in order to win an election, a party must carry the vote in at least two of its main regions, that is Québec, Ontario and Western Canada.[32] Therefore, we suggest that Mulroney, in order to preserve his unusual position as leader of a Conservative majority government, tried to instill a permanent electoral realignment by building a strong electoral base in Québec and Western Canada.[33] For the West, a devotion to free trade represented an ideological reaffirmation of the individual free enterprising mood of the citizens of the region, as well as the demise of a long-standing feeling of alienation. At last, the voice of Westerners would prevail over the concerns of Easterners. They also felt in unison with many in Québec, both among the business elite and the general public, who had confidence in their ability to compete internationally. In other parts of the country, Mulroney could only count on lackluster support. In the Atlantic provinces, the FTA represented a diminution of Canadian government command of its own economy. It meant fewer resources to be allocated for industrial development of this impoverished area of the country. The heavy industry in Ontario was the most likely to be impaired by the rationalization of the Canadian economy following the potential ratification of a regional free trade area. Consequently, backing for the FTA in the province was low when Mulroney decided to give the green light to his chief negotiators.

Armed with a solid electoral majority and strong party discipline, the Conservative Party's chance of implementing the negotiated agreement seemed excellent. That was without taking into account the role of the Leader of the Official Opposition, John Turner, and the Canadian Senate. On 20 July 1988, in what Johnston, Blais, Brady and Crête (1992) call an electoral gamble, Turner persuaded a Liberal dominated Senate to oppose the ratification of the FTA until the issue was brought to the attention of the Canadian electorate.[34] In contrast to the members of the House of Commons, the senators are not elected, but subject to partisan nomination. Since the Liberal party had controlled the government since 1963,[35] the Senate was 'packed' with loyal Liberal senators. Turner faced heavy criticisms for his 'senatorial filibustering.' It was argued that a non-elected Senate had no right to block legislation passed by a democratically elected House of Commons. His reply to those criticisms was that the issue was so fundamental that elected officials had to 'let the people decide' (Wadell, 1988, cited in Johnston *et al.*: 3). After tumultuous debates in the House of Commons regarding the Senate's opposition, Turner's wish was granted: the Parliament was dissolved on October 1, 1988 and general elections ensued.

Did Turner's political gamble throw a wrench in Mulroney's electoral strategic plans? It may have changed the order of things, but it did not change the overall Conservative strategy. Mulroney had hoped to go before the electorate riding on the crest of an implemented FTA, but he would now have to convince the electorate of the beneficial impacts of the FTA. The Senate's filibustering also demonstrate an important disposition of the Canadian polity. Despite its lack of legitimate appeal, the Upper House can forestall policies if a majority of its members perceive that a large segment of the public oppose these policies. Constitutionally, the Canadian Senate has a similar veto power over legislation to its American counterpart. Practically, despite its occasional bouts with the House of Commons, the Senate gives the rubber stamp to legislation originating from the Lower House. It is only for salient pieces of legislation, for those issues – such as the FTA or the Goods and Services Tax (GST) – that question the intrinsic nature of the Canadian identity, that the Senate pursues its prerogatives to the fullest extent of the Canadian constitutional law. As such, Turner's gamble is a revelation of entrenched national resistance to the pursuit of free trade with the United States. In contrast, the American Senate routinely voices support or opposition to policies advocated by other branches of government. While in the United States the FTA was seen as a strict business enterprise, in Canada the ratification of the FTA depended on the break down of a largely popular innate resistance to American economic and cultural invasion of the country.[36]

This begs another question. Why did Brian Mulroney, in the face of significant opposition, shift from a staunch resistance to free trade during the Conservative leadership race in 1983 to an unconditional embrace of the same issue less than a year later? Numerous explanations have been provided for Mulroney's change of heart regarding his country's economic relationship with the United States. It is not our intention to present a lengthy literature review in this short chapter.[37] However, on the basis of those contending explanations, we argue that Mulroney's decision to shift to an increase economic relationship with the United States stems from an electoral calculus, his party's tight dealings with Canadian business, and fear of American trade retaliation.

Despite a landslide electoral victory in 1984, there was room for concerns regarding the next election. Could the Conservatives maintain a stronghold on Ontario's vote where they obtained a plurality of seats for the first time since 1958 or was it simply an accident of history? If the 1958 election was any indication, it demonstrated that the Conservatives could not count on long-term support from Ontario's voters. Their electoral support quickly eroded in the 1962 elections and the Liberal party regained the sympathy of the Ontario electorate. The Liberals would then gain electoral supremacy in five out the next seven elections. Same scenario in Québec: Since 1945, the *Belle Province's* electorate has favored the Conservatives only in 1958 and 1984. In contrast, since 1958, Western Canada had always given an overwhelming support to the Conservatives.

Therefore, Mulroney's strategists had to devise a strategy that would satisfy his party's loyal base in Western Canada, while gaining support in Ontario and/or Québec. The key was to find an issue that would unify either Ontario or Québec with Western Canada. Mulroney also had his hands tied by an electoral promise to the citizens of Québec. He would rectify the affront of 1982 when a Liberal government patriated the Canadian Constitution without the consent of Québec's elected leaders. In practical terms, it meant a series of constitutional discussions between the federal government and the provinces, which goals were to satisfy Québec's demands and bring it back in the constitutional family.

According to Lustzig (1996) and Doern and Tomlin (1991) this explains why Mulroney reverted to the free trade strategy to construct a new winning electoral coalition based on support from Québec and Western Canada. Despite Canada's regional political division, Mulroney may have calculated that he could obtain Western Canada's support for Québec constitutional demands in exchange for side-payments for Western Canada. These side-payments came in the form of 'the deregulation of energy and foreign investment, the creation of a Western Development Fund to help diversify the western economy, and the free trade agreement' (Lusztig, 1996: 78).

Mulroney may have also correctly read the mood of manufacturing and financial entrepreneurs in Québec. Doern and Tomlin (1991) note that despite a substantial share of inefficient Canadian industries in Québec, a new breed of political entrepreneurs in the province would welcome increase international competition and the prospect of a better access to the large American market. Despite initial reluctance, the government of Québec would also follow in its business sector's footsteps.

The United States' Road to the Free Trade Agreement

When President Reagan notified Congress on December 10, 1985, of his intent to negotiate a free trade agreement with Canada. Reagan wanted to reduce a host of tariff barriers between the United States and Canada, with particular emphasis on government procurement practices, air transportation, energy trade, intellectual property rights, and trade in high tech goods. Although the FTA was widely believed to be beneficial to the United States economy, several members of Congress expressed concerns about the potential adverse effects the agreement would have on particular producers in the United States. In fact, members on the Finance Committee expressed their concerns about the adverse effects of liberalization on a variety of import-competing industries, and threatened to reject Reagan's request for Fast Track authority.[38] In particular concerns over adverse effects to the lumber industries and domestic energy industries were highlighted. Thus, the first stage in negotiating the agreement required the Reagan administration to broker several concessions to win pivotal votes. For example, Senator Steven Symms (Republican from Idaho) and Senator Packwood (Republican from Oregon) concerned about the influence of a

FTA on lumber industries in their districts, secured a pledge from the Reagan administration to resolve the lumber dispute (O'Halloran, 1994). Nonetheless, on April 23, 1986, the Senate Finance Committee rejected a resolution of disapproval by a 10-10 vote. The tie granted permission to the White House to begin trade talks with Canada under fast track procedures.

The next step involved in negotiating the FTA required the administration to consult Congress, relevant advisory committees, and special interests in a series of meetings and public hearings. During this period, numerous issues sensitive to domestic interests were discussed in a variety of hearings held before the Senate Finance Committee. Many of the concerns raised by Congress and private sector advisory committees were addressed in the agreement signed by President Reagan and Prime Minister Mulroney on January 2, 1988.

The next step toward ratification of the FTA required the drafting of the implementing legislation. This necessitated agreement between the Senate and Finance Committee and the House Ways and Means committee on the language contained in the FTA. Public hearings (also referred to as non-markup sessions) were held to reconcile differences in the versions of the FTA in the House and Senate. During these non-markup sessions, numerous provisions were introduced to placate constituent interests. One of the most notable provisions was a request by Senators Danforth and Baucus of the Finance Committee. Later referred to as the Danforth-Baucus amendment, this provision requested a subsidy to protect nonferrous metals producers. Later it was extended to other industries faced with similar difficulties such as coal producers and wheat farmers.[39]

In general, Congress sought to compensate constituents and special interests injured by more open import competition. For example, prior to the vote to ratify the agreement Congress repealed the windfall profits tax on oil to compensate oil producers for increased competition from low-priced Canadian oil and crude imports. In addition, the FTA created and expanded existing export enhancement programs designed to aid U.S. producers in their efforts to compete in foreign markets. Moreover, to appease the U.S. lumber industry, which was faced with rising competition from Canadian lumber imports, Congress extended the Agricultural Export Credit Program to include wood products. Thus, prior to passing the implementing legislation, signifying support for the ratification of the free trade agreement, many constituency demands are taken into account. This is precisely why ratification of free trade agreements in the United States is complex.

After the House and Senate committees informally approved of the bill, the President formally introduced the implementing legislation to Congress. Technically the president is not bound by the compromises negotiated during the non-mark-up session. However, because he needs the support of both chambers in Congress, it is unlikely that the president would reverse the committee's recommendations. If he did, he would encounter opposition during the ratification. Therefore to win support for the final legislation, the president often accedes to protectionist demands. On August 9, 1988, the House passed the FTA by a vote of 366 to 40. In early September, The Senate passed the implementing legislation with a vote of 83 to 9 in favor of the agreement. Finally, on September 28, 1988, President Reagan signed the bill implementing CUSFTA.

Conclusion

The goal of this chapter was to demonstrate that the ratification of the FTA was more likely to occur in Canada rather than in the United States, despite institutional arrangements more supportive of trade liberalization in the latter country. The long tradition of protectionism in Canada was rapidly overhauled by a strong desire by the Prime Minister of Canada to foster a new electoral alignment comprising districts from Western Canada and Québec. Political institutions that permit strong party discipline and an important backing by influential business associations allowed Brian Mulroney to propose a new continental vision to his American counterpart. On the other side of the 45th parallel a tough battle awaited President Reagan. In contrast to many Canadian nationalists, a majority of Americans was little interested in the issue of mutual trade liberalization with Canada. However, those in the American business community who believed that Congress was playing a high stake poker game and opposed the agreement perfected the art of lobbying. They were able to take advantage of an electoral system that favors candidates' reputation over party identification. Consequently, even with the Fast Track authority and pro-trade biases in Washington, the ratification of the FTA was not a preordained conclusion.

As our discussion shows, understanding the causes for the formation free trade areas is a difficult task. In the case at hand, we see that different motivations have led to similar outcomes. We have chosen to explain such phenomena by focusing on the preferences of national policymakers and interest groups, and how they are constrained by domestic institutions. More importantly, similar to Mansfield and Milner (1999), we focused our explanation on the interaction of societal and institutional factors in trying to explain why state leaders pursue and ratify free trade agreements. More empirical work needs to be done to conclude with authority, but our study demonstrate that the ratification of a free trade agreement is still possible even if historical trade policies are more conducive to mercantilist guiding principles. The issue is confounded by constitutional arrangements that allows for strong party discipline and, consequently, permits swift policy swings. Conversely, embedded preferences encouraging trade liberalization do not necessarily lead to the expansion of free trade areas. Societal interests that manifest distributive politics and logrolling may impede the march towards liberal trade arrangements.

Notes

[1] In this chapter, international cooperation is defined as the successful domestic ratification of an international free trade agreement among contracting member states.

[2] In particular, (1) the number of political actors with the power to veto policies, (2) the ideological polarization of veto players, and (3) the level of cohesion among collective veto players are three factors which influence the probability of policy change.

[3] This is especially the case when veto players are ideologically polarized and there is a lack of cohesion among collective veto players (Tsebelis, 1995).

[4] Other scholars have also expounded upon this tension. For example see Reed (1994), McCubbins and Rosenbluth (1994), Ames (1992), Cox (1987), and Fiorina (1977).

[5] Carey and Shugart (1995) derive a general model of electoral formulas that rank order the incentives of politicians to cultivate a personal vote that encompasses all existing electoral systems.

[6] For example, Myerson (1993) develops a model that compares how variable electoral systems produce incentives for candidates to cultivate favored minority groups in their districts.

[7] Implicitly, this logic also implies that a state's configuration of electoral institutions also have implications for the strategies that special interests groups adopt to exert influence on legislative behavior. And these strategies should vary according to a candidate's incentives to campaign on a personal rather than a party reputation. For example, in candidate centered structures (weak party discipline), special interests will seek to influence individual candidates directly, while party centered structures (strong party) special interests will seek to acquire access and influence through party organizations. Thus, a politician's decision is in some sense, endogenously determined by the electoral structures of the state. It is logical to assume that the electoral structures of a state will govern campaign finance rules, and that these provisions will induce candidates to adopt particular strategies (e.g. incentives to cultivate the personal reputation over the party or vice versa).

[8] For a complete review of American and Canadian respective trade polices see GATT (1989; 1990).

[9] This explains why the FTA between Canada and the United States required implementing legislation in Canada. In order to ensure ratification, Parliament had to amend some 28 statutes. We are thankful to Michael Hart for pointing that out to us.

[10] Herein lies the root of Western Canada's feeling of alienation towards Central Canada.

[11] Sir John A. Macdonald is the first Prime Minister of Canada (1867-74 and 1878-91) and was leader of the Conservative Party.

[12] The Third Option Policy was made public in an essay written by then External Affairs minister Mitchell Sharp (1972). It came in reaction to the famous 'Nixon measures,' in 1971 when the United States acted unilaterally to cut imports by imposing a 10% surcharge on imported goods, and refused to grant Canada an exemption. In his essay, Sharp claimed that his government had three options: 1) Drift progressively towards greater degrees of dependence on the United States; 2) Promote Canada-U.S. economic integration and seek special treatment; and 3) Diversify Canada's economy and trade away from the United States by increasing contacts with European governments and Japan. As its name indicates, the policy chosen by the Liberal government was the third one. Interestingly, Mulroney later pursued the second option.

[13] The liberal government of William Lyon Mckenzie King negotiated a secret trade initiative with the U.S. but abandoned it because of fear of public scrutiny and a lack of support (Lusztig, 1996; Doern and Tomlin, 1991).

[14] Canadians initiated the discussions and, after initial reservations, American representatives endorsed the Canadian proposal. These initial discussions never came to fruition before the Conservative government was elected in September 1984. For more details see Doern and Tomlin (1991: 15-30) and Smith (1984).

[15] We discuss Mulroney's decision to pursue the FTA with the United States further in this chapter.

[16] For example, the very protectionist Smoot-Hawley Act of 1930 was instigated and passed by the Republicans, while the1934 Reciprocal Trade Agreements Act, often attributed by scholars as institutionalizing trade liberalization in the United States (Bailey, Goldstein and Weingast, 1997; Gilligan, 1997), was passed by the Democrats.

[17] In addition, as Bailey, Goldstein and Weingast (1997) convincingly demonstrate, liberalization was easier to secure because the threshold of political support needed for members of Congress to approve executive tariff-reduction on free trade agreements had been substantially reduced. Prior to the 1934 RTAA a foreign trade agreement, similar to a treaty, required approval by two-thirds of the Senate. Under the RTAA they only required a simple majority in Congress. In effect, protectionist interests would have to muster greater support to block tariff reduction measures.

[18] Cries of protectionism (Destler, 1995) began to be heard in the early 1970's. The rise of protectionism corresponded with a decline in US growth that naturally occurred as Europe and Japan recovered from WWII. In addition, the NIC's later stepped up their development (Bhagwati and Patrick, 1990) and increased the level of international competition for the production of industrial goods.

[19] Despite a dearth of studies on party dissent in Canada, specialists talk with a united voice on the subject. A consensus emerges indicating that on important votes, such as the FTA vote, there exists a negligible number of Members of Parliaments (MPs) voting against the party line. Even on 'free votes' where MPs are allowed to vote according to their conscience or the will of their respective constituency, a large degree of party discipline still exists. For more details see Kam (1998), Overby, Tatalovich, and Studlar (1998), and Wearing (1998).

[20] Donald Savoie (1999) makes a similar argument by indicating that political power in Canada is concentrated in the hands of the Prime Minister and few close advisors.

[21] With the caveat of an unswerving commitment to a social-democratic ideology by the New Democratic party. Yet, members of the NDP are much more open to American investors than were their forebears in the Commonwealth Cooperative Federation (CCF). The CCF was disbanded in 1958 after a disastrous electoral performance and resurrected under the NDP logo in 1961.

[22] The Conservative Party, often referred to as the Liberal-Conservative Party, became the Progressive Conservative Party in 1942 when it joined forces with the Progressive Party.

[23] As suggested by Clarke and his colleagues (1991) the opportunistic nature of the Canadian brokerage system is not limited to trade: 'Canadian brokerage parties differ in several ways from those in most other advanced industrial societies. Rather than having well-defined support from one election to the next based on long-term loyalties of social groups, brokerage parties re-create coalitions at each election […]. Rather than following through on the logic of stances adopted in the past, brokerage parties practise [sic] inconsistency as they search for electorally successful formulae' (pp. 9-10).

[24] This issue is well documented in Doern and Tomlin (1991), especially chapter 5.

[25] In contrast to the American experience, very rarely will interest groups in Canada lobby individual members of parliament. This adds to our contention that the locus of power resides in the hands of Cabinet members. For more on the topic of interest groups representation in Canada, see Paul Pross' (1992) seminal study.

[26] Logically it is plausible to assume that parochial pressures have variable influence on members of the House and Senate because of the difference in the geographical size of the districts they represent. As Senators represent larger geographical constituencies, they may be less susceptible to concentrated parochial interests than members of Congress that represent smaller districts. However, recent studies on trade votes in the Senate indicate that Senators are susceptible to parochial interests such as unions and export interests (Bailey and Brady, 1998).

[27] To be precise, ex ante opportunities include (1) the initial vote over fast track procedures, (2) congressional monitoring and advice, (3) consultations with executive departments, (4) private sector advisory committees and, (5) public hearings. Ex post opportunities include non mark-up sessions (e.g. drafting of implementing legislation), and (2)congressional approval procedures. Thus, Congress has considerable input into the decision making process. For an excellent discussion of these opportunities see O'Halloran (1994).

[28] Tomlin adds that at the beginning of 1981, Canada's under-secretary for external affairs published an article exalting the merits of the Third Option. For the original article see Gotlieb and Kinsman (1981).

[29] In fact, the official date of the ratification is December 24th since the vote was taken well after midnight.

[30] The official result was 141 votes in favor of the agreement, all from the Conservative Party and 111 against, all from the Liberal and New Democratic Party. Forty-three Members of Parliament (MP's) were not present for the vote.

[31] In a landslide election where Mulroney's party obtained 211 out of 282 seats, the PC accumulated a majority of ridings (electoral districts) in all regions of Canada.

[32] Generally speaking, because of a small number of seats available in the Atlantic region (New Brunswick, Nova Scotia, Prince-Edward Island, and Newfoundland), electoral strategists give a short shrift to this region to the benefits of other regions.

[33] That strategy meant that Mulroney would seek to bring Québec back in the "constitutional family" and grant Western Canada's age long pursuit of freer trade with the United States. For a fascinating account of Mulroney's gamble see Lusztig (1996), chapter 4.

[34] In Canada, before a bill becomes law, it must go through three readings and committee scrutiny in both Houses.

[35] Joe Clark's short-lived Conservative government in 1979 constitutes the exception.

[36] This resistance came especially from an intellectual elite. Public opinion on the issue was favorable until a concrete proposal for the FTA was put on the table. Gallup polls indicate that from 1953 until 1984, a little over 50% of respondents believed that Canada would be better off 'if U.S. goods were allowed in [Canada] without tariff or customs charges, and Canadian goods were allowed in the U.S. free' (Clarke et al., 1996: 34). Interestingly, when Mulroney announced his willingness to explore a new reciprocal arrangement on trade with Washington, popular support for the issue started to dwindle.

[37] For a brief overview, the reader should consult Lusztig (1996, 73-76).

[38] The Senate Finance Committee is responsible for drafting up a disapproval resolution, which would effectively veto the executive's authority to negotiate a treaty with another state.

[39] Canadian trade representatives protested the inclusion of the Danforth and Bancus Amendment because they argued that it unilaterally singled out Canada from other countries engaged in similar trade with the United States. The amendment was generalized to trade with other states as part of a compromise.

References

Ames, B. (1992), 'Desperately Seeking Politicians: Strategies and Outcomes in Brazilian Legislative Elections', Paper presented at the Conference of the Latin American Studies Association, Los Angeles.

Bailey, M. and Brady, D. (1998), 'Heterogeneity and Representation: The Senate and Free Trade', *American Journal of Political Science*, vol. 42, no. 2, pp. 524-44.

Bailey, M., Goldstein, J., and Weingast, B. (1997), 'The Institutional Roots of American Trade Policy: Politics, Coalitions, and International Trade', *World Politics*, vol. 49, no. 3, pp. 309-38.

Bennett, S.L. and Smith, R.M. (1999a), 'Representation and Salient Issues: Legislator Responsiveness to the Service Constituency', Paper presented at the 1999 American Political Science Association Meetings in Atlanta, Georgia.

Bennett, S.L. and Smith, R.M.(1999b), 'Domestic Constraints on U.S. Trade', Unpublished manuscript, Rice University.

Bhagwati, J., and Patrick, H.T. (1990), *Aggressive Unilateralism: America's 301 Trade Policy and the World Trading System*, University of Michigan Press, Ann Arbor.

Cain, B., Ferejohn, J., and Fiorina, M. (1987), *The Personal Vote: Constituency Service and Electoral Independence*, Harvard University Press, Cambridge, MA.

Carey, J.M., and Shugart, M.S. (1995), 'Incentives to Cultivate a Personal Vote: A Rank Ordering of Electoral Formulas', *Electoral Studies*, vol. 14, no. 4, pp. 417-39.

Christian, W., and Campbell, C. (1990), *Political Parties and Ideologies in Canada*, 3rd ed., McGraw-Hill Ryerson, Toronto.

Clarke, H.D., Jenson, J., Le Duc, L., and Pammett, J.H. (1996), *Absent Mandate: Canadian Electoral Politics in an Era of Restructuring*, 3rd ed., Gage Educational Publishing, Toronto.

Clarke, H.D., Jenson, J., Le Duc, L., and Pammett, J.H. (1991), *Absent Mandate: Interpreting Change in Canadian Elections*, 2nd ed., Gage Educational Publishing, Toronto.

Clarkson, S. (1985), 'Canada-U.S. Relations and the Changing of the Guard in Ottawa', in B. Tomlin and M. Appel Molot, (eds), *Canada Among Nations, 1984: A Time of Transition*, Lorimer, Toronto.

Clarkson, S. (1982), *Canada and the Reagan Challenge: Crisis in the Canadian-American Relationship*, Lorimer, Toronto.

Conybeare, J. (1991), 'Voting for Protection: An Electoral Model of Tariff Policy', *International Organization*, vol.45, no. 1, pp.57-79.

Cox, G.W. (1987), *The Efficient Secret*, Cambridge University Press, Cambridge, MA.

Cox, G.W. and McCubbins, M. (1993), *Legislative Leviathan*, University of California Press, Berkeley.

Dawson, R.M. (1963), *The Government of Canada*, 4th ed., University of Toronto Press, Toronto.

Destler, I.M. (1995), *American Trade Politics*, 3rd ed., Institute for International Economics, Washington, DC.

Doern, G.B., and Tomlin, B.W. (1991), *Faith & Fear: The Free Trade Story*, Stoddart, Toronto.

Fenno, R.F. (1978), *Home Style: House Members in Their Districts*, Little, Brown, Boston.

Fiorina, M. (1977), *Congress, Keystone of the Washington Establishment*, Yale University Press, New Haven.

GATT (1990), *Trade Policy Review. Canada*, General Agreements on Tariffs and Trade, Geneva.

GATT (1989), *Trade Policy Review. United States of America*, General Agreements on Tariffs and Trade, Geneva.

Gilligan, M.J. (1997), *Empowering Exporters: Reciprocity, Delegation, and Collective Action in American Trade Policy*, University of Michigan Press, Ann Arbor.

Gotlieb, A., and Kinsman, J. (1981), 'Reviving the Third Option', *International Perspectives*, January/February.

Haggard, S. (1988), 'The Institutional Foundations of Hegemony: Explaining the Reciprocal Trade Agreements Act of 1934', *International Organization*, vol.42, pp.91-119.

Hall, P. (1986), *Governing the Economy: The Politics of State Intervention in Britain and France*, Blackwell, New York.

Hartz, L. (1964), *The Founding of New Societies*, Harcourt, Brace and World, New York.

Hillman, A. and Moser, P. (1996), 'Trade Liberalization as Politically Optimal Exchange of Market Access', in M. Canzoneri, W. Ethier, and V. Grilli (eds), *The New Transatlantic Economy*, Cambridge University Press, New York.

Horowitz, G. (1978), 'Notes on Conservatism, Liberalism and Socialism in Canada', *Canadian Journal of Political Science*, June, pp. 383-99.

Horowitz, G. (1966), 'Conservatism, Liberalism and Socialism in Canada: An Interpretation', *Canadian Journal of Economics and Political Science*, May, pp. 143-71.

Irwin, D.A. and Kroszner, R.S. (1999), 'Interests, Institutions, and Ideology in Securing Policy Change: The Republican Conversion to Trade Liberalization after Smoot-Hawley', *Journal of Law and Economics*, forthcoming.

Jacobson, G.C. (1990), *The Electoral Origins of Divided Government: Competition in the U.S. House Elections, 1946-1988*, Westview Press, Boulder, CO.

Johnston, R., Blais, A., Brady, H.E., and Crete, J. (1992), *Letting the People Decide: Dynamics of a Canadian Election*, Stanford University Press, Stanford.

Kam, C. (1998), 'Backbench Dissent in Westminster Parliaments, 1945-1997: A Cross-National Approach', Unpublished manuscript.

Keech, W.R. and Pak, K. (1995), 'Partisanship, Institutions, and Change in American Trade Politics', *Journal of Politics*, vol.57, no. 4 pp. 1130-1142.

Krueger, A. (1990), 'Asymmetries in Policy Between Exportable and Import-Competing Goods', in R.W. Jones and A.O. Krueger (eds), *The Political Economy of International Trade*, Basil Blackwell, Cambridge, MA.

Lijphart, A. (ed) (1992), *Parliamentary versus Presidential Government*, Oxford University Press, New York.

Lohmann, S. (1998), 'An Information Rationale for the Power of Special Interests', *American Political Science Review*, vol. 92, no. 4, pp. 809-27.

Lusztig, M. (1996), *Risking Free Trade: The Politics of Trade in Britain, Canada, Mexico, and the United States*, University of Pittsburgh Press, Pittsburgh.

Mainwaring, S. (1991), 'Politicians, Parties, and Electoral Systems: Brazil in Comparative Perspective', *Comparative Politics*, vol. 24, no. 1, pp. 21-43.

Mallory, J.R. (1971), *The Structure of Canadian Government*, Macmillan, Toronto.

Mansfield, E.D. and Milner, H.V. (1999), 'The New Wave of Regionalism', *International Organization*, vol. 53, no. 3, pp. 589-27.

Mayhew, D.R. (1974), *Congress: The Electoral Connection*, Yale University Press, New Haven, CT.

McCubbins, M.D. and Rosenbluth, F.M. (1994), 'Party Provision for Personal Politics: Dividing the Votes in Japan', in P. Cowhey and M. D. McCubbins (eds), *Structure and Policy in Japan and the United States*, Cambridge University Press, New York.

Milner, H.V. (1997), *Interests, Institutions, and Information: Domestic Politics and International Relations*, Princeton University Press, Princeton.

Myerson, R. (1993), 'Incentives to Cultivate Favored Minorities under Alternative Electoral Systems', *American Political Science Review*, vol. 87, no. 4, pp. 856-69.

O'Halloran, S. (1994), *Politics, Process, and American Trade Policy*, University of Michigan Press, Ann Arbor.

Olson, M. (1968), *The Logic of Collective Action*, Schocken, New York.

Overby, L.M., Tatalovich, R. and Studlar, D.T. (1998), 'Party and Free Votes in Canada: Abortion in the House of Commons', *Party Politics*, vol. 4, no. 3, pp. 381-92.

Pross, A.P. (1992), *Group Politics and Public Policy*, 2nd ed., Oxford University Press, Toronto.

Rae, D.W. (1971), *The Political Consequences of Electoral Laws*, Yale University Press, New Haven, CT.

Reed, S.R. (1994), 'Democracy and the Personal Vote: A Cautionary Tale of Japan', *Electoral Studies*, vol. 13, no. 1, pp. 17-28.

Savoie, D. (1999), *Governing from the Centre: The Concentration of Power in Canadian Politics*, University of Toronto Press, Buffalo.

Schneitz, K. (1998), 'The Institutional Foundations of U.S. Trade Policy: Revisiting Explanations for the 1934 Reciprocal Trade Agreements Act', Unpublished manuscript, Rice University.

Sharp, M. (1972), 'Canada-U.S. Relations: Options for the Future', special issue of *International Perspectives*, Department of External Affairs, Ottawa.

Shepsle, K. and Weingast, B. (1994), 'Positive Theories of Congressional Institutions', *Legislative Studies Quarterly*, vol. 19, pp.149-179.

Smith, M., 1984, 'Sectoral Free Trade with Canada', *International Perspectives*, May/June.

Steinmo, S. (1993), *Taxation and Democracy : Swedish, British, and American Approaches to Financing the Modern State*, Yale University Press, New Haven, CT.

Steinmo, S. (1989), 'Political Institutions and Tax Policy in the United States, Sweden, and Britain', *World Politics*, vol. 41, no. 4, pp. 500-535.

Steinmo, S., Thelen, K., and Longstreth, F. (eds) (1992), *Structuring Politics : Historical Institutionalism in Comparative Analysis*, Cambridge University Press, New York.

Stewart, C. and Weingast, B. (1992), 'Stacking the Senate, Changing the Nation: Republican Rotten Boroughs, Statehood Politics, and American Political Development', *Studies in American Political Development*, vol.6, pp. 223-71.

Taagepera, R., and Shugart, M.S. (1989), *Seats and Votes: The Effects and Determinants of Electoral Systems*, Yale University Press, New Haven, CT.

Tsebelis, G. (1995), 'Decision Making in Political Systems: Veto Players in Presidentialism, Parliamentarism, Multicameralism and Multipartyism', *British Journal of Political Science*, vol. 25, no. 3, pp. 289-326.

Tsebelis, G., and Money, J., 1997, *Bicameralism*, Cambridge University Press, New York.

Waddell, C. (1988), 'Block Free Trade Bill, Turner Tells Senate: Liberal Leader Seeking to Force Election', *Globe and Mail*, 21 July, p. A1.

Wearing, J. (1998), 'Guns, Gays, and Gadflies: Party Dissent in the House of Commons Under Mulroney and Chrétien', Paper presented at the Annual Meeting of the Canadian Political Science Association, University of Ottawa, May/June.

Weaver, R.K. and Rockman, B.A. (eds) (1993), *Do Institutions Matter? Government Capabilities in the United States and Abroad*, The Brookings Institution, Washington, D.C.

Weingast, B.R., Shepsle, K.A. and Johnson, C. (1981), 'The Political Economy of Benefits and Costs: A Neoclassical Approach to Distributive Politics', *Journal of Political Economy*, vol.89, pp. 642-664.

Winn, C. and McMenemy, J. (1976), *Political Parties in Canada*, McGraw-Hill Ryerson, Toronto.

8 Negotiating with Goliath: Cross-national and Cross-level Interactions in NAFTA's Auto and Textile Sectors

DAVID A. LYNCH

Introduction

Like David and Goliath, the fights emerging from the NAFTA negotiations between the giant US and its weaker neighbors hardly seem fair.[1] International relations theories stressing the importance of the distribution of power in determining international outcomes suggest that Goliath will win handily. Yet, like David, Canada and Mexico fared quite well in the negotiations in some economic sectors. In other sectors, Goliath prevailed with few concessions. This calls into question explanatory power of the distribution of power in international negotiations and suggests that others level of analysis needs to be examined. This is not revolutionary. Theorists have long contended that relying primarily on one level of analysis is shortsighted and adding complexity to explain international interactions is necessary. The larger question, however, is how factors at the international and domestic levels of analysis interact.

This chapter uses Robert Putnam's two-level game metaphor to examine the auto and textile and apparel negotiations and explain how the domestic and international levels of analysis interacted in the NAFTA negotiations (Putnam, 1988).[2] More specifically, the chapter will examine two themes. First, how could Canada and Mexico at times turn back the stronger US? In what situations can weaker nations prevail against stronger nations in international negotiations? Or when can weaker nations at least avoid being overwhelmed by the stronger nation? Second, the chapter will examine cross-border and cross-level of analysis strategies and alliances employed by NAFTA actors. How and why did governments and interest groups reach across borders in an attempt to shape the negotiated outcome? Are these dynamics different in trade blocs than in other international negotiations and if so, how?

This chapter finds two explanations for the first theme - how the weaker NAFTA partners were sometimes able to overcome their relative power dearth. The first explanation focuses on the interaction of Canadian and Mexican strategies and goals with those of important US interest groups. The second answer to how the weaker nations could prevail can be found in the institutional arrangements among the NAFTA nations in each economic sector as they entered into negotiations.

One obvious observation about the NAFTA negotiations is the immense asymmetry of power between the US and its much weaker neighbors to the north and south. Realist approaches to international relations suggest that the stronger US would be able to impose its will upon its weaker negotiating partners. The US did indeed fare well in the negotiations. Despite the asymmetry of power, the weaker NAFTA partners were not merely steamrolled in the talks by the US giant. On some issues Canada and Mexico fared quite well. Not surprisingly, their success in the talks varied from economic sector to economic sector. This is theoretically useful because if facilitates exploration of the factors that account for these divergent fortunes. For instance, Canada fared far better in the auto sector than it did in the textile and apparel sector. While the Canadian David did not slay the US Goliath in the auto sector, it did indeed inflict some injury. What accounts for those instances when David (or Davids) can at least injure Goliath?

This chapter finds that a weaker nation can sometimes fare well against a stronger nation by tailoring its strategies to the preferences of the most powerful interest groups within the stronger nation. This, of course, is not always a viable option; the weaker nation's interests may collide with those of the important domestic groups within the stronger nation. Nevertheless, precious political clout can be saved for battles in which there is the possibility for success.

This chapter also finds that the ability of a weaker nation to fare well in trade negotiations with a stronger nation depends upon the existing institutional arrangements between the nations in a given economic sector. More specifically, the ability of a weaker nation to stand credibly up to a stronger nation's demands depends upon whether existing trade institutions give the weaker nation favored access to the stronger nation's markets. If the existing trade institutions provide access to the stronger nation's markets, the smaller nation is afforded some shelter with which it can say 'no'.

The chapter's second focus is on cross-border and cross-level of analysis strategies and alliances (or, interchangeably, alignments) employed by all NAFTA actors, not just the two weaker nations relative to the US The chapter finds numerous cross-border and cross-level of analysis interactions often in unique situations. For instance, even the strongest of interest groups in the strongest nation employed cross-border and cross-level of analysis alliances, even when they could successfully shape the negotiated outcome without such arrangements. Instead of pushing openly for provisions that they wanted, these interest groups would sometimes allow foreign actors to push for the issue and then give these foreign actors 'concessions'. This nicely deflected domestic attention and criticism from their policy desires.

Another interesting cross-border alignment that emerges from the NAFTA auto and textile and apparel sector negotiations is *within* transnational corporations (TNCs) with significant production in all three NAFTA nations. The Big Three automakers, for instance, are the major auto producers in each of the NAFTA nations. US companies dominate the Mexican textile and apparel industry. DuPont, for instance, is a major investor in many Mexican textile producers. In essence, each of these corporations forms its own cross-border alliance. At many turns corporations headquartered in country A were able to get country A's negotiators to give ground to country B's negotiators in such a manner to benefit the corporation in country B. Unions have no such built-in alliance capability and were not able to create effective cross-border alliances in the course of the negotiations.

Are the dynamics of negotiation tactics different in trade bloc negotiations than in other international negotiations? There is some evidence to suggest that the dynamics in trade bloc negotiations are indeed different than either bilateral or multilateral negotiations. The differences between trade bloc negotiations and other international negotiations can be seen on a number of fronts.

The most basic difference is simple arithmetic: the number of negotiating nations differs and this alters negotiation dynamics. In bilateral negotiations, there is less room for cross-national alignments and side-payments by negotiators. For example, weaker nations cannot align together against more powerful nations because, by definition, there are only two nations involved in bilateral negotiations. Relative to bilateral negotiations, bloc negotiations offer greater potential for floating alignments. Negotiators from country A and B might oppose country C negotiators on one issue, but B and C negotiators might be aligned against A on another. Multilateral negotiations, like bloc negotiations, offer the possibility of many such alignments limited, of course, only by the number of countries in the bloc. In addition, the utility of such alignments and side-payments may be diminished by the uncertainty and complexity associated with so many actors in multilateral negotiations.

Another difference between trade bloc negotiations and other international negotiations is that relations among potential trade bloc nations are more apt to be characterized by interdependence than nations in multilateral negotiations. As we have seen in other chapters in this volume, trade blocs usually form through geographic proximity and intensity of interaction, which breeds the desire and need for greater regulatory edifices. Also, given the usual familiarity and interdependence found among trade bloc partners, negotiators, businesses, unions and other actors are more likely engage in cross-border tactical alignments, including alignments within transnational corporations. The payoffs to a trade bloc agreement are likely greater for domestic actors than in bilateral agreements and are more concrete than potential payoffs stemming from multinational agreements. Much of this stems from the high degree of interdependence likely among potential trade bloc nations.

For instance, in NAFTA Mexican President Carlos Salinas was able to link a very clear and important payoff to the Mexican textile and apparel industry (i.e. quota free access to the US) with an unpopular policy that he had long sought (i.e. greater liberalization of the Mexican textile and apparel industry). He could also entice the Mexican textile and apparel industry to take its medicine (great liberalization) by sweetening the deal with access to the US market. Without this important sugar to help the medicine go down – sugar delivered through a trade bloc – the Mexican textile and apparel industry would have fought taking Salinas' medicine. This is also an example of negotiators using the international level of trade bloc negotiations to gain support domestically for otherwise unpopular policies. The ability to use the international level in negotiations to manipulate domestic policy preferences is an important tool that governments have in creating independence from interest groups. Governments are not merely the sum of societal interests.

Another factor that makes trade blocs different than bilateral or multilateral settings is the tide of expectations they can create and the increased economic activity that is based on those expectations. In the years that NAFTA was proposed, negotiated and ratified, trade and investment among NAFTA nations shot up dramatically. This helped create greater pressure for a negotiated agreement and helped soothe fears about founding a formal trade bloc. Governments faced greater pressure to codify rules regarding the closer de facto integration. At the same time, trade and investment increases will tend to demonstrate the benefits of integration. In the NAFTA ratification debate, for instance, a trump card to counter fears of a 'giant sucking sound' as Ross Perot described the loss of US jobs moving to Mexico if NAFTA was passed, was the dramatically increasing export volume to Mexico in numerous economic sectors. This was certainly the case in the auto and textile and apparel sectors.

These factors will of course differ from trade bloc to trade bloc. In fact, they even differ within trade bloc negotiations: the US had very close economic ties with both Canada and Mexico, yet Canadian-Mexican ties were quite weak. Nevertheless, the expectations that NAFTA brought led to an increase in Canadian-Mexican trade, and actors in the two nations did form alignments to shape negotiated outcomes. The expectations in seriously proposed trade bloc negotiations thus are indeed different from multilateral negotiations.

The Two-Level Approach

To understand fully the logic behind cross-border and cross-level of analysis alignment strategies an understanding of Putnam's two-level approach is required.[3] A brief examination will illuminate how a weaker nation can successfully negotiate with a stronger nation and how cross-border government and non-government alignments and strategies develop.

The two-level game approach stresses that successful negotiations between two countries require three agreements.[4] The first agreement is across the negotiating table between negotiators from the different countries. The second and third agreements must be reached between negotiators and their domestic societal actors. Each negotiating team must get sufficient domestic support to ensure the agreement's ratification (either formal or informal ratification). The set of possible negotiation outcomes that generate a winning coalition for the agreement's ratification is called a win-set. The two-level approach therefore stresses the negotiator (or more specifically the Chief of Government, or COG) as the nexus of both international and domestic constraints and opportunities.[5] Negotiators must fashion an agreement acceptable to themselves, their foreign counterparts and to a winning coalition at home and abroad. To conceptualize negotiations as merely between 'nations' is misleading. Negotiations are not simply international events; instead they include complex cross-national and intra-national strategy.

With this in mind, it is easier to see how negotiators can use the opposite negotiator's domestic actors to achieve desired outcomes in negotiations. Instead of convincing the other nation's negotiators through international pressure or persuasion, a nation's negotiators may only have to convince important domestic actors within the other nation. The other nation's negotiators may be forced to be more compliant in the negotiations because of domestic pressure rather than from international pressure.

The two-level approach, like international power approaches, recommends studying the relative negotiating strength between countries. In the two-level approach lexicon this is the COGs' Level I strength. The two-level framework suggests that the strength of each COG within its domestic environment should also be evaluated. Evaluations at the domestic level, called Level II, should be directed toward the following questions: is the 'state' (or COG) strong relative to societal actors? In what manner and to what extent does the system of government (democracy or authoritarian, etc.) and state institutions (presidential or parliamentary, etc.) hamstring the COG's freedom of movement in negotiations? To what extent are societal actors cohesive or divided and over what issues? What are their policy preferences? Whether a state is strong or weak at Levels I and II is likely to influence what negotiating strategies will be employed and which are likely to be successful.

For instance, using the international distribution of power as an explanation for an international agreement outcome would suggest that the weaker nation would follow a 'dovish' negotiating strategy; that is, it would be likely to give ground to the more powerful nation ('cutting slack' in the two-level approach parlance). Conversely the more powerful country would likely follow a 'hawkish' strategy. The policies incorporated into an international agreement would likely be closer to the more powerful nation's policy preferences. But the two-level game logic suggests that merely knowing the distribution of power between given nations is not sufficient to explain and predict the nations' bargaining strategies and the agreement's general policy outcome. In the case of the weaker country, the two-level game logic indicates that the eventuality described by the international distribution of power explanation above (a dovish strategy for the weaker country, a hawkish strategy for the stronger country, and a policy outcome close to the powerful nation's preferences) will indeed come to pass if the COG of the internationally weak nation (Level I) is also strong relative to societal actors domestically (Level II). If, however, the COG of the internationally weaker nation is also weak at Level II, domestic constraints may prevent the COG from yielding ground internationally. This may actually strengthen the hand of the internationally weaker nation in the negotiations. The weaker nation's negotiators can in essence argue with credibility that their hands are tied. This 'tied hands strategy' suggests that the outcome of the international negotiations may be more favorable to the internationally weak nation than indicated by merely using an international distribution of power analysis.[6]

Successfully reaching a bilateral international agreement requires that the two-nations' win-sets and two COGs' acceptability-sets overlap. The COGs' unique position as the confluence of domestic and international forces affords a number of opportunities for the COGs to manipulate win-sets in both countries to reach an agreement favorable to them. There are numerous cross-border strategies that can be employed to manipulate another nation's negotiating position: positive or negative reverberation, synergistic linkages, and COG collusion are three possibilities.[7]

The incentive for COGs to manipulate win-sets at home and abroad can be ascertained following two-level game logic. A COG that is able to enlarge the opposite COG's domestic win-set broadens the set of outcomes that are acceptable to the domestic actors in the opposite country which may facilitate over-lap with its acceptability-set. Therefore, the COG in one country may make side-payments or threats to groups in the opposite nation in order to facilitate support for its positions in the opposite's domestic camp. Because the COG's actions may affect the opposite COG's domestic environment, they are termed 'reverberation'. Side-payments are called 'positive' reverberation and threats 'negative' reverberation; simple persuasion or assurance is called 'suasive' reverberation.'[8] Strengthening the opposite COG's hand relative to its domestic actors may also weaken the opposite COG's international bargaining position. As in the tied hands scenario outlined above (using domestic weakness to gain internationally), domestic constraints lead to a stronger international bargaining position for a nation. Conversely, the lack of domestic constraints will tend to weaken a COG's international bargaining position.[9]

Another tactic is 'COG collusion.' Each COG has an interest in the popularity of the other: a popular opposite COG in the opposite country is less constrained domestically and therefore will not be able to claim 'tied hands' with credibility. Each COG desires popularity at home as well, in order to help manipulate domestic win-sets toward its acceptability-set.

This may lead to 'COG collusion' whereby each uses the international negotiations to shore up their domestic popularity.

A COG can use international bargaining to alter its domestic win-set through the use of 'synergistic linkages.' A synergistic linkage is the linking of a 'losing' domestic policy (a policy that fails to generate a winning coalition domestically) with a 'winning' policy from the international negotiations so as to generate a winning coalition for the otherwise unpalatable policy. The key to successfully employing this strategy is that the winning policy be obtainable only through international negotiations and that the winning policy's success in the international game be dependent upon its linkage to the losing policy.

This can also be seen as the international extension of a practice commonly employed in the US Congress whereby programs or policies that might lose if standing alone are included within larger more popular measures in order to enhance the former's chances of passage. For instance, supporters of gun control successfully included an assault weapons ban into politically popular omnibus crime legislation in the summer of 1994. This structuring of the vote provided political cover for those who otherwise would be more leery of supporting such gun control measures.

These general negotiating strategies and the tactics employed to realize them involve interactions between the international and domestic levels of analysis and represent an advance in the theoretical debate over the levels of analysis. However, the two-level game approach is in its incipient stages. As one of the approach's leading studies puts it (Evans, 1993: 426):

> [There are] myriad leads to be followed up and numerous ambiguities to be resolved. They present themselves as a set of specific challenges to those interested in pushing ahead with the construction of an integrative approach. None of the propositions generated by the project are 'cut and dried'; all point to further inquiry; all offer scope for refinement and extension.

There have been applications of two-level game approach since this call to arms, but it remains accurate. One area ripe for examination is three party negotiations such as those found in NAFTA. This again raises the question whether trade bloc negotiation dynamics are different from other international negotiations.

Case Selection

The auto and textile and apparel sectors were the most contentious in the entire NAFTA talks. This is not surprising, since the industries are very important in terms of trade and employment. The auto industry accounts for more trade among the three NAFTA nations than any other. In the years before NAFTA, autos and auto parts accounted for approximately one-third of US-Canadian trade and over 15% of US-Mexican trade.[10] The textile and apparel industry also accounts for a significant portion of trade among the three nations. For the US and Mexico, much of this trade is comprised of the Mexican assembly plants called *maquiladoras* that dot the border region. The mostly US-owned *maquiladoras* produce garments from US textiles that are re-exported to the US market at low tariff rates. The controversial *maquiladoras* have large employment implications on both sides of the border. Given the size and importance of the sectors in all three nations, it was not surprising that they were the last to be agreed upon in NAFTA.

The two sectors are also among the most important in domestic US politics. They are both hugely important to the US economy and are politically well connected. The two industries have some of the most powerful interest groups on Capitol Hill. The American Automobile Manufactures Association (AAMA-autos) represents the Big Three automakers. These are among the world's largest companies and their clout reflects this. In the textile and apparel industry there are the twin trade groups: the American Apparel Manufacturers Association (AAMA-apparel) and the American Textile Manufacturers' Institute (ATMI). The latter is particularly powerful and is often seen as among the most powerful of interest groups in any issue area. All of these trade associations are strong based upon a number of indices: industry size, financial clout, reputation, expertise, and experience. The unions in both industries are also among the most powerful in the US The United Auto Workers (UAW), the Amalgamated Clothing and Textile Workers Union (ACTWU) and the International Ladies Garment Workers Union (ILGWU) are strong relative to many other unions, but have faced dwindling membership. Therefore, they clearly take a back seat to the industries' trade associations in political clout. The unions' remaining power, however, helps focus congressional attention on trade issues involving the sectors. This, combined with the strong trade associations, heightened the political significance of the sectors' NAFTA negotiations.

With these important interest groups, it is little wonder that some trade scholars believe the two industries to be exceptional. According to I.M. Destler, the auto and textile and apparel sectors are sufficiently powerful that they are exceptions to the US post-World War Two trade regime (Destler, 1995: 24-27). In that structure Congress delegates significant trade responsibilities to the executive branch in order to insulate itself from industry pressures for protectionism. Thus free trade can survive politically. But textiles and apparel, and to a lesser degree autos, are 'special cases.' Why? If they were exposed to the full winds of free trade, they could be sufficiently powerful to bring down the entire US liberal trade structure. Therefore they are often afforded greater trade protection than other industries.

In many regards the automotive and textile and apparel industry are similarly situated. They are both hugely important in economic and political terms. In both sectors the US has the disproportionate share of power, as will be explored below. Despite this, the negotiated outcomes in the two industries included some important differences. Canada fared better in autos than textiles and apparel in achieving its goals in the face of US resistance (Mexico's success was more even). The different negotiated outcomes, coupled with the industries being similarly situated, offer the potential for a better grasp of how less powerful nations can sometimes beat, or more accurately, hold back the more powerful.

Asymmetrical Power

Observers of US relations with Canada and Mexico invariably note the large power imbalance. This power imbalance has become ingrained in the public consciousness in both US neighbors. In Mexico there is the famous lament, 'poor Mexico! So far from God and so close to the United States.' A significant aspect of Canadian nationalism is the shared desire to avoid becoming the 51st state. While this underscores the overall inequality in these nations' relationships with the US, overall inequality is an inadequate guide to the distribution of power among the three nations as they negotiated NAFTA. US military power, to use an obvious example, was not brought to bear on the negotiations.

What areas of power were important to the negotiations? This chapter assumes that power was *not* fungible, even across different economic sectors in the negotiations. This is, of course, only partially accurate: it was the agreement as a whole that had to be signed and ratified. Nevertheless, the negotiations in each economic sector did, to a significant degree, stand alone. This was particularly the case in autos and textiles and apparel because these sectors were viewed as sufficiently important to warrant their own negotiating groups.

What then is the distribution of power among the NAFTA nations in the economic sectors in question? Here too, power is very asymmetrical. Finished vehicle production in the US is typically greater than ten million annually. This is five times greater than Canadian production of two million per year and ten times greater than Mexican production of roughly one million vehicles.[11] Market size is even more asymmetrical. Typically, 35% of Mexico's production is exported, leaving domestic consumption at some 650,000 vehicles (assuming a strong Mexican economy).[12] Much of this flows north to the US Canada is also able to produce more than it consumes in finished vehicles, and most of this goes to the US Despite production of ten million vehicles or more, the US is a net auto importer. Similar patterns exist for auto parts. Simply put, the US has the largest automotive market in the world and it dwarfs those of its NAFTA neighbors. Thus Canada and Mexico are more dependent upon the US market than the US is reliant upon the Canadian or Mexican markets.

A similar picture emerges in the textile and apparel sector. US production is far greater than Canadian or Mexican production. The US textile and apparel industries are roughly ten times that of Canada. The Canadian textile industry is particularly small. US production overshadows Mexican production both in size and in quality. Whereas a significant portion of the Mexican auto industry is quite competitive globally, much of Mexican textile and apparel production lags far behind world standards.

Again, US textile and apparel consumption dwarfs that of the other NAFTA nations. Canadian and Mexican producers are significantly more dependent upon the US market than US producers are upon their neighbors' markets. In 1991 the US received 86% of Canadian apparel exports. The figure for textiles was 64%.[13] The story is similar for Mexico where a significant portion of the Mexican apparel industry consists of *maquiladora* plants. In 1990 *maquiladoras* exports accounted for 90% of all Mexican apparel exports.[14]

Negotiation Results: Overview

In both sectors the negotiations went down to the wire. This is always true in negotiations to some degree, but nowhere in the NAFTA talks was this more the case than in autos and textiles and apparel. Which nations fared better in the two sectors' negotiations and under what circumstances?

There are a number of noteworthy observations regarding the relative success of the negotiating partners. These observations range from those regarding broad sector-wide results, such as the rules of origin, to observations regarding more narrowly focused outcomes with less far ranging repercussions.

In both sectors, the final provisions resembled US negotiators' preferences more closely than those of Canadian and Mexican negotiators. However, NAFTA was not merely a case of the US proposing and Canada and Mexico complying. The US did have to make significant concessions to the weaker NAFTA partners. The US fared better in the textile and apparel sector than in autos, especially relative to Canada. In autos, the Canadian David (and to a lesser degree Mexico) was able to turn back the US Goliath to a considerable degree. In textiles and apparel, the US won with fewer concessions. This opens the door for some theoretical exploration about how a less powerful nation might be able to negotiate successfully with a stronger nation.

Negotiation Results in Autos: David Injures Goliath

That the US had to make significant concessions to its weaker negotiating partners is best demonstrated in the auto sector. Here, the US sought tough rules of origin. The rules of origin determine whether products are to be classified as North American or non-North American under NAFTA and therefore whether they receive NAFTA's low and eventually tariff-free treatment. The US pressed for 65% North American content as the threshold that finished cars must obtain to be considered North American under NAFTA. This would be a considerable increase from the 50% threshold found in the US-Canadian Free Trade Agreement (CUSFTA). This 50% level was the goal of both Canada and Mexico. The US did quite well here, achieving 62.5% in the final NAFTA text, despite united opposition from its negotiating partners.

The US, however, had to cede significant ground to achieve this high threshold. Yes, the content level is the most important aspect of the rules of origin, but other components of the rules of origin are vitally important as well. Privately, US negotiators said that they were willing to give ground on other rules of origin issues, but needed a high content number to ensure NAFTA's passage in Congress: members of Congress might not understand the complex and arcane rules of origin provisions, but they certainly can understand a number.[15]

Thus, Canada and, to a lesser degree, Mexico were given a number of important concessions. First, the US agreed to a long phase-in period for the 62.5% level (eight years, from 1994 until 2002). Second, the Canadian and Mexican governments successfully achieved provisions that addressed a major concern they had regarding the high content level. Both were concerned that a high content level would scare away new foreign investment for auto assembly. Canada has traditionally served as a location for assembly of autos that are then exported to the US A significant portion of the Mexican auto industry is based on this same production strategy. In both nations this often includes more 'non-North American' inputs than found in US-assembled autos. To foreign investors this is precisely the attraction of Canadian and Mexican production: access to the lucrative US market without moving full production to North America. Ottawa and Mexico City reasoned that a high content level would favor US production, where parts production is more extensive. They therefore resisted agreeing to the high content requirement until they obtained a grace period for new investors. Even after the 62.5% is fully phased in for existing North American auto producers, new investors will enjoy a substantially lower content requirement- 50%- during the first five years of their new production.

Third, Canada would not agree to any rules of origin that would classify two controversial Canadian production facilities as non-North American. The US and Canada had a lingering dispute regarding whether two Canadian assembly plants- Honda and CAMI, the latter a General Motors and Suzuki joint investment- qualified for tariff-free treatment under the CUSFTA. Canada regarded these plants' production as North American under CUSFTA rules, but US officials calculated that the Honda and CAMI autos were not sufficiently North American to receive duty-free treatment. The US placed a tariff on the autos, causing a great deal of discord between the two nations. A prominent Canadian negotiator lamented that 'The Americans are bastards. They're behaving like real thugs these days in protecting their interests.'[16] In NAFTA, Canada successfully obtained special provisions ensuring that the Honda and CAMI production would qualify as North American despite NAFTA's higher content level.

Fourth, the Canadians successfully relaxed provisions stipulating which aspects of auto production would count toward the content level. The CUSFTA's 50% content level could be comprised only of the 'direct costs' of production while NAFTA's 62.5% can be comprised of 'net cost' activities such as research and development and interest paid on machinery investment.[17] This aspect of NAFTA's rules of origin makes it easier to meet a given content level than under the CUSFTA's rules.[18]

Thus the US got its way on the automotive content level, but had to cede important rules of origin ground to achieve this goal. These concessions to David (or Davids) lessened Goliath's victory significantly.

Negotiation Results in Textiles and Apparel: Goliath Unscathed

The US fared significantly better in the textile and apparel sector than in autos. In textiles and apparel the US got its way with fewer compromises. In this sector, instead of a content average, NAFTA's rules of origin require that certain production steps be taken within North America to ensure tariff-free treatment. To understand the debate a brief exploration of the textile and apparel production process is needed. First, the fibers must be created (natural fibers such as cotton are harvested or man-made fibers are 'formed'). Second, the fibers must be spun into yarn. Third, the yarn is woven or knitted into fabric (and finished with dyeing and the like). Fourth, the fabric is cut and sewn into a garment (or into nonclothing finished textile products such as auto interiors).

The question in NAFTA was, which of these processes must take place on North American soil to ensure a final product's classification as North American? The CUSFTA served as the status quo and therefore as the point of departure in the NAFTA talks. The CUSFTA's rules of origin stipulated a 'fabric forward' standard. This standard required that apparel had to be cut and sewn in North America (Canada or the US) with North American knit or woven fabric.

Canada's textile industry is much smaller than that of the US, and Canadian apparel producers often use high quality fabrics and yarns imported from Europe. Therefore, it was important to Canada that the CUSFTA allowed non-North America yarn in fabric. Compared to a tougher standard, this aided Canadian producers. Nevertheless, the CUSFTA standard required fabrics to be North American and would have effectively shut out a significant portion of Canadian apparel exports.

To cushion the negative impact this would have on Canadian exports to the US the CUSFTA allowed exceptions to this general rule of origin, called Tariff Preference Levels (TPLs).[19] The TPLs allowed specified levels of some otherwise non-North American products to be classified as North

American for tariff purposes. (These products still had to be cut and sewn in North America.)

The US, with its extensive and politically powerful textile industry, sought a stricter rule of origin in NAFTA – called 'yarn forward.' This would require that all the production steps except the first must take place on North American soil for a good to be considered North American. Thus, apparel items cut and sewn in North America with North American woven or knitted fabric, containing North American spun yarn would qualify as North American, whether or not the fibers were formed within North America.

Because of Canadian producers' tendency to use non-North American yarns and fabrics, Canada sought a rule of origin requiring only that apparel be cut and sewn in North America.[20] This, however, was a less rigorous rule of origin than found in the CUSFTA and was a non-starter with the US Canada, therefore, fought for a rule of origin similar to the CUSFTA's fabric forward; a standard that would still allow products with non-North American yarns to qualify as North American.

The negotiated outcome in NAFTA was very close to US desires. As a general rule, the US-supported yarn forward became the standard in NAFTA. This was a clear victory for the US There are significant deviations from this standard, but these too conform largely to US desires. At US insistence, many products must meet the more stringent 'fiber forward' rule, whereby all aspects of production must take place in North America for the final product to qualify as North American.

The TPL exceptions to the rule of origin also found their way into NAFTA. Importantly, the TPL levels are only slightly higher in NAFTA than they were in the CUSFTA. This is the case despite, or more accurately because, the TPLs in the CUSFTA were rapidly filling. In the CUSFTA, the US did not view the TPLs as a significant concession, at least in many categories. After all, in some of the TPL categories Canadian exports to the US were insignificant. But some Canadian producers viewed the TPLs as an opportunity to expand, and some did so quite successfully. The US therefore ensured that the TPLs would not increase significantly in NAFTA.

On the most important textile and apparel issue the US gave little ground. US negotiators fashioned a tight rule of origin against Canadian preferences. In both autos and textiles and apparel, the US was able to tighten the general rules of origin from the CUSFTA. However, textiles and apparel offer a clearer case of tightening: the general sector rule was tightened and most deviations from this rule were also tighter. In autos the content level is higher than in the CUSFTA, but there are many caveats that significantly dampen its impact. Goliath was substantially turned back in the auto sector, but not in textiles and apparel.

Negotiation Results and Narrow Issues: David and Goliath

There are some instances of victories by weaker nations on narrower issues than those explored above. The first example of one such victory on a less important issue came despite a less powerful nation being opposed by both the stronger nation and the other less powerful nation. Mexico successfully turned back both the US and Canada in one rules of origin issue. Averaging allows non-North American autos produced by a company to qualify as North American if averaged with other qualifying autos produced by that company, so long as the average exceeds the 62.5% threshold. The question was how wide should this averaging be? Should each car rolling off an assembly plant have to meet the 62.5%, or could autos within one plant be averaged together? Could a company average its production across an entire nation, or across the entire NAFTA region?

The US government, at the behest of the Big Three, pressed for nation-wide averaging. Why? The Big Three are the only automakers with extensive production in all three markets, therefore they would benefit from wide averaging. Canada also wanted wide averaging as a way to ensure that the Honda and CAMI production would qualify as North American. Thus Mexico faced a united front. Mexico, however, was very concerned that wide averaging would lead it to merely be an assembler of cars that had significant non-Mexican produced parts. To ensure that Mexico's future would entail full auto production, Mexico stood firm. The final NAFTA provisions allow only narrow averaging: companies can average across a model's production in a given nation. Mexico won the day on this issue. Canada was placated on the issue by being given a special provision for its Honda and CAMI production. The US was turned back. However, not all actors in the US were turned back on the issue. This special provision helped General Motors, which was the US partner in the CAMI joint venture. Not coincidentally, this helped General Motors support a higher content level in NAFTA than it would have without a special provision to include its CAMI production as North American. A side-payment to the Canadian COG was also a side-payment to a very important domestic US actor. This demonstrates the influence that corporations with significant operations in numerous trade bloc nations can have in negotiations and how they can sometimes utilize COGs in multiple nations to support their interests. It should be noted, however, that this was only a small skirmish in the larger battle regarding the rule of origin.

Other victories for Mexico in the negotiations regarded the removal of the 25% US truck tariff and Mexico's inclusion as 'domestic' under US Corporate Average Fuel Efficiency (CAFE) regulations. Among Mexico City's most important auto sector goals were to remove the high US light truck tariff.[21] Why? Light truck production is precisely the area in which the Mexican government believed that Mexico has a comparative advantage relative to its NAFTA partners. Light trucks have a larger labor component than do other autos. Mexico's low wages make it a natural site for light truck production, so long as Mexico has access to the US market.

Similarly, Mexico sought inclusion as 'domestic' for the US CAFE regulations. The CAFE regulations require automakers selling in the US market to meet fuel efficiency standards in their US-sold autos. Each car does not have to meet the standard, rather a company can average together its autos. There is one additional averaging stipulation: automakers must meet the standard in both their domestic and foreign made fleets that are sold in the US US automakers tend to produce their smaller vehicles abroad. Therefore the dual fleet averaging standard ensures that the automakers continue to produce some small cars in the US or in Canada.[22] Mexico City very much wanted to be considered domestic under the CAFE regulations. As with light trucks, small car production has a greater labor component than does large car production. Therefore the Mexican government envisioned Mexico as a locus for production of small cars which would then be exported to the US.

Mexico City won both of these goals from US negotiators. True, it did have to give up concessions on other issues, particularly the phase-out of some of its own onerous regulations regarding trade and investment in the Mexican market. But Mexico City did quite well achieving favorable light truck and CAFE provisions in NAFTA.

Explaining David's Success: Help From Goliath's Domestic Actors

Some of the underdog victories described here are not quite what they seem. Weaker nations seemingly won important concessions from the stronger nation or even thwarted both the stronger nation and the other weak nation. But in some cases, the weaker nations had help from within the stronger nation's domestic camp.

This was the case in some of the examples cited above. Mexico's success achieving elimination of the 25% US light truck tariff and the change in Mexico's status under CAFE regulations can be traced to the Big Three.   Mexico's preferences on these issues mirrored Big Three preferences and therefore the provisions' inclusion in the agreement helped move NAFTA toward a winning coalition in the US.

At first glance, it is curious that the Big Three would want the truck tariff eliminated. In other circumstances they have been very supportive of the tariff's continuation. In fact, they have fought to extend the tariff to other vehicles such as mini-vans. The tariff helps ensure that the Big Three's truck production- one of their strengths- would remain insulated from Japanese competition. But eliminating the 25% tariff for production in Mexico suited the Big Three and furthered their interests against all but one of those same Japanese automakers.   The Big Three are among the largest producers in Mexico, thus they themselves would be the beneficiaries of the tariff reduction. True, Japanese producers could also set up production in Mexico and export to the US But of all the Japanese producers, only Nissan has production facilities and experience in the Mexican market. There is no doubt that the Big Three would gain significantly from the eliminated tariff.[23] This point was not lost on US negotiators.

Similarly, the Big Three would be the primary beneficiaries of Mexico's classification as domestic in CAFE. How so? Because small car manufacturing includes a high labor content, the US automakers tend to produce as much of their small car fleet abroad as possible. This means that their domestically produced vehicles tend to be larger and less efficient, leaving each of the Big Three companies struggling to meet the domestic fleet standard. The Big Three would not have this problem if was there was no two fleet rule, but the UAW and environmental groups have fought to retain this aspect of the CAFE regulations. The Big Three could still alleviate this problem if only there was a low wage nation in which production qualified as domestic under CAFE. Mexico, with the proper NAFTA provisions, would be just such a place.

Thus the concession to Mexico on the truck tariff and CAFE status was also a very significant concession to the Big Three. This is vital for an agreement in which ratification was obviously going to be controversial and in doubt. In these examples, Mexico had friends in high places: the most important US interest groups in the sector. This helped ensure that the concessions would fall within the US win-set and therefore ensured that the US negotiators would be more willing to grant the concession.

Similar to the manner in which Mexico achieved the above NAFTA provisions was Canada's success in favorably resolving the Honda and CAMI incidents. Canada it seems, successfully achieved provisions important to it and detrimental to the US. After all, Honda was among the Japanese companies that successfully penetrated the US market in the 1970s and 1980s. Moreover, the US government was willing to let US-Canadian relations sour in the auto sector during the CUSFTA's implementation to ensure that the Honda and CAMI production remain non-North American and therefore subject to tariffs.

As with Mexico City in the above example, Ottawa had an important ally in this debate: General Motors (GM). GM is the largest of the Big Three companies and wanted its joint investment CAMI plant to be considered North American under NAFTA. GM was willing to stand in the way of the US negotiators' goals as well as those of Chrysler and Ford: a significantly tougher rule of origin. At the beginning of the negotiations, Chrysler and Ford supported 70% North American content, while GM wanted 60%. This weakened the US negotiator's position – a significantly more rigorous rule of origin- because GM would be actively arguing for a lower level. Thus Chrysler and Ford had an incentive to allow grudgingly the Honda and CAMI production to qualify somehow as North American in NAFTA; such a result would facilitate achieving their content level preferences. This is precisely what emerged in the talks. GM, Chrysler, and Ford agreed to present a united front: 65%. GM received assurances that its CAMI facility would qualify as North American in NAFTA.

This was a good issue to give to Ottawa. It was very high on the Canadian agenda in NAFTA and therefore could be used to get Ottawa to agree to a higher content level. Canada did agree to the 62.5%. Honda and CAMI were given special provisions ensuring their classification as North American. Thus in the Honda and CAMI provisions, Canada was able to achieve a considerable negotiating victory, but much of the success came from the support of important domestic interests within the US.

Explaining David's Success: Institutions and the Costs of No-Agreement

In the above examples, the underdog's success was in part due to an ally within the US. This, however, does not explain that in the sector-wide results, Canada fared markedly better in autos than in textiles despite similar levels of US domestic support and opposition. If anything, Canada faced more united US opposition to its rules of origin stance in the auto sector than in the textile and apparel sector. In autos, the Big Three, auto parts producers, and unions were united behind tougher rules of origin. Only foreign producers with auto assembly in the US agreed with Canada's rules of origin preferences. In the textile and apparel rules of origin, Canada faced a less united front, yet fared worse. The ATMI stood strongly against Canada, but Canadian preferences meshed with many US apparel producers and their trade association, the AAMA as well as with US retail companies. Nevertheless Canada was turned back on the textile and apparel rules of origin.

In both sectors, Canada was willing to push the negotiations to the brink of failure in an attempt to get the US to be more forthcoming with concessions. In both sectors, the most important interest groups within the US resisted. Canada met with more success with this strategy in the auto sector than in the textile and apparel sector. Why? Again, the two-level game approach is instructive.

When negotiators make a threat, such as terminating negotiations without an agreement, they are attempting to increase pressure on the opposite nation's negotiators and domestic interests so as to prompt concessions to avoid the no-agreement outcome. How is the threat-targeted nation going to respond to such a threat? While there are many variables that might determine the outcome of this scenario, an essential element is whether the threat is believable to the targeted nation's negotiators and other domestic actors. How might this be determined? Central to this calculation are the costs of no-agreement to the nation issuing the walk-out threat. If the costs of a failure to reach agreement are high to a nation- because it harms important domestic actors, including the negotiators themselves- then the walk-out threat is not likely to be carried out. If, however, the costs of no-agreement are low to the threat-making nation, then the probability that the threat actually will be implemented appears higher.[24] To put it starkly, a mugger is more effective shouting 'give me your money or I'll shoot!' than 'give me your money or I'll shoot *myself*!'

How does this illuminate the case study at hand? Simply put, the costs of no-agreement were higher to Canada in the textile and apparel industry than in the automotive industry. What costs would Canada face in the two sectors if Ottawa really had walked out of the negotiations?[25] The answer can be found in the existing trade institution linking the US and Canada: the CUSFTA. In the CUSFTA, Canada had better access to the lucrative US market in autos than in textiles and apparel. Therefore, the threat of no-agreement was far more credible in the former than the latter.

In the auto sector, the institutional framework preceding even the CUSFTA was quite favorable to Canada. The Auto Pact, signed in 1965, began duty-free access to the US market for Canadian production. In return Canada granted tariff-free access to its market, but only for those automakers that met various Canadian production safeguards. These entailed, among other things, Canadian value added standards. This gave the US automakers an edge in the Canadian market, so long as they met the value added standards. For adhering to the Canadian production safeguards, the Big Three were allowed to export autos into Canada duty- free from anywhere in the world (so long as the average met the safeguard standards). Thus the Big Three came to dominate the Canadian market, but the US exacted no similar production safeguards.

Thus an important precedent was set: Canadian production received ample access to the US market while at the same time was allowed production safeguards. Importantly, this access to the US market was better than that afforded production from elsewhere. Not coincidentally, Canadian auto production grew to be significantly greater than Canadian consumption, with the remainder being shipped to the US.

The CUSFTA altered these Auto Pact provisions, but Canada's favored access to the US market continued. Under the CUSFTA many of the Canadian production safeguards remained. So too did duty-free access to the US market. Importantly, the CUSFTA's rule of origin included a 50% North American (Canada and the US) content requirement. In the NAFTA negotiations, this was precisely the content level that Ottawa sought. Therefore, on this important rule of origin issue, failure to reach an agreement would match Canadian preferences closely. It would leave a 50% content level requirement and would continue Canada's favored access to the US market. Moreover, the Canadian safeguards dating to the Auto Pact made no-agreement still more palatable to Ottawa. This allowed Canada to exact significant concessions from the US to compensate for its agreeing to a higher content level.

This differs from the costs of no-agreement to Canada in the textile and apparel industry. Here too, the CUSFTA would have been the no-agreement status quo. But Canadian access to the US market in textiles and apparel under the CUSFTA was less favorable than in autos. The CUSFTA's general rule of origin excluded a large number of Canadian textiles and apparel because of the Canadian industries' tendency to use non-North American fabrics and yarns. Canada was granted significant exceptions to the CUSFTA's general rule of origin in the form of the above mentioned TPLs. These TPLs, however, were rapidly filling. For instance, during the first two years of the CUSFTA in 1989-1990, Canada utilized 20% of its allotted TPL in one product area: wool apparel. In 1991 this figure was 51%. As the talks unfolded in 1992, the figure neared 70%.[26] In the foreseeable future the TPLs would act as a true ceiling, curtailing increased Canadian exports to the US. The US was well aware of this and was therefore less willing to give in to Canadian threats to leave the textile and apparel talks. Industry officials from both the US and Canada agreed that the US called the Canadian bluff. One US industry official said 'they [the Canadians] were getting rolled. Mexico and the US agreed [and] they had to come along.' According to a Canadian industry official, in essence 'the Americans and Mexicans said 'fine, we can do a deal without you.''[27] Given the costs of no-agreement, it appeared that Canada was shouting 'stop or I'll shoot *myself*!' It was readily apparent to US negotiators and interest groups alike that Canada would be harmed by pulling out of the textile and apparel talks. Canada had little choice but to settle for face saving concessions which fell significantly short of Canadian government preferences.

Other Cross-border and Cross-Level of Analysis Strategies

There were many other cross-border and cross-level of analysis interactions in the auto and textile and apparel sectors of NAFTA. An example of an attempt at suasive reverberation in the NAFTA talks was the Salinas administration's abrupt and tremendously high increases in tariffs on Chinese imports during the negotiations. The tariff rates on some textile and apparel goods shot up to nearly 500% of the value of the goods. The tariff increase, highest on textile and apparel goods, was perceived by US industry officials as intended to demonstrate to US textile and apparel producers that Mexico could be sufficiently tough about Asian imports so as to prevent NAFTA from becoming an 'export platform' into the US[28] This was intended as an assurance to wavering elements within the US textile and apparel industries to support the agreement, thereby hoping to alter the US domestic board. The US retail industry was aghast, but it was a strong NAFTA supporter that would certainly not be turned away from NAFTA by this Mexican government strategy. The move may also have sent comforting signals to domestic Mexican producers as well that had been battered by Asian imports and were fearful of increased US and Canadian competition. Domestic Mexican producers tend to be small and inefficient, although they include larger companies such as Alfa and

Novatex. The domestic Mexican companies are dwarfed by foreign-owned (usually US-owned) producers such as Du Pont.

The Salinas administration used NAFTA as a synergistic linkage to complete its long standing efforts to liberalize the Mexican economy. It had already liberalized the Mexican economy quite a bit, but wanted more than did domestic actors. The selling point to convince skeptical domestic actors was the potential investment such reforms could generate. While Salinas had met with considerable success, full liberalization of many industries dragged because of domestic opposition. NAFTA, however, presented Salinas with the opportunity for synergistic linkages. With NAFTA, further liberalization of the Mexican market became linked with an issue with wide domestic support: access to the US market. Therefore, Salinas was able to liberalize sectors of the Mexican economy to a greater degree than in the absence of this linkage. This was the case in the textile and apparel industries. Access to the US market through the termination of US import quotas was the number one issue for the Mexican domestic textile and apparel makers. Liberalization of the Mexican textile and apparel market, which Salinas had previously sought and only partially accomplished, was the price Mexican textile and apparel producers paid for access to the US market. Salinas used the trade bloc's international table to accomplish what he had not been able to using solely the domestic table.

While the focus of the two-level approach is on the COG, other players may also attempt some of the strategies suggested by the integrative approach. Transnational corporations are well suited to deliver their own side payments or threats, given their strong organizational resources and presence in multiple countries. The head of Nissan's operations in Mexico suggested to Mexican authorities that if NAFTA was not drafted with a high minimum Mexican content level, the company would direct future sourcing of its Mexican assembly operations to the US or Canada.[29] Because Nissan's Mexican production already contained significant Mexican content, the company saw the requirement for Mexican content as a way to hinder newcomers. By threatening to source from NAFTA's northern countries, Nissan was engaging in 'negative reverberation' - a threat. The incident was an instance of reverberation because threatening to source parts from abroad increased the stakes of NAFTA for Mexican-based parts producers, who in turn would pressure the Mexican government, or so Nissan hoped. In essence, Nissan was trying to alter Mexico's domestic win-set toward its own preferences. Mexico City did indeed fight to maintain the Mexican content rule, although Nissan's threat and reverberation may not have been instrumental in this decision. This effort by Nissan is also interesting because Nissan is a Japanese company whose government is not part of the NAFTA negotiations. Companies headquartered in non-bloc nations with operations in North America were indeed active participants in the NAFTA negotiations. This demonstrates the complexity of bloc negotiations and the ability of corporations to cross-border influence.

A strategy that non-governmental actors such as TNCs (and perhaps large domestic producers) or unions can employ is the formation of transnational alignments. In the two-level approach literature, these are formal linkages with groups from the opposite country's domestic arena. However, a more useful definition would include informal linkages as well. Auto parts producers from all three nations formally joined together to promote the issues from their agendas which overlapped. Less formally, the Canadian apparel industry cooperated with US retailers to share information about developments within each other's countries. In the auto sector of NAFTA, each of the Big Three companies had production in all three member countries and was therefore its own transnational alignment. An interesting development arose when General Motor's Canadian subsidiary took a different policy stand on one issue in the talks than that of the parent company. The subsidiary called for lower North American value added than did the US parent company.[30]

There were important examples of cross-border and cross-level of analysis strategies at work in the linkage between access to the Mexican auto market and the reduction of a US light truck tariff and favorable treatment of Mexican auto production in US fuel efficiency standards. The US COG was engaged in a synergistic linkage and, interestingly enough, so was the Big Three. The two-level game literature notes that synergistic linkages will be attempted by COGs, but regarding US CAFE regulations, the Big Three also engaged in a synergistic linkage: they 'conceded' to Mexico on a policy that they themselves wanted but were not able to achieve outside of its linkage to a more domestically popular provision of NAFTA.

An important goal to US negotiators was a more liberal Mexican auto regime that would increase access to the Mexican auto market. Since 1962, the Mexican auto industry was governed by a series of auto decrees. These are presidential decrees that mandate that companies wishing to sell in Mexico must also produce in Mexico. The most recent auto decree, constructed by President Carlos Salinas in 1989, established trade balancing ratios, Mexican content requirements, and investment barriers. The trade balancing ratios stipulated that a company wishing to import autos or auto parts into Mexico had to also export from Mexico a greater value of production. Automakers selling in the Mexican market were required to construct vehicles with 36% Mexican content. The Salinas auto decree of 1989 was more liberal than previous decrees, but still limited US access to the Mexican auto market and would certainly be changed by future Mexican presidents as all its predecessors had been; unless NAFTA permanently replaced the auto decree.

Eventually, the US did gain the market access that it was seeking in a compromise in which the US acquiesced to Mexican demands for the swift elimination of the US 25% truck tariff and for authorization that Mexican produced autos will count as domestic for CAFE purposes.[31] These two concessions were among Mexico's primary goals in the negotiations.[32] Therefore, the US COG was able to use CAFE and the truck tariff as tools to pry open the Mexican market. But important US interests were at stake here as well, and the linkage of CAFE and the US truck tariff termination can only be fully understood by examining the interactions between the US COG and international and domestic spheres.

The linkage is an example of the Bush Administration engaging in a synergistic linkage. In NAFTA the Bush Administration was able to weaken the CAFE provisions somewhat by linking their extension to Mexico with access to the Mexican market. The Bush Administration was not enamored with the CAFE laws; rather it viewed them with suspicion. Bush threatened to veto any increase in the CAFE requirements, but calling for their direct abolishment or weakening would be taking a sizable political risk for the putative 'environmental president.'[33] The Bush Administration would welcome the extension of CAFE to Mexico in the absence of any leverage that it might bring because this would ease the requirements somewhat. As one US negotiator acknowledged, 'generally [on CAFE] all [three sides] had the same objectives.'[34] By linking CAFE's extension to Mexico with the liberalization of and access to the Mexican market, the Bush Administration was able to utilize international factors to advance its own agenda. In the absence of the Mexican market access linkage, weakening CAFE would run counter to the interests of the UAW and environmental groups. However, using NAFTA to obtain a domestically popular political good – access to the Mexican market – and linking this to the domestically unpopular policy – a weakened CAFE – allowed the US COG to diffuse opposition to the latter policy. For instance, one UAW official did admit that in the NAFTA 'Mexico did alter restrictions fundamentally' and that probably wouldn't have happened if not in large-scale talks.[35] However, the UAW still argued that extending domestic status under CAFE to Mexico was one of many flaws in the agreement.

While nominally the CAFE laws are merely environmental regulations, they in fact have extensive trade and production implications. In particular, they force the Big Three to produce small cars in the US (or Canada) in order to meet the domestic mileage requirements they mandate. For over a decade the Big Three have pushed for elimination of the rules altogether and in the context of NAFTA wanted to see the Mexican production count as 'domestic' for CAFE purposes. On the other hand, the UAW stridently wanted Mexican production to remain 'foreign' in CAFE in order to maintain small car production in the US Mexico City strongly desired to stimulate small car production in Mexico by including Mexican production as 'domestic' for CAFE purposes.

NAFTA's final text includes all vehicles with 75% North American content sold in the US as domestic for CAFE standards after ten years, thus easing the 'domestic' CAFE standards somewhat for Big Three companies that produce small cars in Mexico. In the intervening period, after a three year transition, companies that were already operating in Mexico as NAFTA was formed could count Mexican production as either foreign or domestic for CAFE purposes, thus giving automakers greater flexibility in adhering to the CAFE standards.[36] For new Mexican manufacturers, Mexican production will count as domestic during the transition. The CAFE provisions are a victory for Mexico and auto companies that produce in North America, while they are a loss for American labor. As the UAW argued: 'The inclusion of Mexican vehicles as "domestic" under the US fuel efficiency standards will facilitate the transfer of small car production to Mexico.'[37]

The Big Three, interestingly enough, did not fight for the inclusion of Mexican production in domestic CAFE calculations despite their obvious dislike of the CAFE requirements and their desire to liberalize them. The Big Three decided not to push this issue for two reasons. First, they were hesitant to draw domestic political flack on an issue they saw as particularly sensitive. As Big Three officials made clear privately, they were avoiding the wrath of environmental groups as much as avoiding the UAW's opposition on this issue. UAW opposition on a host of other NAFTA issues was seemingly of less consequence to the automakers, or more accurately, was unavoidable. The Big Three regularly spar with environmental groups. Why the hesitation to do so in this case? The Big Three dominated the auto negotiations. With environmental groups, this dominance would be less certain. Including arguments about the environment in the auto negotiations of NAFTA could be a Pandora's Box that was better left shut if possible. Environmental groups had made the passage of 'fast track' negotiating authority for NAFTA and GATT's Uruguay Round difficult. The Big Three were successful in avoiding environmental group attention to the auto provisions. Second, the Big Three did not press actively on CAFE because they knew they did not have to, since Mexican negotiators would push hard on this issue. Mexican negotiators made it clear that the changes to CAFE were among Mexico City's first priorities. Privately, a Ford official said that the Mexicans were 'convinced' that this was 'very important' for them.[38] Outlining these two rationales in a letter to the Bush Administration, the Big Three wrote:

> The government of Mexico has indicated that it considers itself comparatively disadvantaged with Canada because of the disparity of treatment of the two countries under CAFE law, and seeks to negotiate an agreement that Mexican-produced vehicles also be considered 'domestic' for CAFE purposes.
> Given the intense domestic political pressures surrounding the CAFE program and the probable opposition of any change in Mexico's CAFE status from the industry's union, we wish to make clear to the US that our companies do not seek such a change in the status of the CAFE designation of Mexican produced autos in the NAFTA. US CAFE laws are distortive and intrusive regulations which already result in inefficient, and unnecessary investment decisions. However, we see no advantage to complicating the already overburdened domestic political CAFE agenda, by adding another controversial and potentially divisive issue to the ongoing policy debate on the subject.[39]

Mexican negotiators successfully won the inclusion of Mexican production as domestic for CAFE calculations, and further, they won other CAFE-related concessions. The provisions allowing an existing producer to elect to have its Mexican production considered either domestic or foreign for CAFE from three to ten years after NAFTA comes into force (1997-2004) was a concession to the Mexicans. Once a company makes a selection for their Mexican production to be treated as domestic or foreign during the transition period, it will not be able to change its selection. Mexico pressed for the choice during the transition period to provide an option to Mexican producers. This option would allow VW to average its 'dirty' German-made Audis with its smaller, more efficient Mexican produced autos for import into the US ensuring that VW would more easily meet CAFE standards for its 'foreign' fleet.[40] Mexican negotiators had pushed for even greater flexibility: they wanted companies to be able to select annually whether their Mexican production will count as domestic or foreign. Both Canadian and US negotiators rebuffed this proposal, arguing that this would grant Mexican production greater flexibility than exists for either US or Canadian production and that it simply would not float in the US Congress.[41]

As for the three year delay before companies producing in Mexico make the choice regarding their classification during the transition, US negotiators held that this was to ensure that current sourcing patterns not be disturbed. There was, however, a more concrete and specific rationale. The three year delay was sought by Ford.[42] Ford produced some of its large vehicles (the Crown Victoria and the Mercury Grand Marquis) in Canada, but with less than the 75% US and Canadian content that CAFE requires for vehicles to be considered domestic. Therefore, the autos have been considered foreign for CAFE and have been averaged with Ford's more efficient smaller cars imported from around the world. According to a Ford official, to qualify these large vehicles as domestic under CAFE rules, Ford increased offshore sourcing.[43] Including Mexico in CAFE content would push the cars over the 75% level using CAFE's content rules and into the domestic category, a category in which Ford has difficulty meeting CAFE requirements.[44] Therefore the US successfully pressed for the phase-in of the CAFE rules.[45]

On the whole, the US COG successfully used Mexican CAFE status to open the Mexican market. This also achieved the domestic goals of watering down the CAFE rules. The Big Three was equally successful here, using the international negotiation to achieve its CAFE goals, but also using the foreign government to avoid political fallout from trying to achieve its CAFE goals. It is worth noting that not only did this work for the US automakers, but it worked even in very narrow and detailed provisions such as the caveat for Ford outlined above.

As mentioned above, also as part of the compromise that gained access and liberalization of the Mexican market, the US made a number of related tariff concessions. Of particular importance to the Mexican negotiators was the US concession to immediately reduce its 25% tariff on truck imports to 10% followed by a five year phase-out. This was of particular importance to the UAW as well. Just as it feared NAFTA would lead to greater Mexican small car production, the UAW believed that the truck duty had kept truck production in the US NAFTA's rapid erosion of the duty could spur truck production in Mexico at the expense of US production. These truck provisions are particularly galling to labor because trucks at the time were one of the few growing segments of the North American market.

Other US duty concessions are far less consequential because other US automotive duties are low (and, in the case of Canadian production, non-existent for trade qualifying under the CUSFTA).[46] The Big Three, who normally defend the truck tariff and favor extending it to minivans, backed the truck tariff termination for Mexican production. Why? They themselves would be the primary beneficiaries of the provisions, sending Mexican produced trucks to the US duty free. The Big Three's Japanese competitors could not take advantage of Mexican truck options so easily: only Nissan operates in Mexico and newcomers to Mexican production would have difficulty meeting NAFTA requirements initially.[47]

Conclusion

The differences between the negotiated outcomes in the auto and textile and apparel sectors underscore the role of existing trade institutions in trade negotiations. The shadow of existing trade institutions not only helps set the agenda for negotiations, but also plays a significant role in shaping the negotiations' outcome. The parameters of the CUSFTA served as a point of departure for the NAFTA talks in both sectors and made threats by negotiators more or less credible by delimiting the costs of no-agreement. Of course interests- specifically interest groups within the strongest nation- play an essential role in determining negotiated outcomes. They shape the contours of concessions given to the weaker nations, but they too work within the framework of existing trade institutions. Existing trade institutions, therefore, are an important determinant in whether less powerful nations are able to wrest significant concessions from stronger nations.

The two-level approach proves more effective in explaining the NAFTA auto and textile and apparel negotiation outcomes than a traditional distribution of power approach. Moreover, the two-level approach helps explain the many cross-border and cross-level of analysis linkages that took place in the negotiations.

The dynamics of the two-level game are somewhat different in trade bloc negotiations than other international negotiations. Compared to bilateral negotiations the increased number of negotiating nations increases the potential for floating alignments from issue to issue, even within negotiations for a single economic sector. Negotiators from countries may align together on some issues, and against one another on others. So too do interest groups.

This was certainly the case in the automotive and textile and apparel sector negotiations. One area of the auto negotiations where this was evident was the rule of origin. The Canadian and Mexican COGs both wanted a looser rule of origin than did the US COG. The two weaker NAFTA nations sought 50% North American content as the threshold for NAFTA treatment while the US sought 65%. However, on other rule of origin issues, the alignments shifted. On rule of origin averaging – whether each auto had to qualify as North American or if lower North American content cars could be averaged with higher content cars so long as the average was above the NAFTA threshold – the US and Canadian COGs (and automakers) were on the same side of the argument (wide averaging) against the Mexican COG (narrow averaging). Whether shifting alignments are more common in trade bloc negotiations than multilateral negotiations is beyond the scope of this chapter. They are certainly more common than in bilateral negotiations.

Another way in which trade bloc negotiations are different than other trade negotiations is the rising tide of expectations that come with a proposed trade bloc. The rising expectations and concomitant increase in investment and trade levels, increase the cost of no-agreement for *all* actors. For instance, increased investment by US companies in Mexico increases political pressure on the US government to ensure that such investment will be treated fairly. It also increases pressure on the Mexican government to ensure that the regulations that brought in that investment become codified to reassure investors to stay and entice new investors. The increased expectations that trade bloc negotiations bring serves as grease for the gears of those negotiations. The auto and textile and apparel sectors offer some concrete examples of this. Mexican domestic auto consumption was rising rapidly as NAFTA was proposed, negotiated and ratified, thus NAFTA could be more easily portrayed as increasing US auto jobs, not just as a threat to them. A number of wavering textile and apparel state Congressmen were persuaded to support NAFTA after a White House sponsored fact finding trip to NAFTA showed textile and apparel products from their districts on Mexican retailers' shelves.[48] Higher export figures no doubt also helped.

Such expectations may also be found in bilateral and multilateral negotiations, but trade bloc negotiations are more apt to increase the scope of the expectations than do bilateral negotiations and have a greater degree of certainty than to multilateral negotiations. For instance, one reason to negotiate, sign and ratify NAFTA, according to some supporters, was in case the GATT Uruguay Round negotiations failed. This concern was not misplaced: the Uruguay Round took seven years to complete.

Another lesson to be learned from NAFTA's auto and textiles and apparel negotiations is that such negotiations necessarily start from a set of general goals such as increasing the competitiveness of US producers or ensuring liberal economic policies if multilateral negotiations fail. As the negotiations progress, the focus becomes more narrow and practical. How can negotiators draft an agreement that is supported across the negotiating table and back home? The narrow and practical concerns will not always be consistent with the general goals. Negotiations are a balancing act between the two. Can negotiators err on the side of their general goals, whatever they may be, or must they make the practical considerations paramount? This is an old question: how strong is the state? More specifically, how much leeway do COGs have? The lesson from the auto and textile and apparel sectors is that COGs do not stray too far from the desires of the most powerful of domestic interest groups. Nations are not unitary actors. As this chapter has made clear, interest group activities are an essential element to understanding a nation's actions. COGs, however, are not merely conduits of policy desires of interest groups. There are numerous instances in which COGs were able to alter domestic constraints with the trade bloc negotiations. President Salinas using access to the US textile and apparel market through NAFTA to convince the Mexican textile and apparel industry to liberalize is one example. President Bush using NAFTA to weaken CAFE regulations serves as another example. Just as COGs use the 'tied hands' strategy ('That would never be ratified back home') in trade bloc negotiations to gain concessions from negotiating partners, COGs can use a reverse tied hands strategy ('That would never be accepted by our negotiating partners') to manipulate domestic interest groups.

Notes

[1] This chapter is based on David A. Lynch, 'Negotiating with Goliath, Inequality in International Negotiations: Double-Edged Diplomacy in NAFTA's Auto and Textile Sectors,' Annual Meeting of the American Political Science Association, San Francisco, September 1, 1996.

[2] This chapter will not give a comprehensive explanation of the auto and textile and apparel negotiations, nor of the sectors' final texts. For this see Lynch (1995). Both utilize and analyze the two-level game approach.

[3] For more on the approach, see Putnam (1988) and Evans, et. al (1993). The latter work includes varied examples of the two-level game approach at work in different issue areas. See also Lehman and McCoy (1992).

[4] The terms 'country' and 'nation' are used interchangeably here meaning nation-state.

[5] In the case of the NAFTA negotiations, the US COG, in its most basic definition, would be George Bush. A looser definition that is more helpful includes Bush, his chief negotiator who was the United States Trade Representative Carla Hills, and their lieutenants that took part in the negotiations and those close political advisors to Bush active in evaluating the acceptability of the final package. In essence, this definition is equivalent to those definitions of the 'state' which encompass the portions of the executive branch involved in a given issue area. For Canada and Mexico the COG encompasses those actors in the Mulroney and Salinas administrations respectively that were active in the negotiation process or in the final political decisions about the acceptability of the agreement. Primary responsibility rested with the heads of the negotiating teams: in Canada this was Trade Minister Michael Wilson and in Mexico this was Secretary of Commerce Jamie Serra Puche.

[6] Much of this draws upon Lehman and McCoy.

[7] See Moravcsik (1993: 82-83). Much of the following about these tactics draws on this.

[8] The terms 'positive' and 'negative reverberation' are from Jack Snyder (1993: 108).

[9] This assumes that a COG can accurately gauge the opposite COG's domestic strength.

[10] The US-Canadian figure from Paul Wonnacott (1988: 102). The US-Mexican figure from the US Department of Commerce, as cited by the Motor Equipment Manufacturers Association in the February 20, 21, and 28 House Ways and Means Committee hearing, p. 189.

[11] *1993 Market Data Book*, Automotive News.

[12] Ibid.

[13] From 'NAFTA negotiations and the Canadian Textile Manufacturing Industry,' by the Canadian Textile Institute, 3 February 1993, p. 11.

[14] From 'Competitiveness of the Mexican Textile Chain' in *Textile Outlook International*, November, 1992.

[15] Personal interview with an anonymous US negotiator.

[16] *New York Times*, 17 February 1992.

[17] This last issue, as with the Honda and CAMI disputes, was primarily between Canada and the US.

[18] This is an oversimplification. There are other issues that make the rules of origin tighter or looser than indicated here. Those interested in more detail about the final provisions should turn to Hufbauer and Schott (1993), Appel Molot (1993), and Lynch (1995).

[19] Actually, these were called Tariff Rate Quotas (TRQs) in the CUSFTA and Tariff Preference Levels in NAFTA. For simplicity this chapter will use 'TPLs' for both. The difference is only semantic. One US negotiator said this change was because Tariff Rate 'Quota' sounded too much like a 'quota' and thus too protectionist. Anonymous personal interview.

[20] The rule of origin battle was largely a US-Canadian one. Mexican and US negotiators' positions were more harmonious on the rules of origin, with some exceptions of course. US-Mexican debates were more heated in the phase-out of Mexican tariffs. Mexico's primary concern was ending US quotas that limited its access to the US market.

[21] Canadian production was already excluded from this tariff in the CUSFTA.

[22] Canada was already considered 'domestic' under CAFE regulations.

[23] Furthering the disproportionate benefits accruing from the truck tariff reduction is the structure of existing Mexican regulations. These regulations will be phased-out, but during the phase-out period the existing Mexican producers – the Big Three, Nissan and Volkswagen – will continue to be favored over newcomers who would find it difficult and not cost effective to shape their Mexican production to comply with the regulations. This too was at Big Three insistence. Privately, officials from Japanese automakers that were not yet in the Mexican market were irate that the existing automakers in Mexico would be favored by the composition of the Mexican regulations' phase-out.

[24] For more on role played by the costs of no-agreement see Stein (1993), Odell (1993), and Cameron (1992).

[25] The threatened walk-outs in the sectors examined here were independent of one another and independent of the rest of the NAFTA. Canada never threatened pulling out of NAFTA altogether, but instead called for an agreement that excluded either autos, textiles and apparel, or both.

[26] Figures from the Canadian Textile Institute, 'North American Free Trade Agreement,' Submission to the Subcommittee on International Trade, Committee on External Affairs and International Trade, December 10, 1992, p. 18.

[27] Personal interviews with anonymous industry officials. Mexico and the US had already reached an agreement on the rules of origin. Mexico was granted the termination of US quotas in return for Mexico's support of US the supported rules of origin (yarn forward).

[28] Personal interviews.

[29] Shoichi Amemiya, president of Nissan of Mexico as quoted in Orme Jr. (1993: 194).

[30] Personal interview.

[31] *Inside US Trade*, 7 August 1992, pp. 4 and 5. It is worth noting, the US did not want complete and immediate liberalization of the Mexican market for the simple reason that the Big Three already had extensive production there that would be challenged more quickly by newcomers if all barriers were removed quickly. Automakers that did not already have production in Mexico lamented this.

[32] As attested to by negotiators from all three countries in personal interviews.

[33] *Automotive News*, 11 May 1992, 'Auto Lobbyists Mobilize Against Carbon Dioxide Bill.'

[34] Personal interview.

[35] Personal interview.

[36] NAFTA, p. 300-A-11. As the reader may recall, Canadian production already counted as domestic for CAFE purposes before NAFTA.

[37] 'The Potential Impact on the US Economy and Industries of the North American Free Trade Agreement (NAFTA)', Don Stillman, UAW, 25 November 1992, p. 4.

[38] Personal interview.

[39] Big Three letter to US Trade Representative Carla Hills, 9 September 1991, as reprinted in *Inside US Trade*, Special Report, 23 September 1991, p. S-5. Despite the obvious disdain for CAFE in the above passage, officials from all Big Three companies held privately that the extension of CAFE to Mexican production was not a high priority for them in the negotiations.

[40] Specifically, VW will be able to balance its fuel efficient Golfs and Jettas, of which, all sold in the US are made in Mexico, with its German-made Audis which use less efficient V-8 engines. VW pressured the Mexican government for such a provision in NAFTA. After the phase-in is complete, all production in Mexico that is exported to the US will be domestic. Wouldn't this hurt VW if it can't average its Mexican production with other non-Mexican imports? A VW North America official didn't think it would. First, VW sales in

the US have increasingly come from the Mexican market. VW closed its assembly plant in the US in 1988, instead supplying the US market from Mexico. Second, he felt that technological advances would make CAFE requirements obsolete five to ten years after the transition CAFE provisions expire. Personal interview. In fact, this response may have been politic: it is clearly in Mexico's interest to have its production count as domestic for CAFE and the transition provision for VW may have been the most favorable outcome that VW could have realistically won. The Labor Advisory Committee also asserts that Nissan will benefit from this provision, although currently Nissan does not export any built up vehicles to the US from Mexico.

[41] This according to a Canadian negotiator's account. Personal interview.

[42] Motor Equipment Manufacturers Association, 17 September 1992, p. 15.

[43] *Journal of Commerce*, 6 July 1992, p. 10A.

[44] *Automotive News*, 17 September 1992, p. 34.

[45] While the US could have sought to make the one time election earlier, which would allow Ford to consider its Mexican production as foreign for CAFE, this would have locked Ford into classifying its Mexican production as domestic for the entire transition.

[46] The US tariff on autos is 2.5% and is a trade weighted average of 3.1% on parts, however because of the maquiladora program, much Mexican production avoids this and the effective duty is some 2.2% on autos *and* trucks and 0.4% on parts imports. The 2.5% auto tariff was removed immediately and the parts tariffs end at varying times: some immediately, others in five and ten years. US International Trade Commission, 'The Potential Impact of the US economy and selected industries of the North America Free-Trade Agreement,' 1993, p. 4-3. The Canadian parts tariff of 9.2% generally does not apply to Mexican-Canadian trade because under the Auto Pact and CUSFTA the Big Three is able to import duty free into Canada from anywhere it produces.

[47] Not only would newcomers have to meet North American content, but in the early years of NAFTA, they would have to meet Auto Decree requirements such as Mexican content and trade balancing.

[48] Personal interview with a White House official.

References

Appel Molot, M. (1995), *Driving Continentally*, Carleton University Press, Ottawa.

Cameron, M. (1992), 'The Domestic and International Environment of Trade Liberalization in Mexico', paper delivered at the 1992 Latin American Studies Association in Los Angeles, CA.

Destler, I.M. (1995), *American Trade Politics*, Third Edition, Institute for International Economics, Washington DC.

Evans, P.B. (1993), 'Building an Integrative Approach to International and Domestic Politics', in P.B. Evans, H.D. Jacobson, R.D. Putnam, (eds), *Double-Edged Diplomacy, International Bargaining and Domestic Politics*, University of Calfornia Press, Berkeley, pp. 397-430.

Evans, P.B., Jacobson, H.D., Putnam, R.D. (eds) (1993), *Double-Edged Diplomacy, International Bargaining and Domestic Politics*, University of Calfornia Press, Berkeley.

Hufbauer, G.C. and Schott, J.J. (1993), *NAFTA, an Assessment*, Institute for International Economics, Washington DC.

Lehman, H.P. and McCoy, J.L. (1992), 'The Dynamics of the Two-Level Bargaining Game, the 1988 Brazilian Debt Negotiations', in *World Politics*, vol. 44, no. 4, pp. 600-644.

Lynch, D.A. (1995), *National and International Sources of American Foreign Economic Policymaking: The North American Free Trade Agreement (NAFTA)*, Doctoral Dissertation, The University of California, Santa Barbara.

Odell, J.S. (1993), 'International Threats and Internal Politics: Brazil, the European Community, and the United States, 1985-1987', in P.B. Evans, H.D. Jacobson, R.D. Putnam, (eds), *Double-Edged Diplomacy, International Bargaining and Domestic Politics*, University of Calfornia Press, Berkeley, pp. 233-264.

Orme, jr., W.A. (1993), *Continental Shift: Free Trade and the New North America*, The Washington Post Co, Washington DC.

Putnam, R.D. (1988), 'Diplomacy and Domestic Politics: The Logic of Two-Level Games', in *International Organization*, vol. 42, no. 3, pp. 427-460.

Snyder, J. (1993), 'East-West Bargaining over Germany. The Search for Synergy in a Two-Level Game', in P.B. Evans, H.D. Jacobson, R.D. Putnam, (eds), *Double-Edged Diplomacy, International Bargaining and Domestic Politics*, University of Calfornia Press, Berkeley, pp. 104-127.

Stein, J.G. (1993), 'The Political Economy of Security Agreements: the Linked Costs of Failure of Camp David', in P.B. Evans, H.D. Jacobson, R.D. Putnam, (eds), *Double-Edged Diplomacy, International Bargaining and Domestic Politics*, University of Calfornia Press, Berkeley, pp. 77-103.

Wonnacott, P. (1988), 'The Auto Sector', in J.J. Schott and M.G. Smith (eds), *The Canada-United States Free Trade Agreement: the Global Impact*, Institute for International Economics, Washington DC.